IDEAS TO DIE FOR

Ideas to Die For: The Cosmopolitan Challenge seeks to address the kinds of challenges that cosmopolitan perspectives and practices face in a world organized increasingly in relation to a proliferating series of global absolutisms—religious, political, social, and economic. While these challenges are often used to support the claim that cosmopolitanism is impotent to resist such totalizing ideologies because it is either a Western conceit or a globalist fiction, Gunn argues that cosmopolitanism is neither.

Situating his discussion in an emphatically global context, Gunn shows how cosmopolitanism has been effective in resisting such essentialisms and authoritarianisms precisely because it is more pragmatic than prescriptive, more self-critical than self-interested, and finds several of its foremost recent expressions in the work of an Indian philosopher, a Palestinian writer, and South African story-tellers. This kind of cosmopolitanism offers a genuine ethical alternative to the politics of dogmatism and extremism because it is grounded on a new delineation of the human and opens toward a new, indeed, an "other," humanism.

Giles Gunn is Professor of Global and International Studies and of English at the University of California, Santa Barbara, writes on the cultural and ethical study of globalization, and is author or editor, most recently, of *Beyond Solidarity* and *America and the Misshaping of a New World Order*.

GLOBAL HORIZONS
Series Editors: *Richard Falk*
PRINCETON UNIVERSITY, USA AND R. B. J. WALKER, UNIVERSITY OF VICTORIA, CANADA

We live in a moment that urgently calls for a reframing, reconceptualizing, and reconstituting of the political, cultural, and social practices that underpin the enterprises of international relations.

While contemporary developments in international relations are focused upon highly detailed and technical matters, they also demand an engagement with the broader questions of history, ethics, culture, and human subjectivity.

GLOBAL HORIZONS is dedicated to examining these broader questions.

1. **International Relations and the Problem of Difference**
   David Blaney and Naeem Inayatullah

2. **Methods and Nations**
   Cultural governance and the indigenous subject
   Michael J. Shapiro

3. **Declining World Order**
   America's imperial geopolitics
   Richard Falk

4. **Human Rights, Private Wrongs**
   Constructing global civil society
   Alison Brysk

5. **Rethinking Refugees**
   Beyond states of emergency
   Peter Nyers

6. **Beyond the Global Culture War**
   Adam Webb

7. **Cinematic Geopolitics**
   Michael J. Shapiro

8. **The Liberal Way of War**
   Killing to make life live
   Michael Dillon and Julian Reid

9. **After the Globe, Before the World**
   R. B. J. Walker

10. **Ideas to Die For**
    The cosmopolitan challenge
    Giles Gunn

IDEAS TO DIE FOR

The cosmopolitan challenge

Giles Gunn

LONDON AND NEW YORK

First published 2013
by Routledge
2 Park Square, Milton Park, Abingdon, Oxon OX14 4RN

Simultaneously published in the USA and Canada
by Routledge
711 Third Avenue, New York, NY 10017

Routledge is an imprint of the Taylor & Francis Group, an informa business

© 2013 Giles Gunn

The right of Giles Gunn to be identified as author of this work has been asserted by him in accordance with the Copyright, Designs and Patent Act 1988.

All rights reserved. No part of this book may be reprinted or reproduced or utilised in any form or by any electronic, mechanical, or other means, now known or hereafter invented, including photocopying and recording, or in any information storage or retrieval system, without permission in writing from the publishers.

Trademark notice: Product or corporate names may be trademarks or registered trademarks, and are used only for identification and explanation without intent to infringe.

British Library Cataloguing in Publication Data
A catalogue record for this book is available from the British Library

Library of Congress Cataloging in Publication Data
Gunn, Giles B., author.
Ideas to die for : the cosmopolitan challenge / Giles Gunn.
pages ; cm. -- (Global horizons)
Includes bibliographical references and index.
Cosmopolitanism. I. Title.
JZ1308.G86 2013
306--dc23
2012039582

ISBN: 978-0-415-81384-6 (hbk)
ISBN: 978-0-415-81388-4 (pbk)
ISBN: 978-0-203-55091-5 (ebk)

Typeset in Bembo
by Integra Software Services Pvt. Ltd, Pondicherry, India

Printed and bound in Great Britain by
TJ International Ltd, Padstow, Cornwall

For Barbra

A philosopher would be one who seeks a new criteriology to distinguish between comprehending and justifying.

Jacques Derrida

CONTENTS

Preface		viii
Acknowledgments		xiii
Also by Giles Gunn		xvi
1	Introduction: mapping and remapping the global	1
2	Being other-wise: cosmopolitanism and its discontents	14
3	Pragmatist alternatives to absolutist options	39
4	Culture and the misshaping of world order	58
5	America's gods then and now	77
6	War narratives and American exceptionalism	99
7	The transcivilizational, the intercivilizational, and the human	113
8	Globalizing the humanities and an "other" humanism	134
Notes		148
Bibliography		162
Index		171

PREFACE

Ideas to Die For: The Cosmopolitan Challenge attempts to develop the case for a cosmopolitan outlook and practice that is neither a Western conceit nor a globalist fiction. This is a perspective that asks what it would take ethically to transform the necessity of living together, which we cannot escape, into the possibility of living together well, which we dare not abandon.[1] This may indeed represent what some have called a "cosmopolitanism to come," but it is by no means a cosmopolitanism still to be imagined.[2] It depends on an assumption that we are confronted with a world organized less in relation to a hierarchy of solutions than a hierarchy of problems. Unfortunately, most people believe, or prefer to believe, exactly the reverse. Life, they assume, should be about the best answers, not the most intractable problems, and this prejudice, which may have seemed to be diminishing after the collapse of the Soviet Union and the end of the Cold War, only became immensely more extensive and intense as a result of the global event known as "9/11" and the massive set of responses and counter-responses it unleashed. Indeed, the misnamed "War on Terror" generated an equally heated but misleading war of creeds and convictions that now threatens to drown much thinking about the world and its so-called "others" in a sea of fixed ideas. Convictions, as Friedrich Nietzsche warned, are more of a threat to truth than lies. Despite the shift from a bipolar to a multipolar world, it is scarcely an exaggeration to say that ideology of a particularly virulent sort now rules, and doctrines, dogmas, and demagoguery, all filtered through a symbolically mediated fog of words and images, are, to paraphrase Ralph Waldo Emerson, in the saddle.

There is no doubt that religion and sectarianism have played their part in this recourse to inflexible, often authoritarian, thinking worldwide, but its expansion has had as much to do with the decoupling of religion and culture as with their recoupling.[3] The relationship between ideas and the public world is being reshaped by two interrelated forces associated with globalization. The first is deterritorialization, which enables religious and other ideas to circulate in non-territorial spaces that are dissociated from specific locations and disconnected from any specific societal or cultural articulation of their meaning. Floating free of any particular interpretive frame of reference, they in effect spread outside or beyond the circuits of inherited knowledge. The communities that once shaped their formation and determined their applications now have little or no relation to their expression or authority. Their efficacy is related chiefly to their ability to represent themselves as universalist, unchanging, incorruptible antidotes to a world grown strange and frightening because of increasing social, economic, and political inequalities, vast demographic movements, accelerated technological change, heightened violence, the normalization of terror, the collapse of former cultural coherencies, and "the narcissism of minor differences."[4]

While changes such as these are easily lumped together under the umbrella of globalization, this term glosses the terrible price they have exacted from so many throughout the world. People are desperate for certitude in an uncertain world, and absolutisms of almost any kind—right, center, or left; reactionary, traditional, or revolutionary; political, economic, social, or religious—offer the illusion of refuge and reassurance. Whether such conditions will inevitably precipitate the return of new forms of tyranny and oppression, they force us to ask what chances there are for the survival of a view of human beings as potentially capable together, even across immense gulfs of difference, misunderstanding, and grievance, of engaging not in predatory world-rending or world-disordering but in collaborative world-creating and world-extending, in what Jacques Derrida called "mondialization"[5] This is the capacity he believed was endangered by 9/11, and he feared for its recovery in the face of technologies that not only place implements of devastation in the hands of state and non-state actors all too eager to use them, but set off chain reactions, much like the butterfly effect, of reprisals and revenge seemingly without end.

My intention in *Ideas to Die For: The Cosmopolitan Challenge* is to delineate the elements of a pragmatic cosmopolitanism whose commitment to mondialization, to extending the world and the worldwide, matches its commitment to see, if not precisely as others see—which is impossible—then to see as fully as possible what we might see if we could imagine putting ourselves in their place, especially when they see us – which is not impossible. We know—or can know—a good deal more about those we define as "other" or "different" than is assumed either by many of our postmodern epistemologies or by our own indifference or ignorance. The problem is to figure out what we can learn from such knowledge, and this depends far less on accommodating the strangeness of the other to ourselves than on using that same strangeness as a means to confront and possibly revise our own.

"After such knowledge," T. S. Eliot once asked an earlier generation, "what forgiveness?"[6] In light of the grievous injuries caused by subsequent history, we might want to amend that question to read "Before such knowledge, what avowals?" The avowals in this case take the form of a series of issues around which I have organized various chapters in this book, chapters that are intended to move us closer to understanding what, in an era of global absolutisms, a pragmatic cosmopolitanism might look and feel like.

The first issue has to do with what is meant by the "global" itself and whether it represents an actual world process or merely the rationalization for one. Is the word "global" simply a way of flattering those who have the means to move about the world with relative ease, or a description of the frame of reference that more and more of the world's people are forced to use to describe the terms of their own experience, whether that experience is suffered like an affliction, accepted as a responsibility, or embraced as a privilege?

Once this has been clarified, the second problem is what to make of these new absolutisms, religious and secular, that have taken over so much of the global field of discourse, and whether they can be resisted, or at least negotiated with, in any other but the imperious, rigid, and often self-righteous terms they set? The question they pose is whether one can make ultimate sacrifices for any other ideas but those that are assumed to be foundationalist, totalizing, and infallible.

This leads to a third issue, which has to do with how far down into the subsoil of the global the realm of the cultural actually reaches. An issue to which I will be returning throughout this book, I want to explore it here explicitly in terms of the role that culture has played in the recent misshaping of world order led by the Americans.

This fourth issue gives way naturally to a discussion of the relation between absolutism in American religion and the role of religion in American politics, or, rather, the religion that America has tended to make of itself. Why does American religious behavior so easily turn the national imaginary into a religion of righteous imperialism?

The fifth issue pursues the question of religious exceptionalism still further by examining the relationship between America's claims to global uniqueness and its penchant for constructing itself around narratives of war? Why is it so difficult to imagine an American president being re-elected after the loss of a war, and how can narratives of American global identity be constructed without being alternative narratives of war?

The sixth issue then circles back to ask if there are any larger, collective frames of reference that might serve as a check or brake on the hegemonic imaginaries of nation-states. But this raises a further query about what place such transnational constructs reserve for the dimension of the human and the corollary notion of the neighbor.

The seventh issue ultimately attempts to bring the discussion full circle by asking whether questions such as these lead us any closer to discerning the outlines of a new, or at any rate an alternative, kind of world imaginary based at least in part on what the different and the disadvantaged have to teach the rest of us. In what would such a global humanism consist if it is to avoid, on the one side, the risks of solipsism so typical of earlier Western humanisms without becoming susceptible, on the other, to the seductions of relativism or localism so characteristic of more recent international humanisms?

Ideas to Die For: The Cosmopolitan Challenge is composed around these seven issues that illumine what a pragmatic cosmopolitanism might entail. Chapter 1 attempts to reframe the discussion about cosmopolitanism by historicizing some of its global features. To historicize it is not simply to reveal how differently the realm of the global is to be understood if one associates it with the post-World War II compression of space and time as opposed to the formation of the Afro-Eurasian zone of civilization that began to take shape over a period of 4,000 years; it is also to clarify what conceptions not just of time and space but of cultures and civilizations, and of the imagination itself, need to change to accommodate these new understandings.

Chapter 2 then lays out the terms of the overall argument by showing how a pragmatist as opposed to a universalist cosmopolitanism, simultaneously critical and self-reflexive, can be constructed around the heuristic value of the "other" when the notion of the "other" is grounded in a different sense of the worldwide. The sense of the worldwide that I associate with this kind of cosmopolitanism is neither as inclusive as the Stoic embrace of the universal moral community of humankind nor as restricted as Kant's community of individuals who are enabled to step out of their contingent positions and enter a public sphere where they have a right to the free and unrestricted use of their reason. This post-universalistic cosmopolitanism, as some describe it,[7] does, however, assume the possibility of creating public spaces where what is sharable of different peoples' humanity—and clearly not everything of consequence is—can potentially be represented in terms they recognize as their own so long as this does not infringe on the similar rights of others. The difficulty is that it often does, which is why it is so important to cultivate an aptitude for seeing others as they see us and as we might see if we were to exchange places with them, if we were to put their experience on the map of our own self-understanding.

Chapter 3 takes up the question of how to think in a world grown more extremist as well as familiar and seeks to ask whether, in response to new global violences, there are any forms of reflection that can resist the allure of totalizing ideologies. It is my argument that there are—in the development of international human rights from 1945 to the present; in the establishment of the Antarctic Treaty of 1960 that converted an entire continent into a scientific reserve at the height of the Cold War; in the creation of a new national narrative for South Africa that eschewed the politics of victimhood for the politics of reconciliation—and that they reflect a way of thinking that is both anti-essentialist and fallibilist.

Chapter 4 then explores the determinative role that cultural assumptions and values played in the politics that defined—and continue to define—the misnamed "War on Terror." This was, and remains, a war legitimated by the assumption that America was in a position not merely to dictate the conditions and form of its execution but also to refashion realities to support these expectations, and was thus conducted as much by metaphors, images, symbols, tropes, and other figures of speech as by soldiers, weapons, policies, and munitions. Such tactics have left many wondering what to make of new American imperiums that continuously and consciously confuse simulations with facts, symbols with sentiments, artifice with the actual.

Chapters 5 and 6 help clarify this predilection for confusing the fictions of America with the future of the world by detailing how the newest forms of American exceptionalism and absolutism have depended, from long before the administration of President George W. Bush, on the ability, as one of his policy advisors put it, to transform "reality-based communities" into "faith-based communities," a conversion that not only permitted his administration to embark on a global project of revanchism but convinced the country that it could get away with conducting wars on two fronts without anyone actually paying for them.

In the second of these two chapters, I then explore three different kinds of war narratives inspired or threatened by this kind of hubris. The first is a counter-war narrative based on the international human rights revolution that American exceptionalism keeps frustrating by its refusal to recognize crucial elements of it such as the International Criminal Court or, except belatedly, the Convention on Genocide. The second is a potential pro-war narrative that American exceptionalism, bolstered by the Doctrine of Pre-eminence, has written into the "Nuclear Posture Review," a presidential directive that lowers, or now at any rate weakens, the threshold for the use of nuclear weapons. The third is an anti-war narrative that some consider the only hope for any planetary future and is based on the ability of developing a widened and more robust transnational civil society to challenge the prerogatives and policies of a resilient and unrepentant American exceptionalism.

Chapter 7 attempts to deepen the discussion by moving from the national, the international, and the transnational (all subject to the Westphalian system's reliance on regimes of law within and between states) to larger collective frames of reference like the transcivilizational and the intercivilizational, which seem to offer themselves as the only viable source of normative authority not marked by the iron rule of self-interest. But this readjustment of focus can also legitimate new assymetries of power that produce new forms of oppression if it is not grounded on a fresh delineation of the human and the related notion of the neighbor in a global field.

Chapter 8 finally asks whether a new understanding of the human and the neighbor can lead in the direction of an "other," if not a more worldly, humanism. Building on the work of Edward Said, which I bring into conversation with a conservative humanist like George Steiner and a radical humanist like Erich Heller, I attempt to reframe the humanities in a way that shifts its traditional focus from how we read ourselves and others as human to how we read ourselves through the humanity of others. As disciplines of interpretation, the humanities challenge us chiefly not by confirming or reinforcing our sense of ourselves but by putting that sense under some degree of critical pressure. What they seek to help us imagine is what it would be like to think and feel otherwise than we do, to construct an alternative context of experience within which to better comprehend the limitations and inadequacies of our own by attending to the differences between it and the experience of others.[8]

ACKNOWLEDGMENTS

During the course of writing this book, I have accumulated far more debts of assistance, support, and intelligent criticism than I can fully recognize here. Nonetheless, there are a number that are too important to omit. My long absorption with the issues raised in this book has been supported, first and foremost, by my colleagues in Global and International Studies at the University of California, Santa Barbara. They include, from the very beginning, Mark Juergensmeyer and Richard Appelbaum, along with Gurinder Singh Mann and Marguerite Bouraad-Nash, but they were soon joined by Esther Lezra, Aashish Mehta, Richard Falk, Hilal Elver, and then eventually Eve Darian-Smith, Raymond Clemencon, Paul Amar, Alison Brysk, Jan Nederveen Pieterse, Phil McCarty, and Nadege Clitandre. With all of them I have been engaged in an educational and intellectual project that seeks to look beyond conventional academic horizons and begin to explore, and be explored by, worlds elsewhere. Among these colleagues, I owe a very special intellectual debt to Richard Falk from whom I, like so many others, have learned much about what is entailed in attempting to become not just politically but morally accountable to such worlds.

Yet progress on this book would not have been possible without the special friendship and enlightened leadership of Melvin Oliver, Dean of the Social Sciences, who enabled me to keep working on this project amidst heavy administrative responsibilities. I should add that those same responsibilities were made considerably less burdensome and far more enjoyable because of the extraordinary managerial abilities and superb assistance of Cori Montgomery. My two children, Adam and Abigail, have as always provided me with the kind of affectionate and generous, not to say thoughtful and sometimes quizzical, encouragement that inspires me to write, but the book itself would not have taken the form it has, or been completed at all, without the unconditional support, independent thinking and irrepressible candor of my wife, Barbra Gunn, who has given me a new life

I never believed was possible, and so much more, including Sprafkins and Lannins. Dedicating this book to her scarcely does justice to the depth of my gratitude and love.

Along the way I have benefitted enormously from conversations with Emory Elliott, Gunter Lenz, Richard Hecht, Shirley Lim, Ronald Steel, David Palumbo-liu, Gabriele Schwab, Donald Pease, John Carlos Rowe, Isabella Bakker, Stephen Gill, and Michael Jerryson, but no one has shared more acutely my interest in the place of culture in the play of global affairs than my colleague and co-editor, Carl Gutierrez-Jones. Special thanks of a different order are reserved for David Chidester and David Carrasco. Friends of many decades, and each an expert on the inter- and trans-civilizational in historical as well as contemporary perspective, they both played a significant role in assisting me to rethink this book at a crucial stage of its development. At a somewhat later stage in the writing, David Hollinger provided the manuscript with an exceptionally thoughtful reading and made important suggestions for its improvement. And I would be remiss if I didn't also thank Quinn McCreight who helped at the end with proofreading and fact finding. While none of the above bear any responsibility for its deficiencies, they have all helped move this book forward and changed it for the better.

Two events, which framed its initiation and assisted in its completion, deserve special mention. The first was my appointment as a Phi Beta Kappa Lecturer in 2000–2001, which forced me to begin thinking through some of these ideas during visits of at least several days to a number of different college and university campuses in the United States. The challenge and pleasure of these visits was directly related to the fact that they were not sponsored by a single department so much by as an entire institution and therefore required me to explain myself to students and faculty from a variety of different backgrounds and fields. The second was my appointment as a Rockefeller Fellow at its Bellagio Center in the fall of 2010, where I was finally able to begin pulling these ideas together. To anyone fortunate enough to have enjoyed the ideal working conditions and exceptional hospitality and collegiality of the latter, they will appreciate that there are few better places on earth to think and write. Special thanks are due to the Rockefeller Foundation, the Director of the Bellagio Center, Pilar Palacia, and its Residents Assistant, Elena Ongania.

Many of these ideas were first explored with audiences at a number of academic institutions and I am grateful to all for their interest and responses. Those institutions include Indiana University/Purdue University, Sarah Lawrence College, Wake Forest University, the University of Miami, Coral Gables, Rhodes College, the University of the South, Southwestern University, Gustavus Adolphus College, Kalamazoo College, the University of Maine, the University of California, Santa Barbara, the University of Alabama at Tuscaloosa, Stillman College, the University of Capetown, the University of Hong Kong, Bogacizi University in Istanbul, University of Rochester, Macalester College, Carleton College, California Lutheran University, University of California, Riverside, University of Salerno, Bashkent University in Ankara, Fatih University in Istanbul, UCLA, Harvard University, Universidad del

Ceme in Buenos Aires, Rockefeller Study Center in Bellagio, Italy, University of South Florida, Brigham Young University, and Eckerd College.

Earlier versions of material in several of these chapters have been published elsewhere but have here been substantially rewritten. Several paragraphs of Chapter 1 were adapted from my "Introduction" to a special issue of *PMLA* devoted to "Globalizing Literary Studies," *PMLA*, 116/1, 2001, 16–31, for which the Modern Language Association has my thanks. Several pages of Chapter 1 were also published in the "Introduction" to Giles Gunn (ed.), *Global Studies 1*, Dubuque, Iowa: Kendall Hunt Publishing, Co., 2003, ix–xviii. Portions of Chapter 4 are drawn from my "Introduction: The Place of Culture in the Play of International Politics," in Giles Gunn and Carl Gutierrez-Jones (eds.), *America and the Misshaping of a New World Order*, Berkeley: University of California Press, 2010, pp. 1–27, © 2010 by the Regents of the University of California. Reprinted by permission of the University of California Press. Grateful acknowledgement is due to Oxford University Press for permission to republish in Chapter 5 a revised version of "America's Gods," *American Literary History*, 19, Spring 2007, 1–31. Portions of Chapter 6 originally appeared in "War Narratives and American Exceptionalism," in Giles Gunn and Carl Gutierrez-Jones (eds.), *War Narratives and American Culture*, Santa Barbara, CA: American Cultures and Global Contexts Center, 2005, pp. 157–72; permission granted to reprint by the American Cultures and Global Contexts Center of the University of California, Santa Barbara. An earlier and much briefer version of Chapter 7 appeared as "The Trans-civilizational, the Inter-civilizational, and the Human: The Quest for the Normative in the Legitimacy Debate," in Richard Falk, Mark Juergensmeyer, and Vesselin Popovski (eds.), *Legality and Legitimacy in Global Affairs*, New York: Oxford University Press, 2012, pp. 198–215, © Oxford University Press. Reprinted by permission of Oxford University Press, USA. Several pages of Chapter 7 were also published in *The Immanent Frame* to which I am additionally grateful. Portions of Chapter 8, now very substantially revised, were originally published in "On Edward Said," which first appeared in *Raritan*, XXII/4, Spring 2004, 71–8, and I am grateful to *Raritan* for permission to reprint that material here. Additional material from Chapter 8, again much revised, is drawn from "On the New Uses of the 'Secular' and the 'Religious' in Contemporary Criticism: Edward Said, George Steiner, and the Counter-Example of Erich Heller," in Mary Gerhart and Anthony C. Yu (eds.) *Morphologies of Faith: Essays in Religion and Culture in Honor of Nathan A. Scott, Jr.*, Atlanta, GA: Scholars Press, 51–68, with thanks to the American Academy of Religion.

I owe a large debt of gratitude to Craig Fowlie and Nicola Parkin, Editor and Associate Editor, respectively, for Politics and International Affairs at Routledge Press. Their belief in this project has meant a great deal to me, and their thoughtful suggestions have made the book both clearer and stronger. My thanks go as well to Emily Senior, who oversaw the production process, Peter Harris, who stepped in to manage the editorial process, and Rachel Norridge, who improved the manuscript in numerous ways both large and small. It has been a special pleasure to work with a team of people so capable and committed.

ALSO BY GILES GUNN

F.O. Mathiessen: The Critical Achievement
The Interpretation of Otherness: Literature, Religion, and the American Imagination
The Culture of Criticism and the Criticism of Culture
Thinking Across the American Grain: Ideology, Intellect, and the New Pragmatism
Beyond Solidarity: Pragmatism and Difference in a Globalized World

Edited titles

Literature and Religion
Henry James, Senior: A Selection of His Writings
New World Metaphysics: Readings on the Religious Meaning of the American Experience
The Bible and American Arts and Letters
Church, State, and American Culture
Redrawing the Boundaries: The Transformation of English and American Literary Studies (with Stephen J. Greenblatt)
Early American Writing
Pragmatism and Other Writings by William James
War Narratives and American Culture (with Carl Gutierrez-Jones)
A Historical Guide to Herman Melville
America and the Misshaping of a New World Order (with Carl Gutierrez-Jones)

1

INTRODUCTION

Mapping and remapping the global

> The temptation not only to put one's own land in the center of the map, but one's own people in the center of history, seems to be universal.
>
> Marshall G. S. Hodgson, *Rethinking World History*

The terms "global" and "globalization" are fraught with so many complications and confusions that one almost wishes one could substitute others in their place. As now used, globalization conjures up in many minds a spectacle of instantaneous electronic financial transfers, the amoral operations of the capitalist free-market, the erasure of local cultural differences, and the expansion of Western, but most especially American, power. This is hardly an attractive prospect, and when it is coupled with increasing economic inequality throughout the world, continuing degradation of the environment, heightened rivalry among ethnic groups, spreading militarism, the expansion of religious and other nationalisms, normalization of the use of terror, the proliferation of weapons of mass destruction, and other ills, globalization has become associated in many minds with some of the most destructive forces on the planet. In the minds of many of its critics, from Zygmunt Bauman and John Gray to Joseph Stiglitz, Fredric Jameson, and Masao Miyoshi, it has led to the erasure of local differences as well as the integration of more and more of the world's people, as indeed of entire states, into a geopolitical system that inevitably erodes the ability of all but the most privileged to have any influence on their own futures.[1]

In the face of such a prospect, it is small comfort to learn that globalizing trends since World War II have also, by some accounts, made possible a threefold increase in the world's per capita income, reduced by half the number of people living in direst poverty, reinforced the desire to work for nuclear disarmament, helped expand the environmental movement, and encouraged the creation of literally thousands of international groups and non-governmental organizations (NGOs) devoted to addressing various social, political, and economic grievances and the relief of human suffering generally.[2] Yet despite such developments (and sometimes, paradoxically, even because of them), the gap between rich and poor in the world is being widened still further by the forces of economic as well as political and cultural globalization, and these forces, largely but not exclusively reflecting until recently the dominance of the United States and its rich allies in the global North, will have to be addressed if the situation is not to reach catastrophic proportions. As long ago as 1999, the United Nations Development Program asserted that if such developments were not to produce increasing polarization that in the short term benefits only the US and other members mainly of the G7 or the G20, and in the long run virtually no one, the restructuration of "global governance," as the report called it, would have to be accompanied by more massive and efficient debt relief for insolvent nations, the redirection of aid to the poorest countries, the reform of resource allocation of the world's limited resources, the reduction of corruption in countries where economic mismanagement discourages foreign investment, and the redress of continual violations of human rights. But the restructuring of global governance will also have to include reforms far more subtle, such as an alteration of the lenses by and through which cultures perceive one another and an enhancement of opportunities for more and more of the world's people, as well as sovereign states, to shape their own destinies.

However, before we venture too many generalizations about a worldwide process that in its latest phases is changing at a pace rapidly approaching what feels like warp speed, it is important to dispel a few myths about the words "globalization" and the "global" themselves. We can begin by conceding that the term "globalization" is commonly used to refer to the widening and deepening and speeding up of the interconnectedness of the world in many of its aspects, from the economic to the ecological, the cultural to the criminal, the social to the spiritual, the environmental to the pathogenic, but there are still vigorous disputes with very large consequences about just when globalization began, how it is best conceptualized, what its causal dynamics and structural features are, and whether it has, or has not, been good for the world and its peoples. About the only thing on which most students of the term "globalization" are agreed is that it refers to a set of processes by which the world is being threaded ever more tightly together, by which the world is becoming, if not a single place with systematic properties, then an interconnected system of localities whose fate is even more complexly, if also unpredictably, intertwined.[3]

Manfred Steger has combined something of both perspectives in what is probably the most economical definition of globalization as "the expansion and intensification of social relations and consciousness across world-time and world-space."[4] Comprised as much by patterns of transmission, dispersion, exchange, and interconnection that are political, economic, and social but also cultural and historical, globalization refers to a world whose elements and forms are frequently both concatenated, as in an erector set or a Ferris wheel, and polythetic, as in Wittgenstein's concept of family resemblances that describe classes of things whose members are not identical but merely similar. Hence this is neither a system whose parts are all equal or whose movements are all coordinated. If it is a system whose components are multiple and often interactive in unforeseen ways, it is not a system whose components are all interdependent.

Part of this inequity within the global system itself is caused by the different but related system with which it exists in tension and which was created as a result of the Peace of Westphalia in 1648. The Westphalian system, which came into being in the 150 years following the Peace, assumes instead that the world is less a structure of interrelated processes operating in different ways at all levels of experience—and whose constant formations, deformations, and reformations deepen and extend global interconnectivity and conflict—than an association of territorially bounded states claiming sovereignty within their own realm, which renders the system itself vulnerable to the assymetries of power. And with the rise of newer forms of coercive legitimacy, such as capitalism, nationalism, imperialism, colonialism, liberalism, and democracy, not to say socialism, communism, and fascism, the Westphalian system has been rendered still more unstable by forces that were no longer exclusively political. Hence while globalization has not, as some of its most vocal apologists maintain,[5] shattered, much less displaced, the Westphalian system, it has seriously challenged it through the global changes in ideological consciousness that have accompanied it.

But this in turn suggests that the corollary term "global" should not be assumed to represent some seamless whole or unified totality. The term "global" functions merely to suggest the reach and resonance of those processes by which the world is continuously being reconceived and remade as an almost infinitely intricate, but at the same time frequently disjunctive, organism that continues to remain a good deal more than the simple sum of its individual parts. The term "global" did not achieve its meteoric rise until the mid-1980s, when it began to displace cognate terms like "international" and "international relations." Those earlier terms had come into usage toward the end of the eighteenth century to signal the emergence of what in retrospect appears to have been a new world order where territorial nation-states now began to assume responsibility for organizing socio-political and cultural processes and the path was laid for what some call the modern era. But now, at the end of the twentieth century and the beginning of the twenty-first, the ascendancy of the terms "global" and "globalization" seem to forecast the arrival of still another world order, and this time one marked by a reduction rather than expansion of the power of "nation-states" as individuals and communities gain access to sources of information and power that are globally disseminated and thus bypass many of the traditional controls of the political state.

Yet this implies—or at least could imply—that the process of world-making, or re-making, known as globalization, is of comparatively recent vintage, having accelerated to its present velocity only, perhaps, because of the end of the Cold War and the disintegration of the Soviet Union, or, earlier, with the emergence of postmodernism at the end of the 1960s and the beginning of the 1970s.[6] But a number of thinkers push the date of this most recent and vigorous surge of globalization back a good many decades to the beginning of the modern era in the middle of the nineteenth century, when industrial capitalism fueled the original expansion of European nation-states and those nation-states then undertook to acquire and consolidate colonial empires.[7] Other scholars and theorists move the origins of what we call globalization back still further to the Early Modern period, when Europe commenced its initial exploration of the rest of the globe and embarked simultaneously on the development of early world trade.[8]

Those who associate the origins of globalization with this first European Age of Exploration and Discovery are also likely to assume that when the "modern world system," as Immanuel Wallerstein has termed it, first took shape in the early 1600s, it was essentially an economic rather than political system and was built around a series of core states characterized by aggressive commercial growth, strong governmental structures, and a powerful sense of national identity, all of which permitted them to control, for their own benefit, the evolution of those weaker states and regions of the world that developed on their peripheries. Yet even then, in the seventeenth century, it was soon to become apparent that an emergent modern world system based on an extensive system of commodity exchange was also becoming linked as well by systems of exchange that were cultural and symbolic. Just as ideas and ideologies were being traded along with goods, so the new wealth thus accumulated was being defined not only by the size of capital reserves and sailing fleets but also by the production of commodities like buildings, monuments, and paintings reflective of new styles both of affluence and of taste. Commerce, in other words, was going cultural.

This is not, of course, how Wallerstein and other world systems analysts view the matter. While theorists like Roland Robertson, Malcolm Waters, Arjun Appadurai, Frederick Buell, and Manfred Steger have insisted that globalization has always involved interchanges that were symbolic as well as political, discursive as well as economic, Wallerstein has long maintained that even if cultural forms and practices have reinforced this system since it was created, they were only a subsidiary influence in its formation.[9] There is, however, some indication that Wallerstein has begun to modify his position. In response to charges that this conception of the world system is too economistic, together with his more recent assessment that the system may well be on the verge of collapse in the next half century, Wallerstein now concedes that culture plays a much larger role in creating distinctions in cultures as well as between them, though in both these instances he maintains that culture retains its function of mystifying people about the operations of the system itself.[10] For this reason, he maintains that all attempts to resist the system simply help to keep it in place.

The problem is that Wallerstein's view of the way that globalization potentially co-opts even its own critics oversimplifies it by radically foreshortening and consequently misreading its history. Evidence of a world system linking commerce with culture can be found as early as the thirteenth and fourteenth centuries, according to Janet Abu-Lughod, and, more importantly, its origins and trajectory were not European at all but Chinese and Middle Eastern.[11] Indeed, Amartya Sen traces the emergence of such an arc running from East to West rather than, as "world system's theorists contend, West to East, as early as the year 1000."[12] And Joseph Needham has documented numerous inventions, besides the better known magnetic compass, gunpowder, and printing press, that made their way west from China between the first and eighth centuries, which include the crossbow, efficient harness, suspension bridge, cast iron, paper, porcelain, and stern-post rudder.[13] But earliest evidence of cultural and symbolic as well as commercial exchanges spanning out in a global direction can be detected, as a matter of fact, nearly 3,000 years before the creation of any of the so-called modern world systems.

Historians William H. McNeill and Marshall G. S. Hodgson have demonstrated, for example, that an Afro-Eurasian zone of civilization first came into existence over a period of something like a thousand years beginning two millennia before the commencement of the Common Era.[14] Organized initially around four central areas—the northern shores of the Mediterranean, the Fertile Crescent in the Middle East, the Hindu-Kush Range and valleys of the Indus and Ganges rivers, and the Hoang-Ho and Yangtze valleys in China—this zone of civilization was eventually to stretch from the shores of the Atlantic to the waters of the Pacific and the China Sea. Propelled initially by little more than the accumulation of small developments in trade, warfare, governance, religion, and exploration that occasionally enabled people to overcome their natural suspicion of alien ways and begin to reach out toward one another, such contacts were eventually to facilitate not only the exchange of merchandise, services, and technologies but also the much slower, still more consequential transmission of ideas, institutions, customs, diets, rituals, and languages. Such transmissions were, of course, to a considerable degree dependent not simply on the material need for goods or the practical needs of security and survival, but also on the symbolic capacity to create and inhabit, as well as to challenge and revise, symbolic universes of shared, or, at any rate, sharable meaning.[15] Whether such symbolic capacities were, as McNeill now thinks of them, first set in motion by the invention of rhythmic voicing and dance (the progenitors of poetry and perhaps other kinds of symbolic action),[16] "contacts with strangers," as he noted in a retrospective essay on *The Rise of the West* 25 years after its original publication, "is the major motor of social change."[17] This helps explain how cultural conflicts, interactions, and transformations during this long process of development were often to prove as, and sometimes more, fateful than economic or political ones—if only because the former have so frequently determined the way the latter could be understood and actualized. What was in play was not simply people's understanding of others but their understanding of themselves.

As it happens, this history by which the world has, for several thousand years, been continuously woven and rewoven into an increasingly interlinked and often inter-reliant assemblage of life-systems is not one to which, until very recently, the humanities have paid much attention. For all of the relatively recent interest in, say, histories of slavery and racism, or imperialism, or colonialism, or ethnicity, or diasporas, or even sexism, or of our earlier disciplinary involvements in such fields as comparative literature, world history, and the history of religions, or, for that matter, our pedagogical commitment to language programs (the latter of which deserve credit for keeping the possibility of globalism alive even if they could not provide a model for its full conceptualization), globalization is still too often viewed merely as a temporary geopolitical and economic development or as a passing academic fad, and is consequently assessed chiefly in terms of what is taken to be its liabilities and banalities.

Thus despite questions about globalization's evolution and subsequent historicization, or about its varied and complex form and function in different locales, or its association with other historical phenomena, globalization itself is clearly here to stay, no matter how much its contemporary expressions are certain to change. The intellectual challenge is not so much to decide whether globalization and the global deserve to be taken seriously but how best to engage them critically—how, in other words, to assess their implications and consequences, without in the process legitimating their most problematic features. The central questions to be asked, therefore, take a variety of different forms: What are the forces that have brought the world itself into being as an interactive, ever-changing structure of processes and practices? What forms has that densely concatenated, diversely elaborated structure taken over time? What fresh light do such forms, and the factors that bring them into being, throw on such issues as personal and cultural identity formation, mass migration, international terrorism, practices of child rearing, religious violence, human rights reform, the status of women and children, scientific and medical practice, the regulation of international stock markets, the digitalization of information, culinary, and dietary habits, and the new ubiquity of the aesthetic? Is there such a thing as a global perspective? In this new, more global era, has humanity taken on new cosmopolitan forms of expression? To help humanize and manage this new world order, can we develop something like a global parliament of the peoples that can speak to rather than for states?

The answers to such questions will not, and do not, come easily but the questions themselves become more pressing every day. To gain a critical purchase on them, much less to begin to formulate plausible answers to some of them, will require something more than an admission that we now live in a world created by globalizing forces. In addition, it necessitates an understanding that we shall have to develop a new optics for bringing those forces into focus, new histories to understand their provenance and governance, and a new ethics for critically engaging them.

Not least among the challenges to be faced will be the abandonment of some old intellectual habits and the acquisition of several new ones. Among the first to go should be the defense of that barrier both within the academy and outside that currently divides what are thought of as the social sciences from what people like to think of as the humanities. This barrier is not only anachronistic but in many ways indefensible, since its transgression, subversion, and reconstruction has been one of the central intellectual achievements on both sides of this disciplinary divide. During the last several decades, we have witnessed, as a case in point, not only "the humanistic refiguration of social thought," as the anthropologist Clifford Geertz once famously termed it,[18] but also what might be described as a sociopolitical refiguration of humanistic thought, and yet this important conceptual revisioning has done comparatively little, at least at the level of advanced scholarship, to change the way that knowledge is structured or pursued. In most institutions of higher learning, we still divide the College of Arts and Sciences, or its equivalent, into artificial compounds that wall off the so-called harder natural and physical sciences, like Biology, Chemistry, and Physics, from the so-called softer human sciences, like the humanities and the social sciences, and then segregate the latter two from each other on the pretext that the humanities deal with values while the social sciences concern themselves with facts.

Next to go will have to be the practice of thinking primarily in terms of relatively stable entities to be studied, whether they be traditions, periods, institutions, practices, texts, careers, genres, or what-have-you instead of processes, movements, flows to be followed, in manifold directions, at varying degrees of speed, with differing consequences, in specific sites and particular moments. Little can be understood with any degree of accuracy that does not take account of variables such as these and others. But this in turn suggests that our procedures for mapping such developments and their interconnections must change. If global studies is to be something more than a history of globalization, it will have to become genuinely interdisciplinary. Interdisciplinarity, however, is more than a simple practice of redefining one field or method in the image of some other; it is also about what gets reconceptualized in the process. Part of what gets reconceptualized is the way such "transversals," to borrow Roland Barthes's useful term, change the ways these newly reconfigured disciplines makes sense of themselves to themselves.[19] But the corollary of this revision of disciplinary sense-making is that such conversions alter the way each discipline now represents its own knowledge to itself. Thus interdisciplinarity turns out to involve a more drastic and sometimes intellectually destabilizing process than is often understood. What is at issue in such redrawings of the disciplinary map is more than the disciplines themselves and the knowledges they map. What gets altered are the principles of mapping themselves, the way we think about thinking.[20]

Thus where before it was presumed that flows, whether cultural, demographic, financial, or ideological were primarily linear, uniform, and mostly regular, we now appreciate that their operations are better comprehended on the model of a fractal whose patterns can be irregular, haphazard, and multi-directional.[21] We have also come to understand that the arrangement of such processes can be overlapping and imbricated, or, as biologists say, polythetic. Moreover, we now clearly grasp that many changes of a historical nature seem to exhibit what chaos theorists call "the butterfly effect" where, because of the sensitive dependence of certain organisms or phenomena on initial conditions, infinitesimal alterations in complex structures can sometimes produce consequences out of all proportion to their initial causes.

Still a third habit that must be discarded in the social sciences as well as the humanities is our tendency to conceive of cultures, like identities, as homogenous, monolithic, and easily discriminable. Just as globalization has revealed that cultures have the capacity to move across national borders, to adapt to different local conditions, and to recombine, mutate, and re-circulate through various media, so we now assume that the cultural in this context also refers to those assemblages of felt meaning by which people caught up in the webbing of these networks and formations have made sense of their lived experience. Hence the *global* and the *cultural* thus possess a symbiotic relationship or, as we say, are joined at the hip. The global represents in the most general sense that field on which culture exercises itself as an interpretive technology. The cultural represents the instrumentalities by which the global is made more legible or readable and hence intelligible.

A fourth habit in need of rejection is the predisposition to periodize by centuries, as though the life of time can be measured everywhere and at all times in segments of one hundred years. Change occurs at different rates of speed in different cultures and at different moments; shifts in style as well as thought, like the movements of people and the development or reform of institutions, finds or establishes its own pace, and not always according to the calendar but by means of temporal calculuses that are more unruly and diverse. The year 1789 when the French Revolution took place compresses time. The reign of the Tokugawa Shogunate in Japan that ended so abruptly after 250 years with the arrival of Commodore Perry's black ships in 1853 had attempted through Japan's enforced isolation to extend time, as it were, indefinitely. Various populations in the Middle East organize time, not in relation to decades or centuries as we do in the United States, but in relation to the collapse of the Caliphate or the end of the Ottoman Empire.

But if time in effect moves at different rates of speed in different places for different peoples in relation to different trajectories of hope, possibility, custom, and coercion, so place is also a more elastic and unwieldy category than is typically acknowledged. While the city as center has defined the sense of place in many historical communities throughout the world—this imagery is still used in world systems theory to describe the relations between core and periphery—the state and the nation have more recently usurped it as the principal marker of space. But state and nation are now themselves subjected to the ever-shifting coordinates of geographical definition as, on the one hand, states lose much of their definitional outline in the marketplace or the formation of new trans-state organizations like the European Union and, on the other, nations like the United States extend both their hegemony and presence throughout the world through the creation of over 750 military bases, where American territorial sovereignty rules. Merely think of what was involved when the Soviet Union collapsed and 27 states, along with hundreds of communities defining themselves as distinct nationalities, were set free of imperial ligatures that for nearly half a century had held them all together.

But even here—and one could multiply examples *ad infinitum* in East Asia, the Indonesian archipelago, particular regions of the African continent, or the Central Asian plateau—the topography of space conforms to large geopolitical structures. Yet space has not always been so conceived by people and societies that have grown up along river systems or developed their lives in mountain, plain, desert, or forest regions. Then, too, there is the great company of nomadic peoples throughout history, or the equally large group of people in modern times who have been displaced by events beyond their own control and rendered refugees who simply migrate, if they are lucky, from one placeless locale to another. While it becomes less and less likely that any people in the world now live utterly remote from, or untouched by, processes that are in some sense or other global, the fact remains that there are hundreds of millions of people in the world who go about their daily tasks with virtually no active conception of the geographies—urban, national, regional, continental, civilizational—by which we normally delineate space and place. Thus our maps, like our clocks, need to be recalibrated if we are to grasp the way time and space actually function in the life of many of the world's peoples. The geographer David Harvey has said it with his usual succinctness:

> Most of the hegemonic social theories ... that have shaped dominant interpretations and political practices ... over the last three hundred years ... have paid little or no critical attention to how the production of spaces, places, and environments might impinge upon thought and action. In practice, we almost everywhere find tacit assumptions about the nature of space and time, the cohesion of places (the nation-state), and the idea of what is or is not given by nature. ... The effect is like trying to navigate the world with any old map, no matter how arbitrary or erroneous it may be.[22]

Last but not least, if globalization has rendered cultures and the forms and practices that characterize them more mobile and malleable as well as diverse, enabling them to travel across traditional borders and help create and sustain translocal senses of identity, it has also freed the faculty of the imagination, always a potent, if still too often undervalued, force in historical life, to become a principal agent in the construction and reconstruction of the global world itself. By this I mean that we now think and feel in this new informational age as never before in forms whose origination is aesthetic and whose chief material is composed of images, rituals, narratives, ceremonies, myths, music, and performances. Too often associated merely with escape, entertainment, or pure fantasy, the imagination now plays an even larger role in social construction than it has in the past.[23] In addition to possessing the power it has always displayed in peoples' stories, dramas, dances, paintings, and constructions to help them make sense out of the sense of their lives, it has now come to acquire, with the increasingly rapid spread of mass culture, the power to influence, if not determine, not just the kinds of lives people wish to live with themselves but also with others. Hence we shall neither understand how in the past the global has lived its life through time, nor in the present how time itself has become ever more globalized, until we come to terms with the way the imagination has attempted, and continues to attempt, to turn the other logics of life—capital, politics, religion, society—into the shape of its own geographies of desire and discontent.

Benedict Anderson first brought the imagination directly into the sphere of political and social interpretation through his study of nations as "imagined communities."[24]

Cornelius Castoriadis extended such analysis to the imaginative foundation of all societies and turned the notion of the "imaginary" into one of the indispensable terms of intellectual analysis.[25] Johann P. Arnason, Randall Collins, and Chris Rumford have applied this conception to the broader field of civilizations, which they view as overlapping fields of attraction, tension, and repulsion based on multiple and often conflicting frameworks of interpretation that can be appropriated in different ways by social actors both within and outside of particular civilizational complexes.[26] The point to be noted is that the positions in dispute, no less than the interactions among them, are constructed out of, and propelled by, logics of the imagination as much as they are by logics of capital, politics, religion, or any other regime of power and authority because the interpretive energies and capacities of the imagination so often determine the way other logics can be construed and employed.

And so it is with cosmopolitanism or, rather, cosmopolitanisms, which are best understood not in terms of the ideas with which they are associated but the problems with which they have grappled and the aspirations that have propelled them.[27] These aspirations by no means conform to a single pattern any more than they can be understood as responses to a common set of issues. What marks them is the conviction that change depends not on set judgment or belief but on the dialectic of imagined needs that contrast with actual conditions: "It is by a sense of possibilities opening before us that we become aware of constrictions that hem us in and of burdens that oppress."[28] John Dewey's words from *Art as Experience* serve as a reminder that the imagination serves most often as the bridge between individual forms of consciousness and collective modes of mentality. At the same time they raise a question about how exactly this bridge operates and what its traffic consists of.

Dewey's answer, which has large implications for a cultural and civilizational understanding of the global, requires that we dissociate the notion of mind or mindsets, as of consciousness, from any conception of a self-contained entity within the head and thus isolated from the world of persons, processes, and events.[29] Dewey viewed the mind and more general mindsets, like Gilbert Ryle after him, as dispositional in nature and thus best conceived of as a series of capacities, propensities, inclinations, habits, and proclivities rather than a specific set of abilities or ideas.[30] The mind for Dewey was at once cognitive, affective, and volitional; it is a faculty that comes into play and is modified in every interaction between the self and its environment or world. "Whenever anything is undergone in consequence of a doing," Dewey wrote, there is an acquisition not only of new aptitudes and skills but of new "attitudes and interests ... which embody in themselves some deposit of the meaning of things done and undergone."[31] Such deposits of meaning eventually accumulate to become part of the self, its "capital," as it were, on which it draws in all its future contacts with what comprises the environment or world around it. Dewey was thus inclined to view the mind as a kind of background against which the self projects all its relations with the world and in light of which the self is disposed to act in all its future contacts with the world. Yet this metaphor could be misleading unless it was remembered that this background is never entirely fixed but always changing because "in the projection of the new upon it, there is assimilation and reconstruction of both background and what is taken in and digested."[32]

Defining mind in these dynamic terms, Dewey differentiated it from consciousness by arguing that mind refers to the whole funded system of meanings that define the self's dispositional composition, its system of operative or potentially operable meanings, whereas consciousness refers merely to those meanings of which the self is aware, the much more restricted field of apprehended meanings. Mind, therefore, represented to him something contextual and enduring, "a constant luminosity," consciousness of something specific and intermittent, "a series of flashes of varying intensities." While mind extended beyond any individual instantiations of consciousness to the structures of intelligibility that allowed it to make sense, very much like the narrative frame of a story lends coherence and significance to a series of events whose meaning and import would otherwise be lost to us, consciousness could be likened to "the occasional interception of messages continually transmitted" by a "mechanical receiving device [which] selects a few of the vibrations with which the air is filled and renders them audible."[33]

Mind, as Dewey conceived it, changes only slowly, as external circumstances and individual interest compel modifications in the organized body of meanings and aptitudes that dispose the self to respond this way rather than that in the face of new experience, whereas consciousness changes rapidly, since it results from the interaction of a formed disposition and an immediate situation. In relation to mind, then, consciousness "is that phase of a system of meanings which at a given time is undergoing redirection, transitive formation." In relation to consciousness, mind is that "continuum of meaning in process of formation" that binds the intermittent and discrete perceptions of which we are aware at any one time into a cognitively significant series."[34] From this, Dewey rightly concluded that the mind is susceptible to disruption and reorganization in a way that consciousness is not. Destabilize the mind's amorphous but also structured "idea of order" and the whole edifice of thought is potentially endangered, even, perhaps, the constituents of the thinkable. Disrupt consciousness, on the other hand, and what is altered is nothing more than "a particular state of awareness *in its immediacy*."[35]

Such reflections go a long way toward explaining how conscious expressions of thought and feeling are upheld and sustained, not only for individuals but also for cultures, by a larger horizon of mentality and its architecture, but they leave unexplained how the mind, whether individual or collective, responds to the experiences presented to it for disposition. What is the mechanism—we would now call it the software—that enables the mind to assist the self, society, or culture in adjusting its relations with the world it experiences and at the same time develop and change itself as a result of the self's or the society's or culture's experience?

The answer, which Dewey himself could not quite formulate, but a later generation of aesthetic philosophers and cultural theorists from Ernst Cassirer and Susanne K. Langer to Kenneth Burke maintained after her, is that the mind works by translating experiences into symbols which then provide the material for thought and the motivation for action. Essential to both thought and action, symbolization turns the mind into what Langer called a "great transformer," which changes the character of "the current of experience that passes through it, ... not through the agency of the sense by which the perception entered, but by virtue of a primary use which is made of it immediately; it is sucked into the stream of symbols which constitute the human mind."[36]

If these observations tell us anything, they confirm the fact that what Dewey called the mind, and we might describe as thinking, operates on every level of culture, from the intellectually recondite to the subconsciously diffuse, and is to be identified with that continuum of meaningful symbolic activity that enables the self or social group to manage its contacts with the world around it by translating those contacts into construable signs, signs that simultaneously permit the self "to synthesize, delay and modify [its] reactions" to "the gaps and confuses of [its] experience, and by means of these 'signs' to add the experience of other people to [its] own."[37] For another, they allow us to see that if the mind enables human beings to seek a measure of control over their experience by producing symbolic versions of it, culture can be understood as that continually expanding web of symbolic constructions that human beings use to achieve such control hermeneutically. What culture supplies the mind is that set of more or less public and approved versions of human experience that have, for the present, proved efficacious and are thus now available for further use as part of the operative system of meanings of which the mind is a repository. What mind provides culture are the instrumentalities for constantly retesting, modifying, and expanding its networks of operative symbolic meanings so that selves and societies can more effectively negotiate their relations with national, regional, and global surrounds by interpreting them. Culture is therefore no supplement of the mind but an ingredient within it without being identical with it.

But if culture is to be distinguished from mind, so it needs to be differentiated as well from society. Where culture refers to the ordered system of symbolic meaning and significance in terms of which social interaction occurs, society refers to the patterns and imaginaries of social interactions themselves. The relations between culture and society could thus be described, to use Clifford Geertz's distinction, as independently variable but mutually interdependent. Each operates according to its own principle of integration—culture by processes that are more "logical-meaningful," society by processes that are more "causal-functional."[38] But this neat differentiation has been complicated in a world where the business of culture, along with the culture of business, is taking over more and more of the definition and management of both the social and the political. In many of its more predatory geopolitical and market forms, globalization tends to view the social as a mere subset of the cultural, and the local and the global are then reduced to mere counters in a stale game. Cosmopolitanism seeks to recalibrate this game by breaking up the symbiotic and simulated relations of the global and the local, the cultural and the social, the ideological and the subjective, on behalf of extending the worldwide in a direction more humane, or at least less unjust and oppressive, for all. This calls for better cartographies, subtler maps, and more sensitive global navigation systems. Yet as various social, economic, political, and semiotic divides deepen, and the cultural and civilizational imaginaries we have available to us continue to harden, coarsen, or wear out, where are we going to find the better cartographies, subtler maps, more sensitive global navigation systems to prevent them from growing even more ossified? How are we to learn to think and feel not simply about others, or even for them, but with others in the face of global architectures that have become ossified, callous, or obsolete? This is one of the great intellectual and moral tasks that awaits us in the coming century and is taken up in the next chapter.

2

BEING OTHER-WISE

Cosmopolitanism and its discontents

> O wad some Pow'r the giftie gie us
> To see ourselves as others see us!
>
> Robert Burns, "To a Louse" (circa 1785)

"Cosmopolitanism" is a word in bad odor in many parts of the world because it is assumed that citizens do, or at any rate should, share a single socio-cultural identity that is based on a common framework of principles, objectives, and biases. Moreover, it is often believed in addition that this common framework of standards and aims, all upheld by a shared structure of rights and privileges, should be reflected in the congruence between the views of their leaders and of the citizens themselves. There is nothing particularly unusual about these ideas since, with several amendments contributed by nationalism, they constitute basic elements of the Westphalian theory of state identity that is taken in most parts of the world to constitute a territorially bounded sovereign community. Yet this same logic has been strongly challenged throughout the world by a contrary set of beliefs that assume that shared identity is not given but constructed, that most people belong to more than one community of identity at a time, that the sovereignty of states is currently declining rather than increasing, and that national communities, and even hegemons like the United States, are locked in webs of regional and global governance and interdependence.

In theoretical terms, cosmopolitanism is situated between these two positions, the first national, the second global. On the one hand, it recognizes the increasing interconnectedness of political communities in various domains—social, economic, environmental, religious, military, cultural—and encourages the development of understanding overlapping problems that require collective if not necessarily identical solutions, whether regional, local, national, or global. On the other, it celebrates difference, diversity, hybridity, and the need to learn how to reason from the perspective of others, while conceding that multiculturalism as presently understood needs to be revised if we are to elude the dangers of essentialism (my identity is primordial and goes all the way down) on the one side or the perils of reductionism (there are only so many identities possible in the nation-state and this isn't one of them) on the other.[1] What cosmopolitanism then offers is a middle path between the two movements that it views with considerable suspicion—ethnocentric nationalism in the first instance and particularistic multiculturalism in the second. What it assumes is the complexity of affiliations, meaningful attachments, and multiple allegiances to issues, people, places, institutions, regions, and traditions that lie beyond the boundaries of resident nation-states, and the need to create a politics commensurate with this vision of things.

In actual terms, however, cosmopolitanism is a good deal more varied and problematic. Its variations are reflected in the ways cosmopolitanism is often qualified, using such adjectival modifiers as "vernacular," "reflexive," "situated," "discrepant," "patriotic," "realistic," "emancipatory," "working-class," "critical," "thick," or "thin."[2] But such qualifiers also reflect a desire to differentiate contemporary cosmopolitanisms from their more universalistic and Eurocentric forebears and to indicate that they do not apply equally to all people in all situations. This is most obvious in the case of those whose cosmopolitanism of whatever kind is not willed but imposed, not selected but suffered, including migrants, refugees, exiles, the jobless, the homeless, and others who are displaced by globalizing forces and thus experience cosmopolitanism and all it brings with it as a burden or affliction. It is less obvious, and generally less onerous, for many others who experience cosmopolitanism as related in part to the way their horizons of understanding, not to say the conditions of daily life, are being expanded by an increasing awareness of global perils and problematics. Nuclear proliferation, international terrorism, economic instability, climate change, international drug cartels, transnational sex trafficking, desertification, water shortages, the obsession with sustainability, and even the inability of states to deal with natural calamities of which the world as a whole has been made more aware—Hurricane Katrina, the Asian tsunami, flooding in Pakistan—widen everyone's sense of the new ways they have been made vulnerable in a continuously globalizing world. People now live surrounded by hazards that no longer possess a local habitation or a name. The phrase "community of fate" now refers not only to groups of people who suddenly find their futures mutually implicated in the resolution of some temporary social emergency, such as the Severe Acute Respiratory Syndrome (SARS) that broke out in Hong Kong in 2003, but entire global populations, such as those living in low-lying countries or on coastal plains that could easily be threatened within only a matter of decades or less by the continual melting of polar ice caused by the international inability or reluctance to reduce carbon emissions. Horizons have expanded, peoples' sense of the world has broadened and been complicated, because of a deepening realization that they live in something less like a society at risk than a world at risk.

This global re-thematization of the boundaries of people's lives in many parts of the world is surely one of the forms that cosmopolitanism currently takes. Call it, if you will, cosmopolitanism by default; it is indisputably one of the ways that any who are sensible of a world beyond the framework of their own immediate existence experience its reality.[3] While this is a far cry from the kind of cosmopolitanism that Craig Calhoun dismisses as "the class consciousness of frequent travelers," it is apparent that frequent travelers are no more successful than anyone else in escaping some of its consequences.[4] But the consequences, even when they are acknowledged, are clearly not sensed or suffered equally, which is why many theorists shy away from the blanket use of a term that conceals and sometimes distorts as much as it reveals. Calhoun himself is prepared to use the term but only if it is decoupled from the neoliberal capitalist inequities, Western bias, and resistance to radical change with which its many current forms are so often linked. "It needs to approach both cross-cultural relations and the construction of social solidarities with a deeper recognition of diverse starting points and potential outcomes."[5]

David Harvey is suspicious that the new cosmopolitanism is "nothing other than an ethical and humanitarian mask for hegemonic neoliberal practices of class domination and financial and militaristic imperialism," though he is not unsympathetic to the project of a "subaltern cosmopolitanism" if it is informed by geographical, anthropological, and ecological understanding.[6] Timothy Brennan has argued that contemporary cosmopolitanism is in fact inimical to the interests of states still in formation out of the ruins of colonial regimes and often too deeply in thrall to the expansionist policies of the United States and other world powers.[7] Chantal Mouffe finds the whole cosmopolitan project anti-political because it fosters consensuality without contestation, politics without antagonism.[8] While Mouffe does not dispute the fact that any new world order depends on shared ethical-political values such as liberty, equality, and democracy, she is insistent that this consensus reflect the multipolar character of a world where different versions of such a consensus can be debated and rejected.

Less severe in their critique about the possibility of a cosmopolitan framework or outlet, but no less circumspect in their judgments about the shortcoming of contemporary versions, are Homi Bhabha and Paul Gilroy. Bhabha contrasts neoliberal cosmopolitanism with a vernacular cosmopolitanism that focuses on minoritarian perspectives that assert a "right to difference in equality."[9] This is a perspective shaped less by common identities or shared affiliations than by shared practices and ethical commitments—the creation of new forms of representation, accountability, recognition, and cooperation across lines of difference—and is deeply informed by some of the ideas of the American poet Adrienne Rich. Rich argues for the necessity proposed elsewhere in this book of learning how to renarrativize common histories from the starting points of others, to resituate ourselves in the geographies and temporalities of different people, and, indeed, to discover ourselves in their stories as well as our own.

From a perspective no less influenced by the experience of colonialism, Paul Gilroy similarly wonders what kind of alternative cosmopolitanisms will make it possible to live together decently on a deeply divided planet and concludes that it will have to be a vernacular cosmopolitanism from below that sees colonialism as the other side of modernity and replaces the overly exploited and exhausted terms of "multiculturalism" or a Westcentric "globalization" with the ideas of *conviviality* and *planetarity*.[10] Conviviality is associated with the way the "outside" of, in this case, Europe—"strangers, aliens, and blacks"[11]—have in truth lived on the inside of their societies and helped make them what they are. Far from rendering colonial history external to contemporary European history, Europe's colonial others "can be shown to be alive in the interior spaces through which Europe has come to know and interpret itself."[12] Planetarity is thus for Gilroy a way of challenging the "triumphalism" and sense of "ever-expanding imperialist universals" that so often accompanies the term "global."[13] For him it evokes an indispensable element of estrangement that the term "global" collapses but which is consistent with that form of disloyalty to one's own civilization that Montesquieu first suggested we practice "if we seek either to understand it or to interact equitably with others formed elsewhere."[14] In the present, the planetary therefore involves a "consciousness of the tragedy, fragility, and brevity of indivisible human existence that is all the more valuable as a result of its openness to the damage done by racisms."[15]

Such insights confirm what other cosmopolitan theorists like Peng Cheah and Bruce Robbins have concluded about the necessity to think beyond the national or even the civilizational. They display more interest in the politically transgressive than the epistemologically self-critical character of a cosmopolitan framework for politics, but they insist that cosmopolitanism and cosmopolitics exist at the intersections of culture, politics, and economics, "and that we can conceptualize these phenomena adequately only by working in the volatile zone where ethical philosophy, political theory, cultural anthropology, social theory, critical theory, and cultural studies interact."[16] Jan Nederveen Pieterse tends to agree. While he describes the world as a "global mélange" largely reflective of a hybridity that is almost universal—he also sees the worlds of "East" and "West" as braided in complex ways—Pieterse is no less convinced that these perceptions draw from perspectives furnished by everything from cultural anthropology and world history to political economy and development studies.[17]

What all critics of cosmopolitanism seem to agree is that the universalism of what was once assumed to be cosmopolitan has to be radically rethought in relation to a wholly different set of understandings about the way the world actually works in different places, at different times, in relation to different circumstances, through different institutional mechanisms, toward different goals. For another, these changes have brought with them a new set of principles drawing in the West on the Stoic and Kantian cosmopolitan heritages but more circumscribed in nature and application. They are less expansive than the Stoic affirmation of a moral community of humankind in which each person is a citizen and owes a duty to the worldwide community of human beings, and less restricted than the Kantian community of those who are able to step out of their contingent positions and enter a public sphere where they have a right to the free and unrestricted use of their reason.

As David Held rather narrowly articulates them, they are associated with such values as egalitarian individualism, reciprocal recognition, and impartialist reasoning, and where respected, have conspired to create an ethical and political space that not only sets the terms for recognizing people's equal worth but also permits them the freedom to determine how, insofar as this does not infringe on similar rights of others, they shall represent and express themselves.[18] Stephen White substitutes for such values his own trinity of human dignity, equality, and respect, but it comes to pretty much the same thing.[19] Cosmopolitanism in the West is defined in relation to a space where people can work out the terms of their liberty, egalitarianism, and autonomy, but there is considerable disagreement about just how successful they can be or for how long.

Nonetheless, Held has managed to put these cosmopolitan principles and justifications into a broader transnational framework involving both short-term and long-term measures that combine to define the directions of less West-centric cosmopolitan politics. Short and long term, these are recommendations that follow from the principles he has elaborated for everything from governance, security, and economy to the environment, and they range from suggestions as specific as making the UN Security Council more representative, enhancing regional and national political infrastructures, strengthening nuclear arms control, regulating global markets and off-shore financial centers, and instituting a tax on carbon and other GHGs to democratizing global governance, taming global markets through market correcting and promoting instruments, shifting to a low carbon economy, giving global jurisdiction to a new environment court, and the creation of permanent peacekeeping and humanitarian emergency forces.[20] Such proposals as these derive their justification from a more potentially global set of convictions having to do with the structure of the moral universe, techniques for generating public action out of private activities, the orientations for public decisions, and the metaprinciples of justification, but they develop certain difficulties not just because of their potentially Euro-American bias but also because of their very specificity.

Seyla Benhabib agrees that cosmopolitanism concerns "norms that ought to govern relations among individuals in a global civil society," but sees it as "a philosophical project of mediations, not of reductions or of totalizations," particularly when considered in relation to the contrasting claims of democratic nationalisms. While convinced that one of the surest indicators of the emergence of cosmopolitan norms derives from the way certain civil, social, and political rights are being unbundled from a sense of national belonging, she is no less confident that the much touted neoliberal weakening of the nation-state has not necessarily hastened the advent of the cosmopolitanism she seeks. Nonetheless she refuses to believe that the emancipatory possibilities of a post-Westphalian cosmopolitanism are purely illusory and thus speaks of "a cosmopolitanism to come."[21]

The most outspoken advocate of the existence of a cosmopolitan outlook or vision is Ulrich Beck, who as early as 1998 published a "Cosmopolitan Manifesto" announcing the creation of a post-national cosmopolitan world-order as a realistic as well as utopian political project.[22] However, it was not until nearly a decade later that Beck proclaimed that "cosmopolitanism ... has become the defining feature of a new era ... of reflexive modernity."[23] For Beck cosmopolitanism is a dialogical perspective "that explores and exploits the creative contradictions of cultures within and between the imagined communities of nation."[24] A historically novel form of socio-political formation that is to be distinguished from the Westphalian model, Beck offers five principles of a cosmopolitan outlook that has already taken up residence in Europe. They include "the experience of crisis in world society," the "recognition of cosmopolitan differences" and conflict, "cosmopolitan empathy" and "perspective-taking," "the impossibility of living in a world society without borders and the resulting compulsion to redraw old boundaries and rebuild old walls," and "the mélange principle" that "local, national, ethnic, religious and cosmopolitan cultures and traditions interpenetrate, interconnect, and intermingle."[25] Far from being entirely contemporary, Alexis de Tocqueville, along with Adam Smith before him and John Dewey after him, together with a long list of German thinkers from Kant to Simmel, could detect the early development of these principles and they will continue to undergo important modification and change in the future.

More recently, Beck has sought to play off cosmopolitanism against what he calls "cosmopolitization."[26] The latter refers to the uneven, impure, banal, irregular, asymmetric, coercive process going on all around us beyond the "container of the national space," a result of global institutions and agencies plugging into one another and functioning as a kind of "cosmopolitan realpolitik." This cosmopolitization is further producing a second or reflexive modernity defined by new kinds of world risk whose chief features are de-localization, incalculableness, and non-compensability. In order to conceptualize this new world risk society, Beck believes that we must relinquish the dream of building ever more extensive networks of shared assumptions and laws and accept the fact that we are being more actively integrated into webs of shared threats and menaces. This does not diminish the fact that everyday life has become more cosmopolitan, despite the fact that life is now defined by common dangers as opposed to common ideals; people still have to understand themselves and their lives in relation to those of other people.

Beck's new, somewhat more tempered, position on the subject of cosmopolitization, even if not his pessimistic view of the elements which constitute it, bears some affinities with the way Kwame Anthony Appiah thinks about cosmopolitanism. While Appiah's own preference is for a "rooted" or "partial" cosmopolitanism, he also believes that it is going on all around us in ways both banal or casual and formal. However, Appiah differs from many cosmopolitan theorists in not finding cosmopolitan allegiances necessarily in contradiction with more local or particularistic, even national, ones, and he furthermore believes that theoretical agreement on principles and values is not always necessary to achieve a workable consensus on policies and practices. Appiah has considerable faith that the intercultural dialogue that is generated from travel as well as from poems, novels, and films also helps us identify many points of essential agreement with others that are nonetheless local and contingent. In any case, "the challenge ... is to take minds and hearts formed over the long millennia of living in local troops and equip them with ideas and institutions that will allow us to live together as the global tribe we have become."[27]

But what if those "local troops," or at least many members of them, were already living in something like "global tribes" that we have failed to discern because of Western myopia? There is considerable support for the view that cosmopolitanism was initially set in motion as long ago as the origin of the great civilizations of the Axial Age that emerged in the last millennium before the beginning of the Common Era. Each of the civilizations that took root in China, India, Iran, Israel, and Greece, and, later, the Arabian peninsula, were propelled by the creation of religions whose goals, at least in their own terms, were "global" in consequences and whose appeals, at least to the elites responsible for preserving and spreading their message, strove for universalism. This is not to discount the fact that, in the very process of conveying their message to others, the proleptic cosmopolitanism of their visions were all-too-capable of being reduced to dogmas that more easily set people apart than brought them together and that, as a consequence, turned these same embryonic cosmopolitanisms into vehicles of exclusion and oppression rather than inclusion and liberation. But it is also worth observing that some of the chief instruments of their eventual articulation and transmission—Latin replacing Greek in the northern Mediterranean, Sanskrit replacing other languages on the Indian subcontinent—were also capable of furnishing in time a more widespread vernacular basis for new cosmopolitan impulses, just as the spread of Arabic did in the Middle East and Mandarin did in China.

Languages, in other words, could function just as easily as commerce, conquest, or faith to carry new ideas and sensibilities to distant societies, but this vernacular process of diffusion, translation, and appropriation was to produce a somewhat different kind of cosmopolitanism, according to Sheldon Pollock, defined less by concepts than by practice. In the Sanskrit cosmopolis, like the Latin or Arabic, cultural horizons were widened not simply by the expanding state or church but by writers and readers, explorers and traders, whose view of the human was not necessarily restricted to territorial or ideological markers.[28] Such expansions may not have produced the dynamic, potentially transformative interchanges that are sometimes associated with modern cosmopolitanism, but they furthered the spread of axial civilizations while at the same time helping to create new local cultures within them.

In many parts of the world this was to create new sources of tension between vernacular cultures themselves and the civilizational orders that contained them. Thus while axial civilizational complexes helped create the conditions that made it feasible for societies in their midst to become, at least at points, more outward looking and hybrid, they also developed structures of governance and control that encouraged others to resist their hegemony on behalf of different, if not broader, sets of human possibilities. Either way, tension and resistance became almost from the beginning of the Axial Age one of the central components of cosmopolitan inspiration, whether in Asia or Europe, the Middle East or north Africa. Societies, like individuals, acquire widened horizons only through contestation and struggle, only as the imaginaries by which they define themselves and others become more self-critical and vulnerable to revision.

Nonetheless, despite the fact that the historical record suggests otherwise, it has been widely believed in the West that the capacity for civilizational revision and adaptation, for external borrowing, cross-cultural interpenetration, and internal transformations was peculiar to the West. But this presumption has been constantly belied by experience elsewhere. Until the seventeenth century, various Middle Eastern societies of the Islamic world were the most cosmopolitan and internationally sophisticated in the Afro-Eurasian world, not least because of their location in the center of the Afro-Eurasian zone and also because of the opportunities this afforded for diverse peoples to be integrated into this hemispheric nexus of exchange and communication. And with integration came altered perspectives and the release of creative powers that led to the broadening of horizons in everything from literature, philosophy, and architecture to the physical and natural sciences. But the same thing was true of many of the civilizations of Asia, where the emergence of cosmopolitan activity of this sort was "as much a popular phenomenon as an elite project."[29] "Local troops," it turns out, have long been associated with "global tribes," but this has been obscured by the way we have conceived of the local and the global, ourselves and strangers.

If one takes a step back, it is possible to discriminate several kinds of cosmopolitanism. The most common and most self-conscious, but by no means the most ancient, is moral and is based on respect for persons or, more lately, for rights. This is the kind of cosmopolitanism that started with the Stoics' belief that identifications with self, or family, or city and state would eventually enlarge to encompass humanity, and can be traced all the way forward to Hannah Arendt's attempt to re-ground cosmopolitanism on the concept of "crimes against humanity." But Arendt's attempt to found the term on systemic, recurrent offenses so heinous in their violation and degradation of human dignity as to constitute an assault on the very notion of the human itself opened up for her the question about whether there is, in fact, a general human nature that might be placed in gravest danger by the emergence of another regime, such as Nazism, where the banality of evil cancels out the ability to think or feel. Though one could discuss, as she called it in her book by that title, "the human condition," Arendt remained unconvinced that this condition presupposes anything like a common human nature. Human beings could define the essence of much that surrounded them and to which they were subject, but it is "highly unlikely," she believed, that we "should ever be able to do the same for ourselves—this would be like jumping over own shadows." Hence the question of whether there is a human nature that could be desecrated, if not potentially obliterated, remained "unanswerable."[30]

But the most famous of these "moments," as they have been called, in the development of moral cosmopolitanism is associated with Immanuel Kant and his famous 1795 essay entitled "Perpetual Peace."[31] Given its sometimes overly selective interpretations, it should be remembered that "Perpetual Peace" was designed to address problems of state conflict associated with the rise of nationalism in the 150 years following the Peace of Westphalia. Kant defined the prospects for peace in relation to three articles which held that every state should be constitutionally organized according to republican principles, that the relations between nations should be legally founded on a federation of free states, and that world citizenship should be limited legally to conditions of universal hospitality. These articles presupposed the existence of a rule of law operative both within states and, in some universal sense, across them that would guarantee all who claimed membership in this global republic the free and uncoerced use of their reason.

The second kind of cosmopolitanism is political and is closely related to the first among those who base their theories on respect for rights but believe that if we are to translate an aspiration or sentiment into an institutional framework we will need to become actively engaged in social change. Political cosmopolitans range from those interested in promoting a centralized world state and genuine global governance, to those who prefer to limit cosmopolitan politics to the address of particular international concerns, such as environmental protection, nuclear proliferation, or war crimes, to those, often heirs of Kant, who are interested in defining optimal international arrangements in connection either with the theory of justice, such as John Rawls, Robert Novick, and Thomas Pogge, or with the theory of communication, such as Jürgen Habermas and Hans-Otto Appel, or with the theory of democracy, such as David Held and Mary Kaldor.

A third kind of cosmopolitanism, first noted by Marx and Engels and easily the newest, is associated with economics and includes many of the proponents of market capitalism, such as Frederick Hayek, Milton Friedman, and Kenichi Ohmae. Economic cosmopolitanism, especially when linked to a variety of neoliberal principles that include the deregularization of the global economy, the liberalization of trade and industry, massive tax cuts that favor the rich, the reduction of public expenditures and the privatization of public enterprises, the removal of controls on financial flows, and the expansion of international markets has in recent years generated an important backlash of anti-globalist feeling that has then spread to many non-economic issues. Since the end of the 1990s, people have discerned the connection between the predatory spread of the market and the further emergence of such global problems as environmental degradation, the militarization of politics, the spread of the arms industry, the dependence on fossil fuels, and a host of other issues. Anti-globalism is directly related to economic and political cosmopolitanism but also spills over into the largest and most unwieldy, but also most ancient, form of cosmopolitanism, which is cultural.

Cultural cosmopolitanism deals with issues that run the gamut from anti-colonial critiques to resurgent nationalisms, from multicultural disputes to religious conflicts, but its roots run deeper. What is fundamentally at issue in so much of the cosmopolitan controversy over cultural issues is the way that human experience is being constantly reframed in each of these separate but related spheres. And doing the reframing are systems of interpretation that are being brought into conversation with one another. Sometimes these conversations open up discussions; sometimes they confuse or close them; sometimes they aggravate discussions; sometimes they resolve them or at least elucidate what is at stake in them.

Nonetheless, the limitations of these systems, and the problems their potential conflict of interpretation entails, have not deterred interest in exploring the normative dimensions of cosmopolitanism. This interest has centered on the quest for what might be called a global ethics. This quest has taken a variety of forms: from sharply delimited attempts to determine the global outlines and requirements of business ethics, medical ethics, military ethics, or bioethics, to broader inquiries to establish common ground for a theory of international or transnational justice, to a still more general effort to define the philosophical framework for a global code of moral behavior toward others. Whether applied or normative, however, the challenge is to figure out whether agreement can be obtained across broad and complex social, cultural, and political divides on issues affecting our relations with one another. The ultimate hope is that "living together" might extend beyond mere necessity and reach the space of what Derrida called "living together well," but this will often require, as he understood, an "avowal of the wounds caused by irreconcilable differences."[32] Hence the question we should pose to any global ethics is whether its cosmopolitanism is realistic or, as I would say, pragmatist enough: does it envisage how different people with varying grievances and hopes and unequal opportunities living among one another can do so "with some degree of comity"?[33]

The most famous of all attempts to adumbrate a universal standard for global ethics was Kant's association of it with universal hospitality. The purpose of this right was not to alter peoples' understanding of one another but rather to guarantee the stranger protection from being treated as an enemy when visiting the state of someone else on the assumption that in principle everyone is entitled to communal possession of the earth's surface. Kant was also eager to insure the development of commerce that would have been endangered if people were not free to circulate.

Kant's universal was thus always suspect because of its association with the interests of a particular class, but it has also been questioned more recently by Derrida on the grounds that unless universal hospitality is unconditional, it cannot define the unique obligation that each of us has to the other. If universal hospitality is conditional on anything else, Derrida reasoned, then it is defined by the limits of tolerance. But tolerance was for Derrida linked to the Christian notion of charity and therefore tied the acceptance of the other to restrictions and requirements. Implying an invitation proffered, and hence a limit beyond which one must not pass, tolerance struck him as the very opposite of unconditional hospitality, which is best understood not on the analogy of a bidding, request, or summons, he believed, but of a visitation unforeseeably experienced. Unconditional hospitality presupposed openness to the entirely unexpected or even imagined, the wholly other. Whether such an unqualified welcome to or reception of the other as unanticipated is possible for us was less important to Derrida than the realization that impossibility of a certain sort was presumed by the very idea of hospitality itself. Derrida insisted that this impossibility could only be overcome through the establishment of a sense of justice and "the democracy to come," which does not end with the law but in fact goes beyond it.

In referring to the "democracy to come" and the need to use the law to transcend it, Derrida was referring to a kind of impossible perfection or ideal without the imagination of which we will never progress beyond the inevitable frustration of its achievement. Indeed, he went so far as to claim that "it is faith in the possibility of this impossible and, in truth, undecidable thing from the point of view of knowledge, science, and conscience that must govern all our decisions."[34] Thus the notion of impossible functioned for him, both conceptually and morally, as at once a register of the absolute limits of possibility that are permanently embedded in human experience and the morally essential horizon that potentially makes the possible overcoming of impossibility at least imaginatively, if not actually, conceivable.[35]

But the existence of universal values that may function inspirationally as merely impossible or unrealizable ideals has been rejected on other grounds. If people can't agree on ideals that are achievable, how much more unlikely is it that they can come to see eye to eye on ideals that are not? As if traditions were not already too diverse, the world's peoples too various, language always too slippery for there ever to be unanimity, or even uniformity of opinion, on what values matter most for global existence, how much more difficult to achieve consensus on those that should guide thinking even when they are unlikely to be implementable? And even if moral unanimity were universally achievable, the question then would become who should, or could, enforce it short of a world government that almost no one thinks of as possible or desirable. While more people throughout the world are coming to accept that a kind of de facto global governance does operate through such different institutions as the United Nations, the Arab League, the International Monetary Fund, and, say, the International Criminal Court, few people seriously imagine that their different and often conflicting responsibilities and authority can be reorganized under a single system of governance, and most people in the world would find the concentration of power it represented too risky to local interests.

But a great many people, after all, have little or no sense of themselves as citizens of the world even when they feel themselves accountable to various translocal communities. Michael Walzer, a political philosopher of remarkably broad and humanly significant commitments, has declared for many:

> I am not a citizen of the world ... I am not even aware that there is a world such that one could be a citizen of it. No one has ever offered me citizenship, or described the naturalization process, or enlisted me in the world's institutional structures, or given me an account of its decision procedures (I hope they are democratic), or provided me with a list of the benefits and obligations of citizenship, or shown me the world's calendar and the common celebrations and commemorations of its citizens.[36]

Though Walzer is described inaccurately as a communitarian philosopher, he believes with them that people are too deeply rooted in specific structures of local allegiance to support the universalism implied in a global ethics. To be effective, he believes, such an ethics would have to be "thick," whereas commitments of this generality, moral or otherwise, are bound to be "thin." Hence for Walzer and others like him, such as Michael Sandel, and, to a lesser extent, Charles Taylor, loyalties take precedence over principles, solidarities over norms.

David A. Hollinger would dispute this chiefly on the grounds that cosmopolitanism, and thus a moral stance with global reach, is a response to the problem of solidarity. Solidarity he associates most specifically with what is meant by "communities of fate," when circumstances conspire to challenge their senses of identity and force them to ask anew who they are. More specific than the sense of belonging associated with the idea of community itself, solidarity, as Hollinger views it, "is a state of social existence achieved only when parties to an affiliation are understood to exercise at least *some* measure of agency, if only in consciously affirming an affiliation into which they were born." Moreover, this situation has been exacerbated as never before by the forces we have come to identify with globalization, obliging him to suggest that one among the great problems of the twenty-first century is "the problem of willed affiliation, the problem of solidarity."[37]

Cosmopolitanism confronts the crisis of solidarity by opening up more "broadly based, internally complex, multiple solidarities equipped to confront the large-scale dilemmas of a 'globalizing' epoch while attending to the endemic human need for intimate belonging."[38] In this conceptualization of it, cosmopolitanism is to be carefully differentiated from pluralism. Pluralism is concerned to protect boundaries and preserve identities already ascribed. Cosmopolitanism, by contrast, is interested in redrawing boundaries for the sake of enlarging identities. In most of its serious formulations that are not abstract and universalizing, cosmopolitanism simply says: "if you do not take on as much of the world as you can, the world will come to you, and on terms over which you will have less control than you did previously."[39] For the cosmopolitan, then, the global does not start at the water's edge, to refer to a famous metaphor, but at the skin's.[40]

For liberals like John Rawls (and also Walzer for that matter), this is an uncomfortable prospect. While Rawls was committed to developing a theory of justice whose principles could win general assent if everyone was positioned as equals, he rejected the possibility of a global ethics. In his classic *A Theory of Justice*, Rawls argued that self-interested rational persons operating behind "a veil of ignorance" would choose two general principles to structure a just society—the first being that each person should have an equal right to the most extensive liberties compatible with similar liberties for everyone; the second holding that social and economic inequalities should be arranged so that they are responsive both to the greatest benefit of the least advantaged persons and attached to offices and positions open to all under conditions of equality of opportunity.

The problem is that these principles depended on an individualism not broadly shared throughout the world. And so, in his next book, Rawls took fuller account of the "fact of reasonable plurality" among positions that disallow appeals to reason which claim that it is capable of peering through and fully resolving differences among alternative foundational claims. Here, his theory of justice as fairness credited the possibility of different but plausible assumptions about what is good, and therefore promoted the idea that agreement might require no more than an overlapping consensus of opinions.[41] In a still later book Rawls extended the principle of overlapping consensus to define what he called, in his title, a "Law of Peoples" composed around eight principles intended to guarantee their freedom and independence, their right to make their own agreements, their right to self-defense but not war, their duty of non-intervention, their freedom to observe treaties and undertakings, their duty to honor human rights, and their duty to assist other peoples living under unfavorable conditions that prevent them from having a just or decent political and social system. But this "Law of Peoples" was not to be confused with cosmopolitanism. Concern for the justice of societies was not, in Rawls's mind, the same thing as the cosmopolitan concern for the well-being of individuals. According to the latter view, the justice of global institutions still left unaddressed "the need for further global distribution."[42]

This conviction reveals the extent to which Rawls's thinking rested on the fundamentals of social-contract theory and a Western sense of individualism, neither of which in many cultures have much relevance or attraction. Rawls assumed that the center of inquiry should remain the well-ordered society where everyone is presumed to act justly, but Amartya Sen has more recently replied to the contrary that this is to begin from the wrong direction. "If we are to be guided by a theory of justice, then why do we begin with an attempt to define the perfectly just society instead of with the injustices that surround us outside it?" Justice for Sen is anything but abstract; it centers around the way peoples' lives actually work, and where they carry them, as much as it does with the nature of the institutions supporting them. Sen thus rejects the social-contract theory that descends from Hobbes, Locke, and Kant in favor of an alternative tradition that derives from Adam Smith and is carried forward by Jeremy Bentham, John Stuart Mill, and Karl Marx. This alternative tradition is less interested in defining the terms of a well-ordered society than in comparing the kinds of injustice that people actually experience to see what can be done to redress them. What moves us, Sen contends, "is not the realization that the world falls short of being completely just, which few of us expect, but that there are clearly remediable injustices around us which we want to eliminate."[43] Hence his reflections about justice take as one of their starting points Charles Dickens's famous observation in *Great Expectations* that "In this little world in which children have their existence, there is nothing so finely perceived and finely felt, as injustice."[44]

Sen's worry is that the search for the fundamental rules and principles that govern ideally just societies can prevent us from confronting injustice and enhancing justice. While he is not indifferent to the need to bear in mind what justice may consist of and how it might be expressed under ideal circumstances, he is also convinced that the discrimination of actual injustice can also contribute to a theory of justice. The fact that the search for justice seems to commence in the West with Thomas Hobbes's famous description of life as "nasty, brutish, and short" may help to explain why it so often proceeds in a transcendental direction to determine the ideal conditions which might alleviate this situation, but it does little to illumine the situation to which South Indian jurisprudence seeks to be accountable, which turns on the distinction between *niti*, or the specific organizational and legal rules for justice, and *naya*, or the sense of how such rules affect the concrete lives of ordinary people. Without careful attention to the latter, Sen maintains, we have no basis for judging the effectuality or the fairness of the former.

But perhaps justice is not always and everywhere the central issue. This is the radical proposition that Avishai Margalit has made in relation to the problem of compromise. Perfect justice may simply be beyond us in most concrete experiences, forcing us to compromise between what, in a perfect world, should be attainable and what, in a very imperfect one, is achievable. Margalit is, of course, aware that there are certain compromises that are unacceptable, or what Margalit calls "rotten," which must be rejected outright because they are designed to establish or maintain inhuman regimes based on humiliation and cruelty. But what of compromises that have to settle for peace rather than for justice, or that can only achieve peace at the expense of justice? Are they also rotten and evil, or can they be justified as necessary if they don't violate our shared sense of humanity?

While the Talmud describes what appears to be an absolute divide between peace and justice—"When there is strict justice there is no peace and where there is peace there is no strict justice"[45]—Margalit settles for something less unambiguous or severe. Compromise is essential not because perfect justice, or even a just peace, are so elusive, even illusory, but because the most we can often hope for, even at the expense of justice, is just peace. Ideal theory invites us to seek perfection. Actual experience instructs us to settle sometimes for very much less, which can look like failure or betrayal but rarely is if it does not involve a violation of morality itself. Indeed, Margalit is willing to go so far as to claim that we are defined not by our aspirations but by our concessions, and that without compromises there is no humanity that is shared, negotiated, conciliated.[46]

But just how far should the spirit of compromise go? If there are compromises too rotten to make because they jeopardize our shared humanity, are there forms of peace so compromised as to violate all notions of justice? To put this differently, is compromise a moral practice or an ethical standard? If it is the former rather than the latter, doesn't it require something like an interior taboo against the inhumane to help us address issues of conduct, collaboration, and conflict in the global sphere? By global sphere, I mean issues that can be consequential either to individuals, communities, states, transnational organizations, or any combination thereof, and that register on scales of ethical import or significance, which require interpretation within a global as opposed to a national, regional, local, or personal frame? But there is another issue I have already raised in connection with Derrida's notion of hospitality, and to which I will later again return in connection with the application of these reflections to the Palestinian-Israeli relationship, that concerns the dimension of the ideal even when it is unrealizable. Do we need to retain a theory of justice, of the justice to come even if it not yet attainable, in order to determine what compromises, even if not rotten, are acceptable?

Margalit shapes his own answer by associating ethics with the duties we owe to others by virtue of our specific relationships with them, such as family or friendship, but extends morality to encompass the obligations we owe to all who are included within the notion of human. I tend to reverse these distinctions by assuming that morality defines our relations with all those to whom we have particular affiliations; ethics relates to the beliefs, norms, and ideals that affect the quest we share with others for a better life. On this basis, there is always both a theoretical and a practical dimension to ethical reflection, but these two dimensions can produce very different forms of inquiry when projected onto a global background. Those forms concerned with issues already alleged to be global—environmental degradation, nuclear proliferation, refugee relief, international peace, regulation of multinational corporations, violence against women and children, bio-medical questions and protocols—usually tend to focus on the development and implementation of normative guidelines and rules for behavior in specific domains. Those forms concerned instead with the horizon of understanding appropriate for the definition, comprehension, and implications of such issues frequently take a more conceptual direction and seek to elaborate how ethical notions and practices, as well as modes of consciousness, would have to change if brought to bear on global problems.

While the application of ethical perspectives and prescriptions to global problems is an immense and always changing project, the intellectual challenge has basically remained twofold: first, to establish what kind of consensus on principles, rights, duties, values, and obligations an ethics of global scope fundamentally requires; and, second, to determine whether any ethics, consensual or not, can address the diversity of need, suffering, inequality, unfairness, and moral confusion that the world in all its particularity actually represents. The first challenge turns on the question of whether there are any ethical universals to which all societies, and the individuals within them, should or can be held accountable. The second challenge proceeds from the fact that even if certain values are held to be universal, different groups will always disagree about how to construe them, how to interpret their implications and applications, and how to assess and prioritize them.

The argument for the universality of ethical values or norms has often been made with the help of religion, where it is frequently assumed either that all the major religions share an overriding ethical universal, such as the Golden Rule, or that certain ethical principles, such as the injunction to "love thy neighbor as thyself," carry across many religious communions. But if the Golden Rule, which is expressed in almost identical terms in the Analects of Confucius, the Mahabharata, and the New Testament opens up more questions than it resolves—What if that which you would do unto others, because it is that you would have others do unto you, can be described in terms that neither you nor they can accept? Is it clear that everyone in the world wants to be treated as everyone else believes they do?—shared ethical assumptions, such as the importance of law, the dignity of individuals, and the importance of honor, have a way of being variously understood and realized in particular cultural traditions.

This has not prevented many from proposing either that the major religions of the world share recurrent themes—the fundamental equality of all human beings, the idea of human inadequacy and vulnerability, the need to alleviate suffering and mitigate harm—or that one can extrapolate from their diverse expressions certain shared principles, such as respect for all life, tolerance and truthfulness, economic justice and solidarity, and equal rights between men and women. But even when the world, so to speak, has stepped forward to condemn crimes such as genocide—where people can be exterminated simply as a punishment for having been born—this prohibition also runs into difficulty when most of the states that have signed the United Nation's Covenant Against Genocide nonetheless display reluctance to act on it and many people in the world even refuse to acknowledge it.

As already noted, some have argued that unanimity of opinion or common agreement on such matters is less important than identifying areas of overlapping consensus, but here one comes up against the fact that even where people achieve a measure of accord, that accord may be expressed in languages or terms that are very far from being intelligible to or commensurable with one another. Thus the nomination of specific ethical values as candidates for global support often run into the problems involved in all cross-cultural understanding. Even where the meaning of values separated by cultural barriers can be sensed and appreciated, there are always two more problems to be negotiated. The first entails translating what is often expressed in the metaphors, narratives, or figures of speech of one tradition into the idioms of another seeking to make sense of them. The second, if such discursive translations can be achieved, involves an act of appropriation in which one must figure out the difference that such translations make to previous understanding and the internal adjustments that must be made as a consequence. Such negotiations thus depend less on merging or fusing understandings from disparate traditions that may share common assumptions than on enabling different groups of people, through dialogue with one another, to discover in their own terms how they may be traveling separate routes from others toward a similar goal.

For this reason, there has for some years been growing skepticism on the part of many theorists that it is either possible or desirable to base a global ethics on any unity of opinion about principles, perspectives, or practices. For some it may be enough that there is disagreement about the same issues, the terms of the disagreement themselves thus defining the measure of consensus; for others, the key to developing a global ethics capable of being shared across vast cultural differences has less to do with a shared or sharable sense of the issues at stake than with a shared or sharable sense of the needs, both human and social, to be acknowledged, confronted, and engaged. With his exceptional ability to cut through thickets of dispute and sort out competing claims, Charles Taylor has been able to differentiate between ethical norms themselves, the legal forms in which they are expressed and through which they are given force, and the philosophical systems by which they are justified. An unforced consensus may be achievable on certain norms if we allow for, and make a concerted effort to understand, the two crucial legal and philosophical variables that determine their articulation and, to a considerable degree, their comprehension.[47]

But there is another group of theorists and advocates, numbering in the tens, if not hundreds, of millions of people throughout the world, who defend a much more universalist perspective for a global ethics guaranteed by the indisputable authority of their own traditions. Islam in its most extremist and militant forms presents perhaps the most familiar face of this adamantine perspective among those who contend that theirs is the only righteous and infallible faith and all others the work of infidels, but this same doctrinaire, authoritarian stance can also be found within various Christian, Hindu, Jewish, and other religious communities, as well as among various ethnic nationalists and other Holy warriors, and needs to be understood for what it is in the beliefs of its advocates. The members of these communions, whether zealous and violent or merely evangelical and missionary, tend to see themselves as representing a radical form of ethical universalism that seeks the conversion of the world to its own sacred premises.[48] Whether those premises are associated with the re-establishment of the Islamic caliphate or Hindu restoration of Hindutva, radical Zionism's reclamation of the Hebrew homeland or the coming reign of Christ after the victorious battle with the Anti-Christ at Armageddon, these are to be taken seriously as radical, uncompromising assertions of a global ethical absolutism.

Short of such absolutisms, what do, or can, global ethicists build on to frame a perspective that is not merely content with trying to define our obligations to others in a world of difference but seeks to outline the better life to be led in some sense together both for individuals and societies? Can such an enterprise be anything other than a Western attempt to impose its evolving human rights regime on the rest of the world? Does such an ethics require, as we have previously noted about proponents of cosmopolitanism from Kant to Derrida, a shared system of world governance and jurisprudence that people might be inclined to choose if they were free to make such choices? And in what can a global ethics consist if it is not based on a system of belief and value that can be shared in common by the immense variety of cultures and peoples in the world?

Here the arguments tend to unfold in certain predictable patterns. The liberal position holds that even if there aren't any universal goods that all people everywhere recognize and prize, much less espouse, there may be enough common ground among such goods to enable people to cooperate for their mutual development. This requires finding areas of convergence, relationship, or interaction among diverse value systems and then creating ways to articulate them in contexts where their connections, however attenuated and unstable, can nonetheless be productively exploited.

The communitarian position is less sanguine than the liberal because it presumes that the only values capable of securing stable bonds across differences in cultures and societies must be thickly rooted in community. This leads many communitarians to suspect that global ethics is a misnomer since there is no community, actual or hypothetical, from which such general values could be derived. It is one thing to be willing to die for one's country, one's kinsman, or even one's faith, but quite another to imagine this commitment to sacrifice being extended to the world or the planet. One can argue, perhaps, that Doctors Without Borders, or field workers with Human Rights Watch, or even soldiers supporting United Nations' missions tend to refute such an argument, but their sacrifices for values that are seemingly thin may merely prove it: we are most moved by thick values rather than thin because they are associated with the bonds we have to those closest to us in language, custom, culture, and politics.

The main problem with this position is that it fails to acknowledge that our identifications with so-called thick communities, like nations, regions, religions, and ethnicities, are at least as much imagined, invented, and constructed as our identifications with thin ones. And why is this? Because we are no more familiar with most of the people who belong to them than we are certain of the territorial or other limits that define them, or the forms of sovereignty and status that make them so important to us. All we know for certain about such groups, identifications, and meanings, whether our relationship to them is thick or thin, is that they generate forms of horizontal comradeship and senses of solidarity for which people are often willing to make ultimate sacrifices. There is no reason to think that over time these same feelings of belonging, allegiance, and loyalty can't or won't be (for many people throughout the world already are) attached by means of the thinnest materials of sentiment, aspiration, and empathy to entities as abstract and elusive as the global and even planetary.[49] Personal horizons expand as people's identifications change, and thus there is little reason to doubt that as people find circumstances forcing them to relocate themselves on widening maps of experience, whether geopolitical, cultural, social, economic, or technological, so consciousness, albeit more slowly and often with resistance, will also change.

These changes, many of which are not sequestered or containable within any of the categories by which we usually map human experience, have foregrounded the importance of cross-cultural dialogue about the formation of ethical guidelines and strategies for addressing such problems. Among those who have pushed this dialogic alternative, there is some difference of opinion as to whether a global ethics would be substantive or merely procedural. Is it possible to develop any consensus about norms, values, and methods for establishing a global ethical order, or is the order itself to be found in the debates about it which produce, at the very least, a broadened sphere of public discourse where values can be critiqued and reformed? Indeed, some feel that this capacity for self-reflection and self-revision—"fallibilism" as it is called by pragmatists—may be all that is left of the moral amplitude once aimed at in the European Enlightenment, but proponents of the dialogic position still argue that such communicative logics are not to be discounted because they enable people from very different traditions to keep talking with one another, and through talking with one another potentially to listen and perhaps learn from one another.

If this sounds like a minimalist ethical position, it should be remembered that learning from one another need not be restricted to learning more about one another. The key to self-critique and self-revision in a dialogic model of communication is not restricted to what can be learned from what the so-called "Other" reveals concerning itself, important as this may be, but extends to what the so-called self can learn about through such exchanges. While this learning turns all participants in the dialogue, as we shall see in Chapter 7, into potential allies of each other, it also comes so very often at the expense of everyone's inward ease.

Such dialogic tactics may well prove still more significant as a result of what other theorists are learning about the human itself and the nature of moral reasoning. Two of the most promising contributions are coming from capabilities theorists and from experimental social psychologists. Capability theorists argue that the human cannot be defined simply in terms of what is necessary to sustain a recognizably human life—food, shelter, clothing, health—but must also include what is required to make such a life functional. This includes such abilities as feeling, thinking, reasoning, and imagining, which enable all human beings not genetically damaged to achieve, through education, the possibility of self-expression and the power to make choices. The realization of these capabilities is also often thought to require a number of other goods—such as a measure of freedom to select sexual partners, to make friends, to have children, to obtain work, to share in social decisions, to pursue a meaningful life—and the avoidance of certain evils—bodily harm, unnecessary suffering, social humiliation, and other ills.

This a tall order, but it outlines what might be thought of as universals of condition that do, in fact, possess considerable support throughout much of the world. The existence of such human universals has received some reinforcement because of what experimental psychologists seem to have discovered about the moral sentiments. Thus far they have identified as many as six modes of response to situations identified as moral, but whether they are distinct or interrelated, or conflict or cooperate in producing moral feelings, is still an open question.[50] The mere fact that they can be isolated at all is an achievement of some consequence because it suggests that the human mind has over time become hard-wired to respond morally to certain situations: the prevention or mitigation of harm, fairness and reciprocity, purity and pollution, hierarchy and respect, in-group vs. out-group, and awe and elevation.

But the same scientists who have made these claims by no means agree that there is any correlation between the responses human beings make to moral issues and the rationales they give for their actions.[51] It may simply be enough to conclude that these discoveries suggest that we are much closer to an understanding of what moral behavior does for us and why than we are to grasping what measures moral understanding and how. While there will always be disagreement about which moral principles are most efficacious in particular contexts and whether moral principles have to be grounded in the structure of life itself, there are some reasons for believing that "the better life to be led," as Aristotle and Dewey defined the ethical challenge, will in a global world have to bend still more of its energies into turning "living together," to quote Jacques Derrida, into "living together well."[52]

But just how difficult this is to achieve, and what it may require in concrete political situations, Derrida understood only too well. In "Avowing – the Impossible," he attempted to transcend conventional wisdom about the Palestinian-Israeli situation by shifting thinking about politics as the art of the possible to politics as the art of the impossible. By "impossible" he meant, as noted earlier, the horizon of limitations that bounds all human experience but at the same time marks what human potential must attempt to exceed. In such terms as these, the Israeli-Palestinian conflict left him both despondent and narrowly hopeful if an avowal of peace could lead to a responsible quest for its realization. Yet by arguing that "Palestinians will truly live together only on the day when ... peace comes into their bodies and souls," Derrida was at risk of elevating, as Richard Falk called it, "the threshold of peace so high" that he might be "perhaps here unwittingly encouraging a politics of despair."[53]

Falk's response is to take Derrida's proposal for what it is—hints and guidelines rather than policy recommendations for thought—and see if he can recast "impossibility" as a limitation currently beyond plausible realization but not beyond the possibility of fulfillment by wholly unforeseen or predictable developments. His intent is to give Derrida's reservations a slightly less demoralized prospect by paying close attention to roads not yet taken to resolve the Palestinian-Israeli conflict because they are not yet imaginable or plausible. As a longtime student of the conflict, who in 2008 was appointed by the United Nations to a six-year term as Special Rapporteur on Human Rights in the Palestinian territories, Falk's politics are both well known and frequently misinterpreted. A Jewish intellectual who shares Derrida's belief that the Holocaust has cast a long and terrible shadow over understandable Israeli fears for the future, as well as an ardent believer that a just peace cannot be achieved by reliance on the language of politics alone but only by moving outside it toward religion, "the main civilizational custodian of both compassionate and narcissistic ethics," Falk is also widely identified but unfairly criticized for his sympathies over many years with the weaker people in this tragic conflict and for condemning continued Israeli oppression as risking the institution and perpetuation of apartheid and much worse.[54]

But here his opinions on the morality of the conflict, significant as they are and many of which I and many Israelis, not to say other American Jews, share, are not at issue. The point at issue is whether Derrida's hermeneutics of "the impossible" can provide new openings for thinking through, and toward the resolution of, a political and moral conflict that seems to most unprejudiced observers to be stymied. Falk enumerates three possibilities in an ascending order of implausibility. The first is to explore analogous situations of interminable conflict, such as the former stalemate in Northern Ireland, where the change of heart experienced by the main actors outside the state, the United Kingdom and the United States, seemed to derive from a new way of construing the IRA not as a terrorist organization bent on destroying or taking over the state but as a political opponent with grievances and claims of its own. The second "impossible" scenario depends on the further development of global civil society exerting pressure both from within and without, as in the anti-apartheid movement that finally delegitimated the government of South Africa, or the popular uprising that brought down the Marcos regime in the Philippines, or the Velvet Revolution that toppled the Soviets in Eastern Europe. The third, and least likely, "impossibility" would neither be a bottom-up resistance movement nor symbolic legitimacy struggle so much as a wholly unpredictable politics that succeeded not only against all odds but also in the face of completely contrary expectations. This impossibility describes the almost unimaginable triumph of the anti-slavery movement in the mid-nineteenth century and the unforeseen collapse of the Soviet Union at the end of the twentieth, but also the unpredictable democratically-inspired revolutions that have unseated dictators in Tunisia, Egypt, Libya, and possibly Yemen and that are continuing to unsettle regimes throughout the Middle East from Morocco to Jordan and Syria to Saudi Arabia and Bahrain.

Such a politics of the "impossible" may rest on nothing more certain than "our confirmed inability to anticipate the future, and our experience of being consistently surprised by the unanticipated,"[55] but it can still furnish insight into how cosmopolitanism in fact operates, even if it can't ensure when it will come, as beautifully rendered by Sahar Khalifeh in her 1976 novel *Wild Thorns*. Set against the background of Palestinian life in the territories just before the First Intafada, the novel is built around a cosmopolitan moment that cannot last but which remains indelible not only as an image, but also as a template for what is required to produce one. It is a moment when compromise risks the sacrifice of justice for the sake of achieving a moment of peace that serves as a prelude to what the removal of injustice might look and feel like, to what living together well actually entails.

The novel centers around two cousins from a wealthy Palestinian family that has long since lost its landholdings and thus its wealth and status. One of the cousins, Usama al-Karmi, has left the West Bank to look for work in neighboring Arab countries, but after finding none has had to return with the sobering lesson that Palestinians are not welcomed in most Arab countries. Embittered, alienated, and radicalized, he comes back fired with the conviction that the real Palestinian struggle for respect and recognition must begin from within the territories rather than outside them.

But Usama's belief in the necessity of Palestinian resistance and the purity of this cause is brought up short by two interrelated realities that have changed the territories during the ten years since the occupation by Israel in 1967. The first is that while the conditions of occupation have weakened the prospects for a national struggle for liberation, the Palestinian population, and particularly the peasant class that was formerly compelled to labor on the land with no promise of economic improvement, has now found work in the growing economy of Israel, bringing new wealth to a formerly impoverished people. While this prosperity has made more Palestinians acquiescent and, as Usama finds them, submissive, it has also enabled them, even in a society eager to exploit their labor, to live much better than they could under the old Palestinian land system.

The second reality Usama is forced to confront is the class conflict and oppression built into the old Palestianian land system itself, which accorded unusual privileges to the land-owning class while imposing excessive hardship and injustice on those who worked for them. Indeed, much is made of the fact that while the Israelis are no saints, they often make better employers than former Palestinian land barons such as the al-Karmi family itself. It is this second reality which Usama cannot accept since it challenges the terms on which his nationalist revolutionary ideology is based. This nationalist narrative assumes that land is holy and belongs to the people, and that the struggle to reclaim it thus constitutes a sacred mission. The actualities on the ground, however, point instead to the historical fact that the land never belonged to all the people in the first place and thus suggest that those, like Usama, who advocate its violent recovery may simply be seeking to reclaim the former class privilege they enjoyed by exploiting their fellow Palestinians. Unable to accept this fact, or to understand why the situation of fellow Palestinians "inside" no longer conforms to the ideological perspective of those like him from the "outside," Usama resolves on a plan to attack the buses that carry Palestinian laborers into Israel, and this brings him directly into conflict with his al-Karmi cousin, Adil, and his friend, Zuhdi, both of whom will be riding on one of the buses Usama decides to target.

Adil is the older son of the patriarch of the al-Karmi family and has been obliged secretly to take a factory job in Israel to pay for his father's kidney machine and the education of his younger brother and sister while at the same time assisting his fellow Palestinian laborers in surviving the exactions of the Israeli factory system. A good man forced to compromise on behalf of peace even at the expense of justice, Adil knows that there is no way to extricate himself or others from circumstances that are often tragic, but he refuses to relinquish his obligations to others in order to appease his sense of justice. As he tells Zuhdi, one of those others who has himself tried to find work first in the territories, as a mechanic, a taxi driver, and a construction worker, and later in Kuwait, Saudi Arabia, and Germany, before finally returning to join Adil as a lashki worker in Israel,

> "I fight my despair with despair itself. Do you understand? Well, neither do I. I don't really understand this strange mixture of feelings I have, I don't know how to explain what's going through my mind. I'm confused and I can't exactly define my own position. Peace! Brotherhood!—hopes of idiots and dreams of birds. Maybe. I don't know. Yet I still dream. I dream of the impossible. But I ask you, is it possible to grow roses from thorns?"
> "The thorns aren't there to produce roses," Zuhdi answered, "they're there to protect them."
> "Well, I still dream," Adil answered.
> "God's peace be with you, then", said Zuhdi quietly.
> "And with all the world," returned Adil.[56]

But the impossible does, for a moment, become possible, does offer an alternative both to the violence of Usama's grand narrative of nationalist struggle and to the continuing injustice and oppression that follow from the opposition of Israeli and

Palestinian in the daily existence of the territories. It comes as a result of Usama's first act of violence—his second will involve the bombing of the buses carrying Adil and Zuhdi to work in Israel—when in an act of premeditated murder he rushes into an Israeli square to assassinate an Israeli captain in front of his wife and small child. As the child faints to the ground at the sight of her father's murder, Adil's aunt—who despises Israelis in general for their cruelty and indifference to Palestinians and has just taken offense at the ease with which this same Israeli couple, strolling with their child, can afford to buy fruit she cannot provide her own family—is suddenly moved by the sight of the stricken family. Softening in response to the Israeli wife's shock and agony, she instinctively asks for God's mercy on her, and then, noticing that the young Israeli child's legs are exposed, removes her own scarf to cover the girl's naked thighs. At almost the same moment, her nephew Adil arrives. Having seen the assassination but without recognizing the perpetrator, he immediately acts to comfort the widow and splash water on the little girl's face before picking her up and, against the advice of passers-by, leading her grieving mother to safety.

In these two gestures, Adil and his aunt reverse the basic oppositions that define the world of the novel. A sense of shared humanity overrides the distinctions as well as the policies and practices that have set one people against another. Adil and Um Sabir have found ways to put themselves in the place of the victims and to act as they themselves would have wanted someone to act not so much on behalf of themselves as of one of their own. By so doing, they have not only seen from the point of view of others but have simultaneously, against all prejudice and anger, acted in a way they wish to be seen. Here the absolutisms of religious, national, social, ethnic, political, generational, and sexual identities momentarily collapse and another way of constructing and enacting human relations is, however briefly, revealed and represented. Nothing, of course, has been permanently changed, but the tyranny of the old binaries has, in the face of tragedies virtually anyone human can recognize as universal, been shown to be mutable, thus giving a new dignity and resilience to the compromises that Adil and others will have to continue to make.

But do such charitable, selfless gestures actually matter? Can cosmopolitan compromises make any difference in the face of a Palestinian-Israeli conflict defined by these imbalances of power, these inequities of freedom and opportunity, these memories of insecurity, these histories of bad faith, these reservoirs of enmity, abjection, and despair? As almost no place else on earth, politics has transformed itself from the art of the possible into the anarchy of the hopeless and unthinkable, and there is seemingly no way to reverse it:

> Sombre images filled Adil's mind. The dead officer, his grieving widow, the little girl stretched out on the ground, her pale, bare legs partly covered by Um Sabir's veil. People running through the streets, someone yelling, "Leave the pig alone!" Bitterness flooded his heart. My cousin kills a man and I carry off his daughter. Tragedy or farce? Still, the memory of the Israeli woman's

head on his shoulder, despite all the boundaries that divided people, seemed to open the horizons of this narrow world.[57]

And so we, like Adil, dream on—for peace and also for justice, but it will have to be the justice to come, not the inferior, asymmetrical imitation of it available to most people. Because cosmopolitanism cannot by itself bring the impartiality, evenhandedness, and fairness people seek from a just world, much less an end to the inequities that surround them in an unjust one. What it can do is help transcend those narrow absolutist horizons by which our view of others is both blinkered and bound. Those others are not the ones to whom we choose to be neighborly when it is convenient but the ones with whom we are already neighbored, whether convenient or not.

This is the archetypal other who is neighbored by the good Samaritan in the famous story told by Jesus of Nazareth in the New Testament Gospel of Luke. In this story Jesus is not primarily interested in explaining why we should help others in distress but in determining who constitutes the neighbor to whose distress we are accountable. He could have argued with the lawyer that we are obliged to become neighborly whenever we are confronted by someone in need, but instead he shifted the point of the story to address the question of who in need deserves to be considered the neighbor. Here the neighbor is she or he who is found in difficulty in the Samaritan's neighborhood, and the weight of the story is on what that discovery entails for the wounded Israelite, not on how it changes the moral constitution of the Samaritan. "It does not matter," Amartya Sen writes, "whether the Samaritan was moved by charity, or by a 'sense of justice,' or by some deeper 'sense of fairness in treating others as equals.' Once he finds himself in this situation, he is in a new 'neighbourhood.'"[58] And this "new neighbourhood" in turn redefines the Samaritan's relations with any whose lives, because of their shared vulnerability as humans, similarly impinge on his own.

To act like a neighbor, then, is not for the Samaritan to assume a new nature but to exercise a different responsibility commensurate with the recognition of a common identity. This is what requires Adil to rescue the wife and daughter of his enemy from the hands of a violent crowd and what compels his aunt, out of a respect for female modesty, to cover the legs of a child whose parents she despises. These acts by themselves may or may not change anything empirical, but they widen and deepen the emotional and imaginative landscape of the human. Recalling again, as his family's home is about to be demolished by Israeli soldiers as punishment for his little brother's terrorism, Adil recognizes in the face of one of the demolitionists a resemblance to the Israeli captain murdered by his cousin Usama:

> That face! That man! You carried his daughter on your back! You stripped off his stars and carried his daughter. You carried a human being. And you felt your own sense of humanity swell and deepen as you became aware of the Israeli officer as a human being.[59]

This is the recognition on which cosmopolitanism depends, which means something only because of the differences and inequalities it must traverse, the entrenched ideological solidarities it must breach, the injuries of fate and policy it must transcend, if it is to be anything more than an empty gesture of deference that eases the conscience of the favored. The fact that cosmopolitanism is easy to disparage or dismiss does not discount the fact that without a deepened and enlivened sense of what binds us to all those by whom we are neighbored, we will continue to remain hostage to those very conditions mentioned above. The task is not to make cosmopolitanism more universal, context-sensitive, or practical but to make universalisms, contextualisms, and practice more cosmopolitan. This is what in an era of globalized absolutisms makes cosmopolitanism worth fighting for and why many people are willing to die for it.

But how might we get to this pragmatic cosmopolitanism, to the sensibility of Adil and Sen? What does it mean to view the neighbor to whom we are morally answerable as the stranger by whom, at any given moment, we might be bounded? How do we turn the temptation of seeing others as ourselves into the capacity to see ourselves as others? What is the difference between putting others in our place and putting ourselves in theirs? The remaining chapters of this book try to chart a path.

3
PRAGMATIST ALTERNATIVES TO ABSOLUTIST OPTIONS

> If we believe with Raymond Williams, "that however dominant a social system may be, the very meaning of its domination involves a limitation or selection of the activities it covers, so that by definition it cannot exhaust all social experience, which therefore always potentially contains space for aternative acts and alternative intentions which are not yet articulated as a social institution or even project," then criticism belongs in that potential space inside civil society, acting on behalf of those alternative acts and alternative intentions whose advancement is a fundamental human and intellectual obligation.
>
> Edward W. Said, *The World, the Text, and the Critic*, 1983, pp. 29–30

John Dewey once wrote that:

> the business of reflection in determining the true good cannot be done once and for all, as, for instance, making out a table of values arranged in a hierarchical order of higher and lower. It needs to be done, and done over and over and over again, in terms of the conditions of concrete situations as they arise. In short, the need for reflection and insight is perpetually recurring.[1]

As it happens, this passage was quoted in a speech by former Supreme Court Justice John Paul Stevens, whose legal career exemplifies the enduring legacy of Dewey's philosophical orientation almost as accurately as Dewey's words describe Stevens' approach to the law. The quest for certainty in law, as in life, must be relinquished for the sake of applying such rules of governance and acceptable behavior as we have developed over time to the complexities and contingencies of individual cases.

This Deweyan disposition to put once-and-for-all approaches aside in favor of thinking through, on a case-by-case basis, the "true good" of any problem may help explain what lies behind the question that pragmatists have often been asked since the attacks on September 11. Does pragmatism, the query usually goes, really have anything to say in the face of such extreme situations, and, in particular, can pragmatism give anyone a reason to risk their life in a noble cause, whether that cause be the pursuit of the "true" but contingent "good," the battle against injustice, or, for that matter, preventing the "gates of hell" from being opened? When the stakes are really high, doesn't a philosophy like pragmatism, with its Jamesian suspicion of "first principles, closed systems, and pretended absolutes and origins," have to yield to philosophies, theologies, dogmas, and creeds which are not? Is the expedient, in other words, any match for the unconditional?

On first hearing such questions, it is possible to suppose that they proceed from a fairly widespread public perception that pragmatism is essentially neutral with regard to politics, since it can be—and often has been—drafted into the service of agendas that are conservative and reactionary as well as liberal and progressive. The corollary of such opinions is that pragmatism is, at least in its earliest formations, insensible to power and indifferent to politics.

Such perceptions are inaccurate not only on the basis of such historically significant events as James's response to the Spanish American War, Dewey's to the threats to democracy, and Richard Rorty's to cruelty and humiliation, but also because they seem to overlook the importance that pragmatism has always accorded praxis, effects, action, outcomes, and consequences. How could one claim the absence, or at least the impotence, of some dimension of political unconscious in a philosophical orientation like pragmatism, which is so absorbed not only with the active but also relational, provisional, and experimental character of life? Pragmatism assumes that experience is plural, diverse, unpredictable, and messy. It asserts that there are no epistemological positions or philosophical standpoints that are not potentially unstable and thus susceptible to revision and correction. It rather famously holds, in Dewey's formulation, that life does not present us with a hierarchy of answers but only with a hierarchy of problems and goes on to claim that values are no more than prejudices, or at least preferences, that need to be weighed and assessed both against the preferences of others and the practices they promote. Dewey in particular was persuaded that traditional cultural distinctions between high and low, elite and ordinary, refined and common are chiefly concerned with status and need to be democratized, and James added that the understanding of difference—and not just the difference that difference constitutes but the difference that difference makes—is the key to understanding itself. Thus each believed that one of the essential tasks of social as well as political life is to render such differences conversable so that the potential conflicts between them can enhance rather than diminish the wider life of the human community affected by them.

On second thoughts, however, it is clear that certain recent versions of pragmatism lend credence to such opinions. One such version holds that pragmatism reduces all disputes to matters of interpretation since pragmatism is merely a kind of practice like any other, which in this case takes issue with any others that attempt to construct theoretical positions from which to govern practice from a standpoint putatively outside of it and immune to its own contingencies.[2] On the assumption that no such privileged positions exist in a world without ontological or epistemological moorings, a world where language, rhetoric, and discourse simply go all the way down, pragmatism functions to remind us that politics is, like all else, merely a matter of interpretation and dispositions or, in other vocabularies, of taste, sentiment, and desire.

Richard Rorty himself seemed to reinforce this view with his claim that pragmatism is unable to provide us with any basis for saying that what the torturer, the terrorist, or the tyrant do is wicked, criminal, bestial, or evil. While conceding that some may, of course, feel justified in holding such opinions, he insisted that there is nothing in pragmatism that compels us to think so, or, for that matter, compels us to try to put a stop to it. What we do, so this line of argument goes, is not because of where reason leads but because of where feeling does.

This position would be less troublesome if it were simply a result of drinking too deeply at the well of poststructuralism, but it also possesses a measure of support among those who have not. One such view is represented by Louis Menand who concludes his excellent *The Metaphysical Club* with the assertion that "pragmatism explains everything about ideas except why a person would be willing to die for one."[3] If this were simply a reiteration of the familiar complaint that pragmatism is thin on theory while thick on explanation, one might dismiss this observation as just another complaint about pragmatism's aversion to essentialisms of any kinds, but it is clearly intended to highlight what Menand takes to be a serious deficiency of pragmatism itself: pragmatism can tell us everything about ideas, he believes, except whether they ultimately matter and why one would give their life for them.

In a subsequent *New Yorker* review of books responding to the attacks on September 11, 2001, Menand repeated this same claim but gave it an added paradoxical twist. Surveying the spontaneous patriotism and compassion evoked by the attacks, Menand asserted that they add up to a kind of formula in which Americans reveal themselves as simply ready to die for, or at least to defend, the belief "that no one should be made to die for a belief."[4] Or, if this formula is recast in more religious terms, this mixture of patriotism and compassion suggests that "Americans hold it to be a transcendent truth that it is possible to live a good life without loyalty to a transcendent cause."[5]

These assertions, in actuality assessments, would be less disturbing if they did not at one and the same time perpetuate a misunderstanding of pragmatism's intellectual legacy while discounting its relevance to a particularly treacherous moment in the nation's history when, in the aftermath of "9/11," the entire country was rendered more vulnerable to its own residual culture of fear than at any period since the attack on Pearl Harbor. From the day after that murderous attack, it became almost impossible for many to respond to this atrocity in any other but absolutist terms. The country was under siege by a demonic enemy whose apocryphal violence was sustained by a broader "axis of evil" that placed entire civilizations at risk. In the face of such Manichean conflicts, where you are either "for us" or "against us," it was so difficult to trust any theoretical perspective that left open the door to complexity, uncertainty, ambiguity, and nuance. Ideas that were not unequivocally confident of their own ground, assumptions that were less than completely fixed, conceptions and perceptions that are not invulnerable to correction, modification, and revision, were viewed both as ineffectual—and hence in some quarters as effeminate, or at least as unmasculine—and also as duplicitous, and thus by some lights as potentially traitorous or, at any rate, untrustworthy. "The Great Terror War" was therefore unleashed, and the consequences for those countries that found themselves in the cross-hairs may take decades to assess, much less to repair.

From this perspective, Menand's book holds up a particularly illuminating mirror to the intellectual resources that America brings, and has brought, to this fateful global moment. But what exactly is it that *The Metaphysical Club* argues? Does it suggest that America's only home-grown tradition of thinking lacks the philosophical substance, epistemological clarity, and moral decisiveness to confront the challenges posed by the war that global jihad supposedly declared on the US and the US on it? Or does it disclose instead what is still generally misunderstood about the efficacy of pragmatist interventions in a world where the quest for certainty still rules at the expense of human wellbeing?

To answer these questions, I propose to take a fairly detailed look at Menand's symptomatic book, not simply to examine his interpretation of pragmatism as itself a response to the need for assurance, but also to determine, on the basis of Menand's reading, pragmatism's relevance in a world now increasingly organized around the nexus of the insecurities associated with violence, terror, and the rapacities of the market and the seductions and soporifics of unconditional belief. Along the way, it will become apparent that my own view of pragmatism diverges fairly sharply from Menand's, despite my great respect for the lively way he has attempted to historicize some of its most important features. These differences will then permit me to shift the focus of the argument by taking up several historical episodes, widely separated in time, where a pragmatic response prevented situations subjected to violent conflicts of conviction from descending into chaos. In the face of such evidence, the question then becomes, what does a distinctively nineteenth-century way of thinking, as Menand considers pragmatism, have to say to a world riven with doctrinaire ideological and religious divisiveness? Can a theory like pragmatism, which is suspicious of the totalizing claims of all belief systems, all ideological mindsets, have any uses in a world recurrently defined by the clash of such regimes?

Menand's answer has everything to do with where he situates his narrative historically and how he goes about developing it. The question he wants to ask is what difference pragmatism has made to the way people think principally about thinking. The people in question are not only the four major figures responsible for pragmatism's early development—Charles Sanders Peirce, William James, Oliver Wendell Holmes, and John Dewey—but also countless others who either influenced these four or were influenced by them, from Ralph Waldo Emerson, Charles Darwin, Benjamin Peirce, and Henry James, Sr., to Alain Locke, W. E. B. DuBois, Horace Kallen, and Randolph Bourne. The plot of his narrative is anchored by the War Between the States and the way it challenged the contemporary organization of life around a series of absolutes. Indeed, *The Metaphysical Club* might well have been subtitled "The Civil War and the Rejection of the Quest for Certainty," since what motivated each of Menand's major figures was a kind of horror at the results of believing too much rather than too little.

This horror may have been experienced more sharply by Holmes than by his three compatriots, but they all recoiled in one way or another from the view that ideas must reflect the reality to which they refer and thus aspire to become as fixed and stable as the objectively real is itself presumed to be. "The belief that ideas should never become ideologies—either justifying the status quo, or dictating some transcendent imperative for renouncing it—was the essence of what they taught."[6] This conviction encouraged them to take the more emancipated position (though Peirce remains something of an exception in this case) that ideas simply constitute some of our most important "equipment for living."[7] Their truth therefore has less to do either with their concurrence with received wisdom or with their correspondence to perceived fact than with their usefulness as tools designed to provide leverage over circumstances. In this belief, all four of Menand's major figures—"moderns" who conceived of life neither as the reproduction of custom nor as the renewal of tradition but rather as the discovery and creation of new goals for living—essentially concurred.

One of the more original aspects of Menand's reading of the pragmatists is that he is less interested in explaining how Peirce, Dewey, and the others variously came to these conclusions than in showing how, as a result of their different experiences of a world shadowed by war and drastically altered under pressures ranging from the Darwinian revolution to the development of market capitalism, these conclusions, in effect, came to them. But if this makes *The Metaphysical Club* much more than an intellectual history of pragmatism—it is rather a history of the later nineteenth- and early twentieth-century American intellect as pragmatist—it also raises some interesting questions.

The first of these questions derives from the way Menand has constructed his history around an institution named in the title of his book that had already dissolved within a year of its creation but included among its members, in addition to James, Peirce, and Holmes, the lawyers Nicholas St. John Green and Joseph Bangs Warner, the philosopher and historian John Fiske, and the group's resident Socrates, Chauncy Wright. Providing a forum for the discussion of questions about what a later age was to come to call, all-too-prematurely as it has turned out, the "end of ideology" (as well as a display of Chauncey Wright's positivism, which he was supposedly prepared to defend against all comers in a less than pragmatist spirit), it is still not entirely clear how a club of "long-headed youths" who "wrangle grimly and stick to the question" was eventually to shape their thinking so significantly.[8] Even if the single year of the Club's existence constituted the one moment when all the main figures in Menand's narrative but Dewey found themselves in each other's company and were thus at liberty to hear each other out, this image of intellectual influence doesn't square very well with the rather different model of their development assumed in the rest of Menand's book.

According to the latter, the community of mind subsequently created by all four of these philosophers was fashioned less by the cross-fertilization of ideas that occurred during an intensely personal set of colloquies they attended at a formative moment in their development as thinkers than by a complex series of experiences associated with an entire era, which urged minds such as theirs moving along quite different tracks of reflection nonetheless eventually to come to similar conclusions. This impression is reinforced by the fact that the bulk of his history is not organized primarily around a single proleptic year; it is shaped in relation to a sequence of events that runs from the Civil War not only to the Supreme Court's decision in 1919 regarding free speech in U.S. v. Abrams but all the way to, and even beyond, the end of the Cold War. Using this longer time frame still permits one to view the origins of pragmatism as a strategic response to the kinds of self-righteous abstractions that fueled the Civil War, but Menand believes that to carry the story of pragmatism's anti-absolutism much past the capitalist hyperactivity and depression of the interwar period into the postwar oppositions and certitudes of the Cold War era is to make plain why pragmatism was eventually to lose its attractions. How could a perspective so meliorist stand up to the Manichean abstractions of a world grown threatened by totalitarianism? Yet if the decline of pragmatism is essentially to be explained as the extension of a skeptical outlook that sooner or later found itself out of place and out of fashion in a postwar world turned dogmatic, why could pragmatism not just as easily have presented itself in the new postwar age of Cold War dogmatics as again a critical antidote to the logics, whether political or metaphysical, of certitude? To ask the question another way, why is it that after World War II pragmatism afforded a far less appealing interpretive alternative to the rigidities of ideological Manicheanism than after World War I?

Menand's answer is the conventional one. Pragmatism went into steep decline after World War II because its view of ideas was not amenable to appropriation either by the academic modes of critical inquiry and research agendas then in fashion or by a bipolar world supposedly locked in a universal struggle between freedom and tyranny. One could protest that the "deconstructive" habits of mind associated with someone like Dewey, whose chief intellectual tactic, as Menand points out, was to isolate an assumed hierarchy in the way people conventionally think about something and then demonstrate how that hierarchy might be reversed, could have found just as much useful employment after the 1940s and 1950s as it did before then, but this would be a distraction because as Menand well knows, the fortunes of pragmatism in the postwar period were also determined by factors other than its wariness of doctrinaire assurance, unquestioning belief, and self-righteousness. Chief among them, surely, was the way that pragmatism was co-opted by American liberals in the immediate postwar period to justify a new political consensus that, among other things, equated the free enterprise system with a revolutionary potential for social justice, found the key to that potential in economic growth, assumed that increased economic growth was producing a natural harmony of interests among social classes, believed that all the remaining problems caused by lingering social differences could be solved like industrial problems, and sought to export this ideology abroad. In this new dispensation of postwar liberal imperialism, the useful and the expedient were reduced to the level of naked self-interest, or, as it was then often termed, *Realpolitik*, and in the minds of many then as now, pragmatism was rendered as no more than a theory of the relative perception of advantage.

Another of the factors that altered the fortunes of pragmatism in the postwar period was the fact that in reaction to US exceptionalism, various disciplines within the humanities and some of the social sciences developed a strong aversion to almost any intellectual traditions that were markedly American. Couple this with what Menand notes about the effects of the American academy's turning away from public issues and toward professionalism during much of this same period, and the reasons for pragmatism's eclipse by other conceptual and methodological traditions of reflection, more narrow, specialized, and self-protective, become even more apparent.

In addition to questions about the form or shape of Menand's history, however, there are also questions that need to be raised about its content. The story he tells, with some exceptions, is almost completely restricted to developments within the United States even though several generations of historians of pragmatism have been at pains to show that pragmatism was from the beginning part of a trans-Atlantic movement of philosophical and political discourse that swept through European and American intellectual life from the last two-thirds of the nineteenth century through the first quarter of the twentieth.[9] Quite apart from James's relations with Charles Renouvoir in France, the Papini circle in Italy, or F. S. C. Schiller in England, pragmatism contributed to the search for alternatives to the mid-nineteenth-century philosophies of idealism and naturalism where ideas functioned as something more than mechanisms of adjustment and something other than pure templates of desire. Moreover, it brought to the fore a number of European intellectuals like Max Weber and Wilhelm Dilthey who believed, as Dewey did, that the "results of reflection" should not be allowed to separate "the subject matter experienced and the operations and states of experiencing [it]" and who were again to be reprised in the 1960s and 1970s as part of the immigration of Continental ideas from without, which helped pave the way for part of the post-Cold War revival of interest in pragmatism itself.[10]

From the perspective of the present, one can also see that if pragmatism has now been repossessed not only by philosophers, literary critics, cultural historians, and students of religion but also by legal theorists and intellectual historians, so it has always circulated, at least since William James's brother Henry began to write stories, in mediums other than discursive thought. As Henry informed William upon the receipt of the latter's gift of his new book entitled *Pragmatism*, he found himself "lost in wonder of the extent to which all my life I have … unconsciously pragmatised."[11] And upon finishing *The Meaning of Truth*, Henry was even more effusive:

> Thank the powers—that is thank yours—for a relevant and assailable and referable philosophy, which is related to the rest of one's intellectual life

otherwise and more conventionally than a fowl is related to a fish. In short, dearest William, the effect of these collected papers of your present volume ... seems to me exquisitely and adorably cumulative and, so to speak, consecrating; so that I, for my part feel Pragmatic invulnerability constituted.[12]

But as various literary and cultural critics have shown, the list of unconscious pragmatisers has also included Gertrude Stein, Charlotte Perkins Gilman, Robert Frost, Wallace Stevens, Marianne Moore, Zora Neale Hurston, William Carlos Williams, Kenneth Burke, Ralph Ellison, Frank O'Hara, Elizabeth Bishop, and a host of others.[13]

The fact that Menand overlooks, or at least downplays, the extent of pragmatism's significant cultural diffusion at the beginning of the twentieth century tends to distort his view of its subsequent nature and, particularly, of its theory of ideas. Far from being, as Menand contends, merely a philosophy of adaptation in the crude or simple sense, where ideas are mere tools of convenience "like forks, knives, or microchips," pragmatism is better understood, as Dewey first articulated it and others have later amplified, as a theory of situated creativity.[14] For example, Dewey held that the purpose of every act, "creative" or otherwise, is not solely to reach a goal in which, at least for the time being, action is presumably terminated but, in addition, to liberate the capacity for new action. Yet this in turn makes action itself something more than the pursuit of tasks and something different than the overcoming of obstacles. Action becomes the means by which experience generates from within itself the means to transcend its former terms and modes of expression without transcending experience as such. In short, action is not defined solely by the goals it achieves or serves but by the process it enables, thus making pragmatism a "theory of the creativity of human action."[15] To quote Dewey:

> The pragmatic theory of intelligence means that the function of mind is to project new and more complex ends—to free experience from routine and from caprice. Not the use of thought to accomplish purposes already given either in the mechanism of the body or in that of the existent state of society, but the use of intelligence to liberate and liberalize action, is the pragmatic lesson.[16]

This prompts a further question about why Menand has comparatively so little to say about the role of the imagination in thought. Peirce in effect argued that the imagination is the agency that we often and necessarily rely on to bring difficult sets of reflections to satisfactory closure; intellectual matters are ultimately resolved for Peirce not logically in terms of what follows but aesthetically in terms of what fits. James then proceeded to install the imaginative even more deeply at the center of all intellectual operations by arguing that thought is not only rational but by necessity inferential, since so much of the time we must make decisions less on the basis of the proven, the confirmed, or the established and more in relation to what is the likely, the possible, or the probable. Dewey then took this one step further by insisting that the critical dimension of thought is in fact dependent on, and enabled by, the aesthetic. This encourages one, as Dewey recast the pragmatic rule, to determine the meaning of anything in terms both of the probable, as opposed to merely verifiable, causes from which it emerged and the potential, as opposed to inevitable or predictable, consequences in which it may result. To think critically about anything requires a double movement backward toward the past to determine the presumable, as opposed to the verifiable, conditions from which something emerges, and forward toward the future to calculate the potential, as opposed to the assumed, or even the predictable, outcomes in which something may issue.

But this raises a still more serious issue because of the way Menand minimizes the entire critical thrust of the theory of intellectual inquiry that pragmatism has always represented. It is worth recalling that Peirce first used the term "pragmatism" to define a procedure for determining the rational meaning of ideas and concepts. For Peirce, that meaning could only be established by relating an idea or concept to its implications for human conduct, on the grounds that all distinctions in kind, no matter how fine, are nothing more than possible differences in practice. James then took Peirce's perception of the connection between ideas and effects and turned pragmatism both into a critical method and a theory of truth. As a critical method, James argued that if the full meaning of any proposition is not to be found in some particular to which it points, then for pragmatism it depends as well on what would have to change in experience if it were true. As a theory of truth, on the other hand, James maintained that the "true" for pragmatism can neither be reduced to an inherent property of ideas, nor identified with a reflection or copy of the real, but can only ultimately be understood as an expression of something's working relations with whatever is already held to be true in whole or in part.

Since these convictions about truth, and the procedures for ascertaining it, carried with them a number of implications for understanding experience in general, it is no coincidence that pragmatism quickly developed for James and Dewey (and also for many others both in the United States and abroad) into a more generalized perspective on life itself. And as pragmatism acquired this larger sense of itself as a general perspective, it also became in time, and especially as a result of its transnational reformulations, more pluralized and heterogenous, making it now more accurate to speak of pragmatisms in the plural rather than the singular. A pragmatist outlook or perspective thus acknowledges that if truth is always partially hostage to the past, to the assemblage of things already conceded or accepted as true, thought never commences from a position of complete neutrality and can never yield conclusions that are entirely objective. Claims for the disinterestedness, detachment, or impartiality of thought are at best only ideals, at worst a smokescreen for deception and manipulation. Thinking for the pragmatist is a process better described as tentative, provisional, improvisatory, experimental, even hypothetical, and always open to revision and self-correction, a process directed less at resolving doubt or securing assurance than in sorting out and assessing alternative options. In testing hypotheses about experience against experience, pragmatism is a technique—this was one of Dewey's chief contributions—not only for overcoming obstacles and smoothing out difficulties but for actually enriching the qualities of life itself.

As a general perspective or orientation, then, pragmatism shares with aspects of late modernism or postmodernism a conviction that absolute certainty in thought is almost always out of reach. It moreover holds that if "the quest for certainty," as Dewey termed it, has run its course, that quest needs to be replaced, or at any rate be complemented by, something like an aesthetic reconceptualization of experience itself as a form of art and the moral purpose of that art as, following Nietzsche, life's continuous revaluation of itself. At the same time, however, pragmatism is very clear that we can develop or attain varying degrees of acceptable or warrantable knowledge about any number of things. Hence it neither asserts that the search for truth is ultimately futile nor that all truths are relative and, in effect, equal. If it insists that no one possesses the whole truth either all or even most of the time, it also assumes that the only way we can correct our ideas about any truths is by referring those truths back to experience and particularly to what those others on whom they might bear similarly make of them.

In this sense, while pragmatism is wary of foundationalism, it does not, as in some versions of postmodernism, reduce all our negotiations with reality to a dispute between sentences or metaphors that provide no basis for comparison. Through its reference back to what has, or can, or might happen, it provides ways to establish standards of evaluation that can be fairly widely shared and publically contested. Truth for pragmatism is therefore inevitably social. Just as Peirce was looking originally for a test of truth that would convince all investigators, rather than just one, by standing up to the laboratory's requirements for exactitude, consistency, and coherence, so James and Dewey believed that the search for the true is in the end always a communal rather than an individual undertaking and that its value can only be established in relation to its impact on others.

One way of defining pragmatism is to call it a philosophy of difference—a philosophy, that is, designed to measure and gauge the different kinds of difference that difference makes, whether this difference refers to distinctions of identity, expression, action, principle, sentiment, or taste. Such difference is quite obviously the basic signature of a pluralistic world, but this does not mean that pragmatism merely replicates or legitimates in its procedures the ideology of multiculturalism. From a pragmatic point of view, multiculturalism, at least in America, has long been in danger of foundering on the contradictions between the centrifugal pressures it generates for the recognition of cultural diversity and the centripetal pressures it creates for a uniform sense of cultural identity.[17] The only way out of this contradiction is to rethink the meaning of our multicultural, multicentered world in a way that takes serious account of what William James meant by "a certain blindness in human beings." He was referring to our inability to think our way into the feelings of other people without succumbing to the contrary belief, as we might now put it, that all our views of others are always already merely forms of ourselves. The alternatives we are left with are neither insensibility nor solipsism. While differences are ineluctable, this does not mean that they are utterly incommensurable or just another version of ourselves. There is as much danger in dismissing such differences because they seem so alien as in presuming to think they can be reconciled or regulated. The question is whether they can be made conversable without anyone "presuming to regulate the rest of the vast field."[18]

But are there some differences too deep for words or comprehension, too sacred or private to be discussed? Many would argue that religion itself poses such a challenge, which is why some, like Rorty, have suggested that we might be better off without it. A topic now very much at the center of the new atheism debate,[19] it begs a question about whether there is a distinction to be made between those religions, or religious formations, that think they can provide absolute certainty in the face of the world's deception and evil and those that seek instead to provide moral guidance and succor in the face of the world's insecurity and injustice. A distinction that often accounts for those religions, or traditions within them, that seek to command, rule, and coerce as opposed to those that seek to console, reconcile, and reform, it also helps illumine the relation between religion and violence. Those religious traditions that wish to command and rule tend to turn the religiously and culturally different into the absolutely and totally other, and are thus tempted to resort to the ancient religious practice of scapegoating, where people attempt to cleanse or purge themselves by ritualistically projecting onto others the burdens of their own undesired fears and pollution. Those traditions dedicated, on the other hand, to consolation and transformation try to reverse, or at least counter, these processes by reconceiving the absolutely other as the radically different and then employ another religious practice that turns the different not into an opposite but instead into an ally who can help the self become better acquainted with aspects of itself.[20]

Pragmatism thus furnishes not one but two ways of approaching the deep diversity at work in the world today. Negatively, it presents itself as a cautionary philosophy that seeks to warn us against the evils of absolutism, and particularly the deprecation of the different that absolutism breeds. More positively, it offers the record of its own genesis as a philosophy initially developed by James as a method for settling otherwise interminable ideological and metaphysical disputes and furnishes an intellectual instrument that can be, and frequently is, employed to sort out and evaluate the comparative moral and religious merits of different perspectives— James called them "world-formulas"—in the new globalized world in which we now find ourselves.

Toward the end of his book, Menand attempts to sum up what he takes to be the two deficiencies of the turn-of-the-century pragmatism in which Dewey shared. The first derives from pragmatism's inability to explain where people get their wants and desires, merely clarifying instead what outcomes might result if they were to act on them. The second, related to the first, is that pragmatism cannot account for why people would ever act in ways contrary to their own self-interest and thus risk putting their lives on the line.

In response to the first claim, Menand glosses the role of inter-subjective relations in pragmatism's understanding of the formation of selfhood and thus fails to do justice to Dewey and Mead's convictions that a sense of desire, like a perception of need, is socially constructed as well as biologically inherited. Moreover, unless the sense of desire is unrelated to the sense of need, this charge also overlooks the fact that Dewey and James both expended considerable energy—James most self-consciously in *The Principles of Psychology* and *The Varieties of Religious Experience*, Dewey in *Human Nature and Conduct* as well as, later, in *Art as Experience*—pondering the significance that the second might have for the first. While there is no getting around the fact that Dewey paid far less attention than James did to the anatomy of personal life or the grammar of human motives, it was Mead who connected the social with the psychological through his pragmatic philosophy of the act.

While this is not the place to rehearse all the details of Mead's thinking, it is worth remembering that his philosophy is based on the reflexive capacity of the self to communicate with others through gestures that, as they assume meaning and significance over time, are intended to elicit a particular response. In other words, communication is possible only because the self has the ability, through the use of such symbols, to assume the attitude of the other with respect to its own gesture. By creating in those employing them the same attitudes they generate in those responding to them, such significant symbols enable, and indeed require, any who use them also to internalize what others take them to mean. Thus as the vocabulary of significant symbols broadens, so do the various ways that the self, by taking the attitude of others toward it, can know itself. Self-formation and self-knowledge is thus to a considerable extent dependent on what has subsequently become known as the Social Scriptorum produced by such exchanges, that assemblage of different attitudes and roles that people can assume in relation to each other.[21] While this hardly reduces selfhood to society, it does suggest that pragmatism has a good deal to say about where people get their yearnings and wishes, feeling inevitably framed by, even if not confined to, the repertoire of social roles that are available to them.

As for Menand's second claim that turn-of-the-century pragmatism lacks an explanation for how people act in ways that are often indifferent to, or in defiance of, a prudential, self-interested calculation of consequences, the evidence seems to run in the opposite direction. While pragmatism places strong emphasis on the instrumental importance of ideas or, as James preferred to put it, on their ability to put us in better touch with the rest of our experience, this is due in no small measure to what James and Dewey both believed to be the conservative nature of truth itself. Likening truth to a kind of credit system on which our thoughts and beliefs pass along with relative ease until some new experience challenges them, they assumed that we immediately respond to the discomfort this causes by modifying the body of already accepted opinion only as much as we feel is absolutely necessary. But if or when this tactic fails to alleviate our sense of inward unease, we then look for some new truth that may either force the stock of received opinions to be reseen in a new light or compel it to be abandoned altogether. Whichever the case, the mind needs to find relief from the unsettlement of received and approved ideas as well as it can, and if this ultimately necessitates the embrace of an opinion or belief so new that a radical revisioning of much that was formerly assumed to be true must be made, generating as a result actions contrary to those previously understood as natural or self-interested, there is nothing in Dewey or in James that says this couldn't, and in fact does not, happen all the time.

Is this not what almost certainly does occur in the case of religious conversions or intellectual, artistic, and emotional epiphanies? Such momentous internal transformations tend to find their justification in an entirely different, sometimes even an opposite or contrary, logic of explanation than the one they have displaced, but it is a logic of explanation, nonetheless, which still owes its credibility to the way it puts the mind in more effective working relations with those parts of its experience that it presently deems decisive and leads to actions assumed to be consistent with that perception. But this, in turn, helps explain what Menand thinks pragmatism cannot explain about ideas. People are willing to die in defense of ideas they do not regard as immutable because, however far "the sense of purposes" they keep alive "outrun evidence," and the meanings they establish "transcend indurated habit," as Dewey noted about artistic experience, those ideas still enable people to keep faith with the truth of whatever else they have experienced, even when it defies their own self-interest.[22] Hence the erasure of any contradiction, to go back to Dewey's statement at the beginning, between something called "true good" and the need to rethink and revise its meaning again and again "in terms of the conditions of concrete situations as they arise."[23]

This means that pragmatism can explain why one might die for an idea and that it can provide us with reasons to defend values when the stakes are high. We do not have to believe that values are immutable or ideas absolute, as I shall soon show, to make sacrifices for them. As far as the pragmatist is concerned, all we need to believe is that this value or idea is validated by the rest of our experience. Pragmatism can easily concede that certain truths have held up over very long periods of time and been broadly supported. At the same time, it acknowledges that few truths have lasted for ever and gained assent from everyone. In this sense, "universality," like "timelessness," are relative terms. But the point is not whether certain truths have been widely shared, for they most certainly have; nor is it to achieve consensus on how they are construed and practiced, for we certainly will not. The point, rather, is to understand that while the universality of certain truths and values will always be deeply contested around the world, the disputes they attract nonetheless attest to the enormous investments almost all of us everywhere have in their interpretation and application. While we clearly need to find better ways of saying what we mean by such values even when there is a measure of overlapping consensus in how we describe them, we still more urgently need to find better ways of safeguarding what they variously represent to people throughout the world. An excellent example of this challenge is represented by the subject of human rights, an idea for which many people have been willing to die without any absolute assurance, except in the language of various famous Declarations, that they are built into the very structure of things.

This is particularly true in the case of international human rights, which in the form in which we now know them did not even come into existence until after World War II. Part of a larger effort to reorder the entire world of postwar international relations which had begun in 1945 when the United Nations itself was chartered to outlaw aggressive war between states, the movement for international human rights was born out of the attempt to protect individuals, and particularly those victimized by war, from abuse by setting appropriate standards for their treatment. While its principal authors were under no illusions about how far down those rights went or how likely they were to be honored, Eleanor Roosevelt, Rene Cassin, John Humphrey, and Charles Malik, all of whom played an important role in the formulation of the Declaration, knew that in a world of global violence, power rules through the relentless and merciless use of force to intimidate, panic, maim, and slaughter. They also clearly realized that the governments who initially agreed to become signatories to the Declaration did so only because they were confident that it would not constitute any threat to their own sovereignty. Nonetheless, the drafters also comprehended, in a manner wholly consistent with Dewey's understanding of the creative power of ideas, that once the Declaration was established, its very existence would begin to increase awareness and appreciation of the legitimacy of human rights around the world and thus become an instrument that might, if not deter the worst violations of rights, at least begin to bring them to international attention.

But the creation of the Universal Declaration of Human Rights in 1948 was only the first stage in a process initiated by the chartering of the United Nations in 1945 to create a new legal and moral architecture that would protect individuals from the kinds of atrocities that so many millions suffered in World War II. The second stage of this process emerged the same year the Universal Declaration was signed when the Genocide Convention was established to protect religious, racial, and ethnic groups from extermination. The third stage materialized a year later with the revision of the Geneva Conventions (the Geneva Conventions were first produced in 1864), which attempted to strengthen immunity for non-combatants, and the fourth stage appeared with the establishment of the international convention on asylum, which sought to protect the rights of refugees.

However, the full significance of these developments can only be gauged by remembering that before World War II international law did not apply to individuals but only to states or to individuals as citizens of states. Thus when the protections of the Universal Declaration of Human Rights were enfolded in 1966 into the two Covenants on Political and Human Rights and Social, Economic, and Cultural Rights, something unprecedented was accomplished. Even if many of the states that had originally signed the Universal Declaration had no intention of legally honoring at home the protections and prohibitions they were prepared to support abroad—the United States, for example, still maintained a system of racial segregation in the South, actively discriminated against women in the workplace and elsewhere, and perpetrated housing restrictions in the North as well as the South—it unwittingly enabled individual rights language to take on something like a life of its own as an international norm and helped shape both the anti-colonial revolution abroad and the civil rights revolution in the United States.[24] Yet the effects of these ideas, what Dewey might have called their creative afterlife, did not stop here. Rights discourse and its remedies were subsequently incorporated during the postwar period into the structure of various new state constitutions and were eventually employed as a measure both to determine the legal qualifications applicable to older states for admission to such organizations as the European Union and for new states from the developing world to seek membership in the family of nations.

Nonetheless, this fairly positive interpretation of human rights developments has been challenged on a variety of grounds: that the tradition of rights inscribed in most international covenants is derived from philosophical traditions that are essentially Eurocentric and elitist, or at least Enlightened and thus privileged; that human rights have been used in the post-colonial era to justify diplomatic and military interventions by Western powers in non-Western countries; that the West has been, at best, inconsistent and at worst hypocritical in applying rights standards to its own societies; that when such standards have been applied at all in the West, they have frequently been restricted to the civil and political sphere without being extended to the social, economic, sexual, cultural, or domestic spheres; that the United States has set its own interests above the need to stop genocide not only in Armenia and Western and Central Europe before World War II but in Cambodia, Iraq and, most especially, Rwanda and Darfur since World War II; and that, perhaps most intractable of all, different parts and cultures of the world clearly honor very different and often conflicting, if not at points incompatible, traditions of human rights.

It also must be acknowledged that countries within the Atlantic community, say, whose conception of rights derives from the European Enlightenment—France, Great Britain, Canada, and the United States—differ sharply even amongst themselves over everything from which rights most matter, to what institutions should implement them, to how they should be enforced. Moreover, it is hardly irrelevant that the necessity of extending international rights from states to individuals only became obvious when the people of the West, like everyone else, could see for themselves the horrors to which certain Enlightenment traditions in Europe had actually led. Hence while efforts on all fronts and on all levels must continue if human rights are to be brought more fully into line with the diverse experiences and needs of the world's many peoples and cultures, few would argue that a movement intended to protect individuals against cruelty and oppression should be altogether abandoned simply because it has clearly been shaped by European interests and just as clearly misused by Western as well as non-Western states.

Surely one of the more positive results of the human rights revolution has been the subsequent development of a parallel advocacy revolution where a vast network of non-governmental human rights organizations now numbering in the tens of thousands have not only given voice to individual victims but developed structures of accountability and agency that currently comprise some of the lineaments of what has come to be known as a global civil society. This is not to pretend that all NGOs dedicated to human rights are in agreement with one another or act in concert to relieve suffering and promote justice. It is merely to say that without the advocacy revolution, and the monitoring function that NGOs perform, states would have been able to violate human rights with far more impunity than they have since World War II, and many of the rights instruments that were signed into law during the last half century would have lacked any real power.

But real power is indeed what at least some human rights instruments now possess, a power that extends well beyond the ability to censure those who violate human rights covenants and now includes various mechanisms to bring such violators into compliance and actually punish them. The International Tribunal at Arusha, for example, secured the first convictions under the Genocide Convention. The International Court at the Hague enabled the first international convictions for war crimes since the Nuremberg Trials. And now, with the indictment of Slobodan Milošević, James Taylor, and Radovan Karadžić, the first war crimes trials in history are being conducted to convict sitting heads of major states. Call this record of human rights achievement sporadic and irregular, as we must; call it unevenly honored and practiced between the North and South, between the West and the rest, as we should; call it woefully inadequate in its applications to the condition of, say, women, children, the elderly, refugees, or immigrants, as we will—it becomes most problematic when, as an instrument of enforcement, human rights discourse has been transformed into an ideology of last resort.

This conversion is exactly what the early pragmatists, as Menand rightly notes, sought to discourage. But opposition to the hardening of ideologies does not have to be grounded in the belief that ideas are merely disposable tools capable of being discarded when something more useful turns up. Far from viewing ideas purely as implements of adaptation, Dewey and James thought of them instead more along the lines of what Kenneth Burke calls symbolic actions: responses to the questions raised by problematic situations that are designed not so much to answer those questions as to strategically cope with them by reinterpreting them in a way that simultaneously constructs a critical perspective on them and contains an implicit attitude toward them. Viewed as strategic responses to the problematics of particular situations, then, ideas are the products of the situations that generate them but can, and do, change as quickly and profoundly as the situation itself changes. The larger the stakes those situations presuppose, the more radical must become the intellectual strategies for addressing them. In this equation, there is nothing to prevent ideas developed in response to the most transient and, as Menand characterizes them, "nonproducable of circumstances," from becoming, depending on what is at issue, beliefs for which, without being taken as unconditional, people will nonetheless be prepared to make ultimate sacrifices.[25]

A second example of a moment when, for pragmatic reasons, many of the leading states of the world refused to subsume their own notions of the "true good" in the tyrannical abstractions that defined them during the Cold War, and rethought its meanings on equal terms with all others who might have a vested interest in its interpretations and applications, is furnished by the Antarctic Treaty of 1959. Eventually signed by 48 countries, this Treaty set aside Antarctica as a scientific preserve and banned military activity and, after the signing of the Madrid Protocol in 1991, also prohibited mineral exploration and extraction on the continent. Here an international order uneasily poised on the brink of nuclear Armageddon decided to suspend its hostilities at the edge of the Antarctic not only to prevent Cold War politics from turning the "lost continent" into a war zone but also to convert at least one global space into a realm of civic activity where rival states could exist and cooperate for the sake of scientific advancement and environmental protection.[26]

The key to these developments was the establishment in 1957 and 1958 of the International Geophysical Year. A scientific rather than a political undertaking, it organized tens of thousands of scientists from 66 nations into a coordinated inquiry that focused much of its attention on the study of Antarctica. The largest scientific enterprise ever initiated, it involved twelve countries, seven of which had earlier asserted territorial claims over the continent itself (Argentina, Britain, France, Chile, New Zealand, Norway, and Australia) and five new ones eager to join in the exploration of Antarctica (Belgium, Japan, South Africa, the United States, and the Soviet Union). This set the stage for a very dangerous competition on the least populated and most underdeveloped continent on the face of the earth but it yielded instead one of the most extraordinary cooperations among nations in the history of the world.

That spirit of cooperation was codified when at President Eisenhower's invitation, the twelve nations whose scientists had been involved in research on the continent during the International Geophysical Year were asked to meet in Washington, DC in October 1959 to produce a treaty regulating its development. It took 18 months to hammer out an agreement on provisions guaranteeing that Antarctica would be used for peaceful purposes only, that scientific investigation and cooperation in Antarctica would be free, and that results from this research would be exchanged and made available to all the signatories, but the most symbolic article of the Treaty was no doubt the one barring all military activity on the continent, which made the Antarctica Treaty the first arms control agreement of the Cold War. Little wonder that a Norwegian delegate said of the Washington conference: "The thrilling saga of Antarctica has inspired men everywhere with its emphasis on basic human values—courage, patience and willingness to work together towards a common goal."[27] Since the signing of the Treaty in June 1961, all the consultative nations, which encompass roughly two-thirds of the world's people, have met at least every other year and produced agreements on environmental protection, the conservation of living resources, and even the safeguarding of seals. As a treaty governing a territory to which seven nations have claims and another two, the United States and Russia, consider themselves to possess the "basis for claims," it has not survived without challenges that may drastically intensify when it comes up for renewal. But the more extraordinary fact is that it was created at all and that it has lasted throughout the turbulence of the Cold War and beyond as an example of how pragmatic foresight and reasoning trumped the most intractable ideological oppositions and absolutisms.

As a third example of pragmatic thinking, and its applicability to a world of violence where people are still willing to put their lives on the line for causes that are not couched in fixed or doctrinaire terms, let me turn to the nationalist narrative that is continuing to emerge in postapartheid South Africa. This is a narrative crafted in response to the horrors of centuries of racial oppression and naturalized cruelty that could have left its victims wanting either to avenge their suffering or to refashion themselves in the image of their victimization. But in places like Cape Town's Robben Island, which served from the sixteenth century on as a place of exile, incarceration, and banishment for South Africa's political enemies and social outcasts and was most famously home to President Nelson Mandela for 18 years, this temptation was consciously resisted and, for the most part, overcome. And it was overcome by nothing so much as an idea that confronted the absolutisms of racial prejudice with a belief that such convictions debase not only those they are intended to oppress but also those who seek to oppress them. This was a belief for which the prisoners of Robben Island were willing to risk their lives and by means of which, according to their own testimony, they were able over the years to transform their prison into a kind of university, to turn a site of banishment and inhumane treatment into a symbol of the regeneration of the human.

We cannot forget, however, that in the years between the end of apartheid and the beginning of the new South African government under Nelson Mandela, more than 10,000 people were casualties of violent reprisals, nor that in the years since, the state has made comparatively little progress in bringing economic or political relief to the great majority of South Africa's people. But the bloodletting that could have exploded into a civil war of retribution like America's own War Between the States was avoided because the new South African leaders, like many South African citizens of all races and mixtures, refused to allow ideas to be turned into weapons or belief to become an instrument of retribution. Instead, and at great risk of arousing the demons of reprisal, the people of South Africa created a Truth and Reconciliation Commission intended to bring into the light deeds of darkness that were committed on both sides of the struggle over apartheid. Writing in 2007, the philosopher Charles Taylor admitted that it is still not possible to know "if this will ultimately work":

> A move like this goes against the utterly understandable desire for revenge by those who have suffered, as well as all the reflexes of self-righteousness. But with this, and even more the extraordinary stance of Mandela from his first release from prison, what one might call his reununciation of the rights of victimhood, the new South Africa might never have even begun to emerge from the temptations to civil war which threatened and are not yet quite stilled.[28]

While the wounds from almost two centuries of racial persecution will always remain and perhaps never fully be healed, those wounds were prevented from continuing to suppurate by a conviction that the only way to escape the grip of ideas in the service of racial discrimination was, and is, by refusing to think in terms of the dogmatic and vicious racist oppositions on which they are grounded. The "freedom fighters" of Robben Island and their supporters were willing to die for their beliefs, even though their beliefs were often supported by nothing more essentialist than a pragmatic conviction that the "true good" is always in danger of being turned into a totalizing abstraction unless those who seek to pursue it are willing to rethink its meanings on terms of equality with all those others who also have a vested interest in its interpretation and applications.

4

CULTURE AND THE MISSHAPING OF WORLD ORDER

> But perhaps the most fateful change is, again, the pervasive raggedness of the world with which, so suddenly, we now are faced. The shattering of larger coherences, or seeming such, into smaller ones, uncertainly connected with one another, has made relating local realities with overarching ones, "the world around here" ... with the world overall, extremely difficult.
>
> Clifford Geertz, *Available Light: Anthropological Reflections on Philosophical Topics*, 2000, p.221

> The conquest of the earth, which mostly means the taking it away from those who have a different complexion or slightly flatter noses than ourselves, is not a pretty thing when you look into it too much. What redeems it is the idea only. An idea at the back of it; not a sentimental pretense but an idea; and an unselfish belief in the idea—something you can set up, and bow down before, and offer a sacrifice to.
>
> Joseph Conrad, *Heart of Darkness*, 1995, p.20

What role have, or do, cultural assumptions, principles, and aspirations play in international politics? In the American academy as well as the public arena, the traditional answer to this question has been "fairly minimal." Not that anyone has considered international affairs immune to the influence of ideologies, values, or even symbols, but only that the conventional orthodoxy in international relations has tended either to downplay the effects of such factors or, more likely, to presume that the best way to understand their importance is by determining how they have been expressed within the terms and constraints of the state system. In much of the scholarship devoted to the study of international relations, "culture talk" has often been held to be at best a diversion or distraction, at worst a distortion or even a delusion; and given some of its recurrent exaggerations, one can rather easily see why. It is scarcely necessary to cite the notoriety of something like the "clash thesis" by Samuel P. Huntington, much less the more widespread obsession in the

United States and elsewhere with "culture wars," to realize that the term *culture* has been as susceptible to misrepresentation and deformation as the word *politics*. Where culture is held to explain everything, it illumines almost nothing. And yet the cultural component has worked its way back into the discourse of international politics, not simply as a necessary way of accounting for the temper, tension, and force of particular policies and practices, but also as a way of comprehending the political or, for that matter, the economic itself. One can no more divorce political interests or economic issues from cultural prejudices than one can separate the history of institutions, diplomacy, and war from the history of consciousness.

Such elemental linkages have, of course, long been acknowledged in the writings of everyone from Adam Smith, David Ricardo, and Karl Marx to Max Weber, Hannah Arendt, Karl Polanyi, and Immanuel Wallerstein, but they have been given new applications in the work of, among countless others, Judith Sklar, Robert Cox, and Paul Krugman. Culture in their work is not simply a tool kit but a template or blueprint and road map for how people think and act, and above all, interpret their world to themselves and to others. In this sense, cultural systems as they operate in the international sphere are neither simply framed nor delimited by politics; as Edmund Burke knew as well as Antonio Gramsci, not to mention Sayid Qutb, they generate the emotional and cognitive weather of which at various levels politics is both the consequence and sometimes the corrective.

This assumption has not been lost on a series of scholars who are particularly interested in which cultural system or set of values is to be preferred if one wants to promote what they term "human progress." By "progress" they mean such things as democratic participation and economic development. "Culture matters," as one collection has been titled, because it establishes the horizon of expectations and the grammar of motives that enable people to act on behalf of their own wellbeing and perhaps that of others.[1] This is by no means an idle ambition but it tends to restrict the case to be made here for why culture counts for so much. *Culture* as the term is employed here will not be confined only to those values, assumptions, beliefs, perspectives, and dispositions conducive to the creation of economic advancement and political democratization, but will be widened to include all the practices, subjective as well as empirical, by which people make their lives not simply productive (according to some economic or political calculus) but meaningful.

This wider understanding of the place and play of culture in international affairs has become increasingly self-evident since the end of the Cold War, which caught so many students of global politics by surprise. Itself a battle between ideological mindsets and their many variations projected onto the field of superpower rivalry, the end of the Cold War suddenly revealed many international structures to be ineffective and outworn, others to be surprisingly resilient, and everyone scrambling to define the different ordering of the world that might take its place. James Rosenau spoke for many when he suggested that the Cold War now appeared "more a collage of perceptions than a confrontation of powers, ... more a shadow play than a stark drama." If, as he continued, "weapons build-ups and arms races were perpetuated more by unwarranted perceptions and distorted intelligence reports than by actual plans for military offences," one was now compelled to grasp "how fully the course of events are fictions of convergent imaginations, of inter-subjectivities rather than objective conditions."[2]

"The tyranny of metaphor," as the historian Robert Dallek calls it, is not confined, however, to the illusions spawned by the Cold War. It has guided American foreign policy from its beginnings to the present, allowing virtually all subsequent American presidents, according to Dallek, to perpetuate three postwar myths: that the United States has the power to transform the world; that compromise and conciliation always represent a sign of weakness, and that American military strength and readiness is the only effectual way of meeting every major international conflict. Such illusions bedeviled even those few presidents like Eisenhower and Kennedy who actually knew better, but the figurative forms in which such illusions and misconceptions were couched and defended made their appeals as conventional wisdom almost impossible to resist.[3]

But culture's ubiquity in shaping and controlling perception is not restricted to politics but is also apparent in economics, as the money managers and financial executives at Bear Stearns eventually realized when the gigantic investment bank and securities trading and brokerage firm was brought down not by a lack of cash but rather by a surplus of it. Bear Stearns was done in—and the world economy in turn seriously threatened—not by bad bets or corporate malfeasance so much as by cultural misreadings, symbolic and otherwise, of its true condition. When the run on Bear Stearns began in early 2008, the Federal Reserve along with J. P. Morgan Chase threw it a lifeline amounting to a multibillion-dollar line of credit that suddenly made it absolutely flush with cash. But the news that Bear Stearns had obtained this lifeline, amounting to a cash cushion of $17 billion, had an effect on Wall Street that was the very opposite of its intention. One insider detailed the confusion this way:

> This line of credit, the stop-gap measure that was supposed to solve the problem that hadn't really existed in the first place had done nothing but worsen it. When we started the week, we had no liquidity issues. But because people had said that we did have problems with our capital, it became true, even though it wasn't true when people started saying it. ... So we were forced to find capital to offset the losses we'd sustained because somebody decided we didn't have capital when we really did. So when we finally got more capital to replace the capital we'd lost, people took that as a bad sign and pointed to the fact that we had no capital and had to get a loan to cover it, even when we did have the capital they said we didn't have.[4]

So much for mathematical models of market behavior. The mistakes, which were catastrophic for Bear Stearns and contributed to the near collapse of the entire global economy, had nothing to do with econometrics, market laws, or "invisible hands," but solely with perceptions based on interpretive frames that were not only mistaken but cultural through and through.

The language in these two examples is telling. In the first, the Cold War not only turns out to have been represented by figurative forms but also in some profound sense to have partially been fictive in its conduct. In the second, the collapse of one of the premier firms on Wall Street, which helped trigger the recession of 2008, resulted from a simple misreading of signals that was then compounded by interpretive spin. This merely underlines what international relations scholars, like members of the informed public generally, have now relearned from the current wars in Iraq and Afghanistan: global politics and the global economy are threaded with cultural assumptions that profoundly affect not only how we conceive and enact our relations with others but also how we imagine that the world should be reshaped. Hence constructing images of world order and models of global governance is not an exercise solely reserved for the select few who make or propose policy. Rather, it is rooted in what might be called the telos of culture itself, which tends to make imperialists of us all, and nowhere is this more obvious than in the United States.

The genealogy of America's own imperial destiny goes back to a time long before there was a nation or a people. It begins, one could argue, with the founding of the ill-fated Jamestown colony in 1584, but conventional histories of American adventurism usually associate its origins, if very tardily, with the Spanish American War of 1898. A poorly disguised grab for territory and trade in the Caribbean and the Pacific, the Spanish American War drew some of its sharpest criticism from America's then most internationally renowned author. Mark Twain's response was characteristically prescient:

> I left these shores, at Vancouver, a red-hot imperialist. I wanted the American eagle to go screaming into the Pacific. It seemed tiresome and tame for it to content itself with the Rockies. Why not spread its wings over the Philippines, I asked myself? And I said to myself, here are a people who have suffered for three centuries. We can make them as free as ourselves, give them a government and country of their own, put a miniature of the American constitution afloat in the Pacific, start a brand new republic to take its place among the free nations of the world. It seemed to me a great task to which we had addressed ourselves. But I have thought some more, since then, and I have read carefully the treaty of Paris, and I have seen that we do not intend to free, but to subjugate the people of the Philippines. We have gone there to conquer, not to redeem ... It should, it seems to me, be our pleasure and duty to make those people free, and let them deal with their own domestic questions in their own way. And so I am an anti-imperialist. I am opposed to having the eagle put its talons on any other land.[5]

Others, like President William McKinley, saw this preemptive move rather differently. Insistent that the Philippine people could not be left to themselves, as "they were unfit for self-government—and would soon have anarchy and misrule over there worse than Spain's was,"[6] McKinley was incredulous and outraged that detractors [presumably like Mark Twain] could challenge the "virtue," "capacity," "high purpose," and "good faith" which qualified "this free people as a civilizing agency." Believing that a century and more of "free government" has uniquely qualified the people of the United States "for the great task of lifting up and assisting to better conditions and large liberty those distant peoples who, through the issue of battle, have become our wards," McKinley embraced colonialism, like so many of his imperialist kinsmen throughout the nineteenth and twentieth centuries, as a moral challenge.[7]

McKinley did not think of himself as patronizing but instead as large-minded and patriotic; yet his kind of condescension is so often merely another mask of coercion of the sort that has guided much American thinking and behavior ever since. Referring to Kant's notion of radical evil, the cultural critic Lionel Trilling warned in the 1950s that there is no moral danger greater than the process by which, "when once we have made our fellow men the objects of our enlightened interest, [we] ... go on to make them the objects of our pity, then of our wisdom, ultimately of our coercion."[8]

There is, nevertheless, another school of thought, now most vigorously defended by the British historian Niall Ferguson, which suggests that America has long been an imperial power and should not be ashamed of admitting it. Ferguson contends that America's centrality to the stability and wellbeing of international order has been an accepted truth for well over a century, and now the US cannot allow its reluctance to be perceived as an empire prevent it from fulfilling its global responsibilities. The only real issue, say the defenders of what they view as a too hesitant American imperialism, is how to do it well. And doing it well requires acting multilaterally when it can and unilaterally when it must.

The most dramatic recent threat to global governance and America's hand in guiding it is associated with the attacks on the Twin Towers and the Pentagon on September 11, 2001. Those attacks, which were perceived by the American administration and, at least in the beginning, by a considerable percentage not only of the American people but also of the world's as assaults not just on the US but on some of the supports of the world system itself, set in motion a massive, far-reaching counter-response whose purpose, it was soon to become apparent, was at once to preserve world order as it was constructed on September 10, 2001 and simultaneously to reconfigure it. One can speculate about whether al-Qaeda actually believed that its targeting of some of the symbolic foundations of world order would be so successful, much less foresee the reaction that those attacks would subsequently generate, but there is little doubt that the counteraction they produced by the so-called "Coalition of the Willing" led to consequences that far exceeded its expectations. Actions taken by the United States and its allies have thus far succeeded not in strengthening world order but in further endangering it, at once destabilizing the Middle East, bringing new and terrible suffering to millions of people displaced by the violence, alienating many of America's friends and potential global partners in the future, saddling the American Treasury with a debt of trillions and trillions of dollars, and discrediting the reputation of the United States for generations to come.

This paradox might seem obvious, but reducing its global meaning to the self-contradiction of failed American politics clearly misses the role that cultural forms played in producing it. It effaces the way the symbolic in our so-called postmodern world has taken over much of the definition of the real by compelling us to see the real through images of itself. This is not to propose that reality is composed of nothing but copies or forgeries. But it is to suggest, let us say, that the terror of which 9/11 was the expression, and the terror it unleashed, as I will explain more fully in due course, cannot be comprehended without understanding their nature and function as cultural expressions of a very special sort. As has already been mentioned in the Preface, the transformation of life into spectacle, horror into the image almost of a movie, merely made it easier to hide the reality of which the events of 9/11 were a grotesque realization. What was hidden in plain sight was American responsibility not so much for the perpetration of this crime (though the United States had had plenty of warning) but for its creation. The United States had trained and armed those who turned against it and the image of world order it thought it could protect using elements of its own destructive potential. Thus what made the event so frightening is that whether we do or do not live in the kind of postmodern hyperreal of the sort defined by Jean Baudrillard, we now do inhabit a kind of global surreal where the terror of the real made symbolic can be magnified many times over by the terror of the symbolic made real.

But the meaning of the word "terror" is in fact extremely difficult to pin down. While states have used spectacular violence as a political strategy to spread fear and panic among their own citizens from, if not before, the time of the French Revolution, the first "global" attempt to define terror sought to decouple the practice of terrorism from the policies of states. Hence the League of Nations restricted terrorism to "criminal acts directed against a state and intended or calculated to create a state of terror in the minds of particular persons, or a group of persons, or a general public," and this definition finds its echo a half century later in a recent FBI publication, which defines terrorism as "unlawful use of force and violence against persons or property to intimidate or coerce a government, the civilian population, or any segment thereof in furtherance of political and social objectives."[9] While "one person's terrorist is," as the old adage has it, "another person's freedom-fighter," such definitions have helped reinforce the mistaken view, now widely held by the American public, that terrorism involves no more than illegitimate violence directed by disenfranchised groups at innocent civilians.

The problem with this view is that it erases too much of the past. While the full history of such matters is beyond the scope of this chapter, it is essential to remember that the United States, along with other world powers and, to be sure, numerous dissident groups, bears responsibility during the postwar period for the creation of an international climate favorable to the use of terror.[10] This occurred most dramatically during the administration of Ronald Reagan when, in response to the overthrow of friendly dictatorships in places like Iran and Nicaragua, the United States began to regard various forms of militant nationalism as proxies of the Soviet Union and thus determined to employ "all means necessary," to invoke the operative phrase, not merely to contain Soviet expansionism but to reverse it. Terror became the weapon of choice both for the Contras in Nicaragua and for the *mujahideen* in Afghanistan, and the justification of its covert use culminated in the labeling of all nations then suspected of sponsoring terrorism—Iran, Iraq, Libya, Sudan, Cuba, North Korea—as "rogue states."

This is not to imply that all terrorism and terrorists are the same—there are crucial distinctions to be made between the genocidal murders of the Khmer Rouge in Cambodia and ethnic cleansing in Bosnia and Kosovo, mass murder in Central Africa and separatist terrorism in Chechnya, "shock and awe" employed by the American military in the invasion of Iraq, and the bombing of abortion clinics in the United States—but rather to claim that this most recent global expansion of the use of terror, by state and non-state actors alike, probably had its origins in the later phases of Cold War and thus did not, as many people presume, arise suddenly with the emergence of Islamic jihadism. Terror was used by Timothy McVeigh, Theodore Kaczynski, and the nameless perpetrator (or perpetrators) of the anthrax attack on members of the United States Congress, no less than by, say, Kurdish nationalists in Turkey, the Tamil Tigers in Sri Lanka, or the Revolutionary Armed Forces of Colombia (FARC), and this should caution against the use of any discourse that associates terror only with non-Western others and rarely if ever with states. Christian terrorism, for example, has again made a return to the United States, though it is important to remember that its ideological justification has been present since the 1980s and 1990s in the preaching of the Reverend Jerry Falwell and Pat Robertson about the End-Time of Rapture promised by the New Testament Book of Revelation.[11] Indeed, threats of right-wing violence in the United States, according to the Southern Poverty Law Center, rose by 200 percent between 2009 and 2010, and the plan developed by Christian Hutaree militia in Ohio and Michigan to use the assassination of a policeman for the purpose of killing hundreds of his or her fellow officers using an IED (Improvised Explosive Device), planted at the funeral in order to trigger an armed revolt against the government, was clearly inspired by al-Qaeda tactics and nearly succeeded before it was detected.

Nonetheless, terror has now acquired various new sponsors, adopted different methods, and developed altered if far from uniform enhanced ambitions.[12] The terror we now face as what could be, and certainly feels like, a recurrent condition of global life, may have its most immediate roots in the Cold War era, but it is now different not only in scale but also in scope, purpose, and, perhaps, in nature from what preceded it. If terror is at bottom no more than a strategy for using excessive, seemingly gratuitous violence to gain attention and intimidate populations, it has become infinitely more lethal, disruptive, and psychically disabling as it has learned how to exploit the tools of the modern media, availed itself of more destructive weapons, and joined its tactics to causes that are not only ethnic and national but also religious.

This has led some experts to differentiate between the "old terrorism" of the Cold War era—where the goal was the expulsion of colonialist regimes, the overthrow of capitalist imperialism, or the desire for ethnic or regional separatism, and the object was to ensure that many people watched while only comparatively few died—and the "new terrorism" of the post-Cold War period, which is more often but by no means always linked to vague religious or apocalyptic aims and seeks to inflict as much pain as possible. At least until 9/11, the new terrorism seemed to be best represented by Aum Shinrikyo, the sect led by Shoko Asahara, which first employed weapons of mass destruction in March 1995 when it released sarin gas into the Tokyo subway system. Miraculously killing only 12 people while injuring several thousand, Aum Shinrikyo actually possessed enough sarin gas to cause hundreds of thousands of deaths and hoped to succeed in the destruction of entire major cities.[13]

But the full impact of the difference between the new terrorism and the old was not fully absorbed worldwide until the attack on the World Trade Center and the Pentagon. Here, it became clear, terror had escalated to a new mega-level where the symbolic, if not also substantial, harm it was intended to inflict was meant to equal or surpass the kinds of social injury once associated with large-scale military attacks by state actors, and the assailant now was something other than a nation-state itself. "Megaterrorism," as Richard Falk calls this newest form of violence, operates outside the legal framework of states (thus remaining to a certain extent "invisible" or only partially visible), indiscriminately targets entire populations, and measures success chiefly in terms of the destabilization caused both by the fear it inspires and the excessive, defensive counter-reaction it is intended to create.[14] Turning the assailant from a sovereign state or dissident community or group into a global network, the assailed becomes any and all who are rendered vulnerable by its stratagems of cruelty and carnage.

In the process, the atrocities of 9/11 brought something still more dreadful into play. This new element was a result not only of the world stage on which they were performed but of the world, or rather conception of the world itself, that their performance sought to menace. Though the attacks of 9/11 did not, like Aum Shinrikyo's assault on the Tokyo subway system, rely on weapons of mass destruction, the abyss they opened was just as potentially bottomless. It was the abyss revealed when terror becomes more than a violent instrument of intimidation and coercion and is converted into a technology devoted to disrupting, in truth disabling, mentality itself and the affective circuits that make it work. Far from merely shocking the mind, megaterror seeks utterly to enfeeble it; and with that enfeeblement is threatened the possibility of imagining much of any future at all beyond the present of its own ravages. In this new era, terror seems at times, especially if it were to involve the use of weapons of mass destruction, to open onto a futureless present bereft of the hope of any other destiny but the one defined by its own mechanisms of unpredictable mayhem.

The late Jacques Derrida went still further, arguing that 9/11 became uniquely lethal because of its perverse autoimmunitary effects. Operating like an organism seeking to protect itself from a perceived threat by suicidally destroying its own system of defense, 9/11 actually succeeded in reproducing aspects of the very evil it was seeking to resist. First of all, this was revealed when the United States found itself on 9/11 being attacked from within, as it were, by militants associated none too distantly with the forces it had itself helped train and supply to fight the Soviet Union before the end of the Cold War. Moreover, that earlier training of the *mujahideen* in Afghanistan not only created many of the conditions that supported the development of al-Qaeda but may have, in turn, helped focus al-Qaeda's interest in targeting two of the most potent symbolic expressions of American power.

Second, this autoimmunitary logic enabled 9/11 to acquire the status of a calamity worse than the Cold War itself by threatening Americans and others with the loss of something less tangible, but almost more irreplaceable, than the world of institutions and structures and even individual lives that were preserved for more than 40 years by the nuclear balance of terror. What was put at risk by this auto-immunitary logic was "nothing less than the existence of the world ... [or the] worldwide itself," that process, by turns legal, economic, linguistic, political, legal, ethical, and spiritual, through which we seek to extend the world's meaning as well as materiality by bringing ever widening spheres of experience, both here on earth and beyond, within its range of significance. Derrida referred to this multi-disciplinary process of world-making and world-extending as *mondialization*, and assumed that there is no more crucial component of the global than this.[15]

Third and finally, this autoimmunitary logic suggested that repression might be circular, that revenge may quite possibly become insatiable, that reprisings and reprisals could feed off each other *ad infinitum*. Were this to occur—and Derrida believed that the repressed always return to unsettle constructions whose exclusions compel and enforce it—he was fearful that the relationship between what he referred to as "earth, *terra*, territory, and terror" might be permanently altered, further blurring distinctions between combatant and non-combatant, civilian and soldier, insurgent, citizen, occupier, and peace keeper, especially in a world where nanotechnologies now make their operations less visible or controllable.[16]

Whether the potentially suicidal logics of autoimmunology can be extended to the entire global system—megaterror as the global system under attack by its own antibodies—they demonstrate, with all the modern technological resources available to it, that death is not simply the source and sign of the global system's power, nor the symbol of its destiny, but also—and emphatically—its nemesis. That is, the sacrificial violence of the terrorist attacks assaulted the system at the one point where the system cannot defend itself. By portraying death as preferable to life, death gains dominion in the very act in which it simultaneously displays itself, like life, as disposable. In addition, these logics pose a series of hard questions: Where, beyond the wars in Afghanistan and Iraq, and possibly Iran and Pakistan, may these actions and counteractions potentially take us? What in the way of costs to international structures and practices will they, or could they, exact? Who among the world's people are likely to bear the largest burdens for paying for them? What they will do to our senses of ourselves as members of a global and not just a national community? And how can these actions be explained and justified in relation to international covenants, global understandings, and widely shared human standards? All this, and a great deal more, is very far from clear.

Yet, there is less of a mystery about what is meant by the phrase *world order*. This term is most often associated with the international architecture that began to take form in the century and a half after the Peace of Westphalia, when the Thirty Years' War that effectively brought to an end the Holy Roman Empire and devastated most of Europe was concluded in 1648. The new international system of governance that slowly emerged, and that was eventually to replace the myriad independent states as well as hundreds of semi-independent principalities that existed previously, was organized around territorially bounded states whose sovereignty within their own realm encouraged a disposition to advance their own interests at the expense of other states. This potential for conflict meant that the Westphalian system of state-based sovereignty was inherently precarious and unequal. While the sovereign statism on which it was premised was intended to provide a measure of parity among its participants, the hegemonic nature of their relations created vast imbalances that rendered the existence of the system itself dependent on the maintenance, through alliances, treaties, and other compacts, of a tolerable but always shaky balance of power.[17]

This "realist" description of international order was originally articulated in the United States in the Cold War writings of political thinkers like George F. Kennan and Hans Morgenthau, and is currently linked with a wide array of figures from Henry Kissinger and Zbigniew Brzezinski to Donald Mearsheimer and Kenneth Waltz. Defining global governance as a process of managing potential and actual international conflicts between sovereign states seeking to extend their own power and influence with the help of transnational agreements and juridical practices, as well as through the use of brute force, has made it appear as though world order was almost wholly dependent on political, legal, and military determinants. But this portrayal of world order was already becoming outdated by the early nineteenth century when the international order, defined by state-based sovereignty, began to be influenced by the rise of ideologies like nationalism, imperialism, colonialism, racism, communism, and fascism—ideologies that spread like wildfire due to revolutions in everything from communications to armaments. Suddenly it became apparent that political factors alone, even when coupled with economic and social factors, were not capable by themselves of explaining the dynamics of global change. Transformation and innovation in the international arena were also the result of forces, often long at work in the interstices of global architecture, which affected everything from the establishment and transmission of belief systems and normative regimes to the shaping of symbolic systems of feeling and desire.

Nowhere has this been demonstrated more clearly than in the United States itself, where a predisposition to define its own place within the Westphalian system has always found expression in terms that were as semiotic as they were geopolitical, as ideological as they were strategic. Indeed, from the time of its earliest messianic beginnings in the theocratic aspirations of some of its first European settlers, America has rather consistently exhibited a tendency to define its own political ambitions in a language heavily laden with cultural premises and has recurrently conceived of those ambitions as constituting a model, archetype, or paradigm that others might well emulate. The Puritan John Winthrop may have been the first of his kind to call upon his prospective fellow voyagers to think of themselves as building an exemplary "City upon a Hill," but he was certainly far from the last. Just as Americans have always tended to treat their own view of themselves and their "New World" experiment as normative and prescriptive, so do Americans continue to believe that this model of governance and aspiration is a replicable, not to say exportable, commodity.

One consequence of this conviction has been the creation in the United States of a discursive environment where it has currently become nearly impossible to distinguish between putative recommendations for revising world order in light of the threats posed by the new "War on Terror," as the last US administration insisted on misnaming it, and the forms that American exceptionalism now takes in the global reshaping of international relations. The neo-Wilsonian ambition to spread democracy to the Middle East and elsewhere—in the thinking of some, all the way to East Asia—was, and still is, understood by many of its neo-conservative apologists and defenders to possess its idealistic precedent in Thomas Jefferson's dream to couple freedom with national expansion by constructing, as Jefferson termed it, an "empire of liberty." Such imperialist rhetoric goes back still further to the spiritual impulses that activated the first colonists in tidewater Virginia. Never ones to resist the opportunity for conversion, conquest, and commerce, these colonists observed as early as 1610 that if the Indians would not submit to Christian conversion "apostolically, without the helpe of man," they would have to be compelled "imperiallie, [as] when a Prince, hath conquered their bodies, that the Preachers may feede their souls."[18] Physical domination, then, both economic and political, along with ideological control, would henceforth tend to be yoked together as the components most indispensable for fashioning what American Protestants actually liked to imagine as a "righteous empire," and this utopian ambition, geo-religious as well as political, continues to inform what, for many contemporary US citizens and policymakers alike, is their international imaginary.[19]

Recent discussion of a "new world order" did not originate with George W. Bush but rather, as it happens, with his father, George H. W. Bush. The senior Bush revived a phrase first associated with Woodrow Wilson's "Fourteen Points" speech and then later applied it himself to the fashioning of the Bretton Woods agreements and the founding of the United Nations. Bush *père* again retrieved it to describe the new world both he and Mikhail Gorbachev hoped would emerge after the Cold War from collaboration between the US and the Soviet Union. It is nonetheless not without significance that subsequent credit for ending the Cold War, and thus for bringing into being a new world order, was immediately taken by the United States, even though President Gorbachev clearly remembers it differently. "If the new Soviet leadership and its new foreign policy [of perestroika] had not existed," President Gorbachev has insisted, "nothing would have happened." The end of the Cold War thus did not result from the collapse of the Soviet Union, as Americans like to imagine, but from what he calls "a process":

Bush and I made the declaration at Malta, but Reagan would have had no less grounds for saying that he played a crucial role, because he, together with us, had a fundamental change of attitude. Therefore we were all victors: we all won the cold war because we put a stop to spending $10 trillion on the cold war, on each side.[20]

In this case President Gorbachev was suffering as severely as his American counterparts from a case of presidential personalism. The Soviet Union imploded because Gorbachev couldn't control the "process." If the Cold War was ended because of "a fundamental change of attitude," what might be called "perestroika" on both sides, President Gorbachev was as much a captive, even victim, as captain of it, and nothing he did or did not do would have prevented President George H. W. Bush from claiming responsibility for the new possibilities of global governance it opened up, when he specifically utilized the phrase in a speech he delivered to a joint session of Congress on September 11, 1990, almost immediately following Saddam Hussein's invasion of Kuwait in August 1990, entitled "Toward a New World Order." However, the vagueness of the phrase's reference—was this about the restoration of the rule of law, US military leadership, a more active UN?—was not finally resolved until it came to be identified with what in particular George H. W. Bush thought would emerge from the collective international response to Iraqi aggression during the first Gulf War.

In the aftermath of that war, there was considerable public commentary about whether such a new world order had in fact already emerged, or had been replaced by enduring elements of the old post-World War II world order that had preceded it, or had been overwhelmed by the forces of globalization. Two among a number of books that kept alive the belief in a newly emergent world order were Huntington's *The Clash of Civilizations and the Remaking of World Order* and Francis Fukuyama's *End of History*, but the real work of reprising this phrase had been going on elsewhere for a number of years. It was actually set in motion as far back as the late 1960s when a group of conservatives associated with the State of Washington's Senator Henry "Scoop" Jackson began to argue that America was losing its backbone abroad. In the 1970s, alarm among those on the Right only increased following America's humiliating defeat in Vietnam, the Iranian Revolution in 1979, and the Soviet invasion of Afghanistan the same year; all this led to the creation of the Committee on the Present Danger, which was designed to broadcast its concerns about American infirmity of purpose and further commitment to the spread of democracy.

In 1980 with the election of President Ronald Reagan, these ideas immediately found their way into policies that, within a decade, were to lead (so neoconservatives argued) to the collapse of the Soviet Union. While that collapse later emboldened some, like Fukuyama, to argue that history in its previous bipolar form was now in effect coming to a close with the victory of the capitalist order, it encouraged others, such as Robert Kagan and Paul Wolfowitz, to wonder if the time had not now finally arrived for America to begin more aggressively to spread the Good

News of democracy throughout the world. To ensure the protection and support of this all-important mission alongside other American "assets," Dick Cheney, then Secretary of Defense, subsequently commissioned, with support from Wolfowitz, the creation of a policy statement in 1992 entitled the "Defense Planning Guidance" (its authors were Zalmay Khalilzad, America's former Ambassador to the United Nations and former Ambassador to Iraq, and Abram Shulsky), which proclaimed America's need to remain pre-eminent as a beacon of democracy in an unstable world.

This doctrine seemed to be confirmed by the first Gulf War, but it also left a number of its most ardent supporters (many of whom were now affiliated with the swelling number of conservative think-tanks that had grown up in Washington in the 1970s and 1980s) more convinced than ever that the US should have gone all the way to Baghdad to overthrow Saddam Hussein and to secure the country and its oil. But regime change and the pursuit of US economic designs in the region were merely several among a number of agendas associated with America's global interests and ambitions that, by 1997, would be systematically articulated in the creation of the Project of the New American Century. Here, Wolfowitz and other neoconservatives like Richard Perle, Elliott Abrams, and fellow traveler Donald Rumsfeld began to consolidate their convictions about America's simultaneous need to expand its global governance and solidify its global dominance.

As early as 1996, in fact, Perle and some of his friends had begun to bruit about the possibility of removing Saddam Hussein from Iraq, but it was not until the events of September 11, 2001 that they and others found the rationale for such a mission. That rationale was more than a policy objective; it was what Robert Kagan tellingly described as "a ready-made approach to the world."[21] Indeed, by March 2001, nearly six months before the attack on the Twin Towers and the Pentagon, the conservative columnist for the *Washington Post,* Charles Krauthammer, had found the terms to define this "ready-made approach to the world" when he declared that "America is in a position to reshape norms, alter expectations and create new realities."[22]

Such language, as we shall see in Chapter 5, was almost immediately to find its way into American policymaking in the administration of the second President Bush, decisively shaping both the political and the religious terms in which it would restate the case of American exceptionalism. But neither the new Bush administration, nor its supporters like Krauthammer, were in a position to realize that by spring 2001 this monopolar global moment had, in various ways, already passed them by and was rapidly disappearing behind them. The faith to which this belief in the power of the United States to fashion new realities, remake norms, and revise expectations for the world operated in a way reminiscent of the illusions that addled the imagination of F. Scott Fitzgerald's Jay Gatsby. They already belonged, as should have been realized long ago, to what Fitzgerald called "the orgiastic future that year by year recedes before us," that hegemonic prospect that was already disappearing into the republic behind them as the second Bush administration and its defenders reached out to grasp it. But Fitzgerald's language captures perfectly the unacknowledged elegiac character of that moment that connected post-9/11 America and "the old island here that flowered once for Dutch sailors' eyes" and "once pandered in whispers to the last and greatest of all human dreams":

> It eluded us then, but that's no matter—tomorrow we will run faster, stretch out our arms farther. ... And one fine morning—So we beat on, boats against the current, borne back ceaselessly into the past.[23]

As the United States embarked after 9/11 on a series of policies myopically indifferent to the way the world was actually already rearranging itself, new centers of power were emerging not only among states but also above and below them. Regions like South America, the Middle East, East Asia, Southeast Asia, and Africa were reorganizing themselves around local states; states within states like California, New York, and Texas, and global cities like Tokyo, London, and Mumbai were taking on larger roles in the global economy; global organizations such as the United Nations; the International Monetary Fund, OPEC, and the World Bank were establishing guidelines for the operations of everything from international finance and energy production to development; NGOs from Human Rights Watch, Oxfam, and the International Red Cross to the Bill and Melinda Gates Foundation were addressing issues everywhere that transcended state power; terrorist organizations like al-Qaeda, and militias like Hezbollah and the Taliban, were pursuing agendas that owed allegiance to religions and ideologies rather than to nationalisms and states. In the vacuum caused by the end of the Cold War and the erosion of communism, power was redistributing itself in ways that would prevent what many thought of as the strongest state the world has ever known either from acting in its own self-interest or from being able to impose its will on the world. A new world order was in the process of emerging even before George H. W. Bush was elected, which looked—and would eventually begin to operate—in a very different manner than was assumed in the White House.

What the administration of George W. Bush did or did not do in relation to these developments is almost less important than why and how it went about it. Believing itself to be the world's only real hegemon and thus able after 9/11 to dictate to allied world powers the course of action it wished to take, the United States acted as though all other nations would, in the other sense of hegemony, accept its values and priorities as their own. There was, to be sure, considerable precedence for this high-handedness. From the end of the Cold War, American elites had been enamored of the possibility of global hegemony and Bush's predecessor, President Bill Clinton, had, like those before him, continued to extend American power and influence largely through economic expansion and the broadening of NATO powers.[24]

George W. Bush's route to ensuring global dominance was by declaring a "War on Terror," and thus the United States immediately set out to invade Afghanistan for the purpose of destroying the Taliban and capturing Osama bin Ladin. The result of that effort only succeeded for a time in preventing the return and resurgence of the Taliban who now, more than a decade into this war, control much of the southern and eastern section of the country and threaten to take over much of the rest, are firmly established in parts of Pakistan, and risk demonstrating that American might, now deployed by President Bush's successor, President Barack Obama, is no match (either as the Soviets learned themselves in Afghanistan or the United States learned more than five decades before in South Vietnam), against a determined force of militant fighters in a weak state bent on resisting foreign occupation.

Mistakenly convinced that the Taliban had been successfully routed in the initial phase of the Afghanistan War, the Bush administration then, according to the famous "Downing Street memo" of July 23, 2002, cooked the evidence in order to justify its predetermined decision to invade Iraq, falsely alleging in the process that there was a connection between Saddam Hussein and al-Qaeda.[25] The initial success of the invasion of Iraq itself, which employed terror tactics of "shock and awe" widely praised by Secretary of Defense Rumsfeld, was supposed to produce a grateful and compliant populace, but when the ensuing occupation proved incapable of providing even the most minimum levels of security or essential services, the mood of the population quickly began to sour and within a matter of months produced suspicion, fear, dread, resentment, and eventually the insurgency, militias, assassinations, and chaos.

The creation of the insurgency that followed was made almost inevitable by the recklessness of L. Paul Bremer, head of the Provisional Coalition Authority, when he fired all the members of the Ba'ath Party and at the same time disbanded the entire armed forces. With two strokes of the pen, Bremer not only created the conditions that would lead unemployed and increasingly desperate men to resort to violence and terror to redress grievances and eventually begin settling scores, especially religious conflict, but also turned over the promised reconstruction of a shattered Iraq to cohorts of American bureaucrats completely inexperienced at nation-building whose ranks were supplemented by tens of thousands of almost always American private contractors and security personnel. It was the latter who then, along with members of the American military, and acting on orders going to the very top of the chain of command, compounded the catastrophic bungling of the Iraqi occupation by the perpetration of atrocities that came to be associated with places like Abu Ghraib, Bagram Air Base, and Guantanamo, and with practices such as rendition and extreme forms of physical and psychological torture. Although the Bush administration initially excused these egregious violations of its own laws as the inappropriate behavior of a few "bad apples," these barbarities were accompanied by a suspension of many other legal protections affecting the treatment of prisoners and created a climate for extending this abuse not only to other foreign nationals but also to American citizens.

If governmental authorization of warrantless wiretapping and other threats to civil liberties have now begun to awaken the American people (and not just those who have suffered the loss or fearful wounding of loved ones) to some of the domestic "unintended consequences" of the Iraq War, it did surprisingly little, beyond generating among a majority of the populace a desire to end the war and bring home the troops as soon as is reasonable, and to produce the kind of massive resistance one would expect from those who consider themselves a "free people." Yet, what has for many defined their sense of freedom has been their apparent exemption from any of the war's greatest costs, at least until the recession of 2008, when the near total collapse of the American, if not the global, economy, publically blamed on the manipulations of bankers, brokers, and other finance people, finally began to reveal the costs of the nation's military overextension. But even as millions of Americans have suffered mortgage foreclosures, lost jobs, bankruptcy, and despair, they have generally tolerated, under the Obama administration as well, the continual erosion of civil liberties for the elusive prospect of international security. Suspending the rule of *habeas corpus* for anyone suspected of a connection with terrorist sentiments or groups; refusing, except under extreme pressure, to investigate human rights violations; narrowing the terms of legitimate dissent by viewing almost any act of criticism of the government as "aiding and abetting the enemy"; employing "signing statements" to protect the president's right to disregard Congressional legislation if it conflicts with his interpretation of the law; and exploiting the "fear card" while defending secrecy, profiling, and the surveillance of fellow citizens—in all these ways the federal government has continuously appealed to and exploited America's weakness rather than its strength, and the American people have gone along with it.

One of the more flagrant examples of this occurred on September 14, 2006—in its lead editorial the next day the *Washington Post* described it as "A Defining Moment for America"—when the President of the United States made a personal journey to Congress to lobby for the use of torture in the interests of protecting national security. Scarcely more than one week later, on September 24, 2006, a classified National Intelligence Estimate entitled "Trends in Global Terrorism: Implications for the United States" came to light—it was completed in April 2006—which confirmed that all 16 spy agencies of the federal government were in agreement that America had been made *more* vulnerable to terrorism rather than less by the invasion and occupation of Iraq. Nonetheless, on September 29, 2006, the Bush administration won a major legislative victory with the passage of a Senate bill (echoing a similar bill previously passed by the House) that not only stripped detainees of the right of *habeas corpus*—this was barely mentioned in the debates on the Senate floor!—but gave the President broad powers to conduct military tribunals for terrorism suspects and determine permissible techniques for interrogation. Years later in another administration, many of those same powers, broadly challenged in the courts, are still being defended by the Executive Office. Indeed, it eventually came to light in a series of articles, again published in the *Washington Post*, that the chief sponsor of many of these and other secret proposals and policies was Dick Cheney, the Vice President of the United States, clearly acting on President Bush's behalf.[26]

It thus became obvious over the course of the second Bush administration that the utopianism underlying its rhetoric promoted something considerably more dangerous, possibly even more feral, than the conquest of the real by the representational, of the actual by the imaginary. Because this discourse was frequently justified by recourse to terms that were by turns incipiently religious and militantly unconditional, it reinforced—and was reinforced by—America's recurrent tendency to conceive itself, albeit sometimes grudgingly, as a warrior state whose calling is to convert as much of the rest of the world as possible—by force if necessary, by persuasion if possible—to its own salvific theology of democratic liberty and free enterprise. That this theology often masks the meretricious politics that frequently inform and express it is part of its purpose. Spreading democracy in a world seen through Manichean lenses that divide its states and peoples into good and evil, virtuous and iniquitous, light and dark, ally and opponent, friend and enemy then becomes a license to turn the empire of liberty into an imperium of power and privilege.

Nor has the new American administration, while clearly inclined to distance itself from this crude triumphalism, been able—or even been willing—to shed much of its exceptionalist bias. Despite the sobering experience of an almost catastrophic global financial meltdown and the discouraging realities of one war that is currently being lost in Afghanistan and another that may break out again when the United States withdraws the bulk of its forces from Iraq, President Obama, like his predecessor, continues to allow, indeed to encourage, if with noticeably less appetite, the discursive fashions of today's politics to shape the conduct, if not exactly the conscience, of his policies. Despite widespread evidence that the economic stimulus package of 2008 assisted for the most part those same individuals and institutions that put the international market at risk, President Obama insists on defending it, or permitting others to defend it, with arguments that are still basically self-serving, and refuses to bring anyone to account. Or, again, even where he separates himself from practices such as torture and rendition, he has continued to violate Pakistan's sovereignty through the undeclared war he is waging with Special Forces and predator drones against the Taliban and al-Qaeda in the tribal territories of North and South Waziristan, infuriating ordinary Pakistanis and Pashtuns alike, and he justifies the continued operation of interrogation facilities at Bagram Air Base and elsewhere as, against all evidence, an indispensable instrument in America's fight against terror. Indeed, it has been alleged but not confirmed that key intelligence leading to the assassination of Osama bin Laden was produced by such methods, but even if it were, this would not detract from the fact that practices such as these have done much to discredit the United States in the eyes of the world. While President Obama prides himself on the putative difference between his policies and those of his predecessor, there is discernible overlap in the questionable assumptions on which they are based—the United States is in a global struggle with radical jihadism; if the world cannot count on American consistency in the economic as in the military sphere, who can it trust; American pre-eminence in world affairs is the surest guarantee of international security—and the myths used to support them.[27] Such canards remain the staple of American political discourse, but they have come to seem more and more out of touch with a world order that the United States still acts as though it was responsible for, but which is actually in the process of being radically rebalanced.

The actual degree or extent and pace of that global rebalancing may be a matter of opinion, or at least of perception, but so is the symbolically freighted idea of "world order" itself and who is assumed to legislate it. While no one would seriously dispute that such a notion possesses historical provenance, power, and validity, it also carries huge imaginative implications and resonance. For one, it conveys a sense of stability, coherence, and legitimacy that is belied by the violent struggles of the last hundred years to control and manage it. For another, it lends to those who use the term an impression of authority, mastery, and reasonableness that is often, as in the present, illusory. More significant still is the fact that it discounts everything that tends to fall outside its presumed range of governance, and now, given its identification with the model of state-based sovereignty and international relations, obstructs a comprehension that global design and governance is currently being challenged and reconstructed by various non-state actors who have little respect for Westphalian sovereignty. The term "world order" can easily blind one to the actual decentering and disorder that it seeks, often only provisionally and intermittently, to contain and manage. Hence the idea of world, both as philosophical concept and as political construct, is more fragile and fluid than it sounds and also more diverse and heterogenous in its formations and dispositions than is portrayed. Just ask President Obama.

American policymakers have had their own response to these issues for more than half a century. World order is based on a set of norms defining the appropriate relationships among and the administration of the community of nations, and the United States is uniquely qualified to uphold it and compelled to enforce it. A doctrine first articulated in a celebrated article in *Life* magazine in 1941 by its publisher Henry R. Luce, who announced the dawning of "The American Century," Luce urged his fellow Americans to "accept wholeheartedly our duty to exert upon the world the full impact of our influence for such purposes as we see fit and by such means as we see fit."[28] This axiomatic belief, together with its corollary that America's unique responsibility for global leadership requires it to support "the sacred trinity" of "global military presence," "global power projection," and "global interventionism" has become "so deeply embedded in the American collective consciousness as to have all but disappeared from view."[29]

The danger in all this is not simply, or even chiefly, that such discourse is figurative through and through. The danger is rather that, far from representing mere verbal embellishments in debates about global governance, such figures, and the tropes on which they depend, are now part and parcel of what is at issue in its revision and reform. This danger is far from new. In response to the recurrent penchant in the United States to prefer reproductions to originals, imitations to realities, fakes to the genuine article, the historian Daniel Boorstin subtitled his 1961 book *The Image*, "a guide to pseudo-events in America." While this was scarcely a new disability in American social and political life even then, it is now markedly more pervasive, perverse, and potentially fateful. One critical intellectual challenge therefore becomes how to penetrate this fog of words, images, metaphors, and tropes before we drown in them. A second challenge is to determine where to find the conceptual and moral leverage to bring this nearly impenetrable fog under intellectual scrutiny. Still a third involves what to make of the new imperiums that continuously and consciously confuse simulations with facts, symbols with sentiments, artifice with the actual. And fourth, there remains the question of how one is to conduct a conversation in political cultures so indifferent to nuance, so resistant to alternative perspectives, so insensible of the feelings of others, so bent on confounding the fictions of America with the future of the world.

The remainder of this book is an attempt to probe questions such as these in the interests of delineating some other ways to think about humanity and human interconnectedness in a time when political discourse is often as ideologically over-determined as the political action it tries to explain, rationalize, or revise.

5

AMERICA'S GODS THEN AND NOW

> America, I do not call your name without hope
> Pablo Neruda, from "America, I do not call your name without hope" (tr. Robert Bly) in Bly, 1971, pp. 94–5

Among the several motives that Herman Melville's Ishmael gives for going to sea in *Moby-Dick*, one stands out among all the rest for reasons of prudence. "Not ignoring what is good," Ishmael confesses, "I am quick to perceive a horror, and could still be social with it—would they let me—since it is well to be on friendly terms with all the inmates of the place one lodges in."[1] Whether or not Americans inhabit some sort of common asylum, sanitarium, or convalescent home, there is no denying that many of the inmates believe that they are sharing this residence with what strikes them as a kind of horror. To a majority of the religious, that horror is to be found in the secularism of the US's public and popular culture; to numerous secular modernists and their many sympathizers, it is represented instead by the piety and politics of the US's more ardent believers. The difficulty is that, unlike Ishmael, neither group displays much interest in becoming social with what it abhors, though both might profit from a dose of Ishmael's "genial, desperado philosophy," which holds that "doubts of all things earthy, and intimations of some things heavenly; this combination makes neither believer nor infidel, but makes a man who regards them both with equal eye."[2]

The inmates need to get to know each other better if only because the distinction they think divides them between the godly and the ungodly is in the US highly unstable. While more than one-third of the US population is eagerly bent on theocratizing the politics of the state, most of those same citizens are just as intensely interested in ensuring that this confection of the ethico-political, the religious, and the national is fashioned in a way that is congruent, or at least compatible, with the putatively godless culture that surrounds it. If this often makes it difficult in the US to differentiate the religious from the secular, the sacred from the profane, this is not because the much-touted renewal of faith in the US—what many claim to be a fourth religious awakening—has led to a repudiation of the realms of the public and the popular; it is rather because the realms of the public and popular have now, as part of this revival, been asked not only to work *for* religion but to do much of the work *of* religion.

Nonetheless, one should be wary of what people make of this fact since the US remains, as Henry James and Mark Twain both warned, a bad country to be stupid in. Whenever the US's need for beliefs and values has exceeded its current supply, the temptation has often been to assume, both writers insisted, that their appearance must then somehow be faked. What you cannot retrieve or produce, you must pretend or counterfeit. And it is just such fakery, the simulation rather than the substance of belief—"soul-butter and hogwash," in Twain's terms; "the triumph of the superficial and the apotheosis of the raw," in James's—which makes the American case so tricky to assess. What is profane in the US, one might ask, that cannot be, and has not been, transcended upward into the sacred or religious—baseball, the Almighty Dollar, Disneyland, Graceland, the Super Bowl, Tupperware parties, the virtual Church of the Bunny, the Internet's Kick-Ass Post-Apocalyptic Doomsday Cult of Love? And what is religious or sacred in the US that has not also been transcended downward into the terms of the profane or secular—brocading the covers of Bibles, putting the image of Jesus on wearing apparel, making religious rock or rap music?[3]

This is not to claim that the materialization of faith is necessarily suspect. All religions depend on and encourage the creation of forms and shapes to assist the faithful in internalizing their beliefs. This is merely the other side of the need to make faith palpable, to render it sensuously as well as mentally available. The sacred is not alien to the profane but in fact reliant on it for its very manifestation. Objectifying belief does not result from some spiritual deficiency but rather from the nearly universal need to give tangibility to one's deepest feelings. Religion can no more do without the support of vernacular and popular as well as high culture than it can survive in a vacuum. The physicality of religion constitutes the medium through which it does much of its breathing and offers much of its sustenance. Religious souvenirs, relics, shrines, prints, art, wearing apparel, and even some of the commercialization of faith that goes along with them, are perfectly consistent with a sacramentalism latent in all but the most severely iconoclastic expressions of faith.

Serious issues arise not with the materialization or even the proselytizing of religion but rather with its commodification and marketing in a global mass culture dedicated ever more zealously not simply to helping the consumer get what he or she wants but actually dictating it. The tyranny of the global market is no fiction and its predatory nature no exaggeration. When desire is almost wholly a creature of manufacture by industries of simulation that specialize in widening the gap between belief and experience, this leaves many of the faithful suspended at that late modern intersection where the differentiation between the sacred and the secular no longer reduces, if it ever did, to Max Weber's distinction between enchantment and disenchantment, but rather suggests the somewhat less magical distinction between being converted and possibly being conned, between detecting in the "blessed rage for order," to quote Wallace Stevens, "ghostlier demarcations, keener sounds,"[4] or only descrying what Milan Kundera calls "the beautifying lie" that moves us to tears of gratitude when we find ourselves mirrored in its own reflections.[5]

As a case in point, merely consider the Harris poll that reported in 1998 that 66 percent of non-Christians believed in miracles and 47 percent accepted the Virgin Birth. *Newsweek* stated at roughly the same time that 79 percent of Americans are convinced that biblical miracles actually occurred, and another 40 percent of the population generally (though surely this number must now be higher), and 71 percent of evangelical Protestants specifically, are certain that the world will end in a battle at Armageddon between Jesus and the Anti-Christ. At the same time, nearly 20 percent of American adults imagine that they belong to the richest 1 percent of the population and another 20 percent believe that they will join that 1 percent before they die. While it would be easy to dismiss such statistics if they were not so compelling, those pertaining to economics no less than those to religion, it is also easy to be fooled by them. For as alarming as it is to discover that nearly 40 percent of the American people who live in a country where the gulf between rich and poor is greater than anywhere else in the developed world nonetheless assume that they now are, or are soon going to be, wealthier than 99 percent of their fellow citizens, it is truly astonishing to learn how completely at home the great majority of these same religious people feel themselves to be in the world of NASCAR and the Internet.

We have often been told that evangelical Protestants, like charismatic Catholics and orthodox Jews, to say nothing of traditional Muslims, Buddhists, Sikhs, and members of other communions, are adamantly opposed to the invasion of the precincts of belief by popular culture, but to judge from the way they live their faith, this could not be further off the mark. The key to this anomaly is to be found in the nature of American individualism, and that individualism is best expressed by the manner in which people have taken aspects of religion—worship, fellowship, doctrine, tradition, morality, sin, witness, and identity—into their own hands.[6] This does not mean that Americans have turned religion into a solipsistic form of self-expression so much as that they have turned themselves into experts at refashioning religion to meet their own needs. The spiritual challenge in the US, and for most religious Americans, is not to get right with God but to make God right for themselves, to find a form of religion that furnishes the requisite opportunities not only for devotion and support but for the expression of the personal and the private. Such habits of belief, for all but the querulous or the pedantic, usually leave questions of dogma or doctrine far behind and concentrate attention instead on what is experienced as most congenial. If it feels right, then, echoing of Ralph Waldo Emerson's famous dictum, it must be right.

There are, of course, plenty of Christians, to take only one communion, who would vehemently object to this description of the relationship between American religion and modern secular culture. Convinced that popular culture in the US, like the public sphere as a whole, remains a snare and a delusion, they describe themselves as "resident aliens" comprising a Christian colony within liberal society (the language belongs to Methodist theologian, Stanley Hauerwas) that seeks to redeem it, or at least to avoid its contaminations, by disavowing all or most of its ways. Such traditionalists see themselves holding the line against a godless democratic secularism that has exchanged Christian soteriology for the culture of the therapeutic. Here salvation is not construed as personal regeneration or spiritual rebirth but rather as, in Philip Rieff's famous formulation, amplitude in living.[7] Religion to such Christian apologists must therefore remain a thing apart, uncompromising and uncompromised, if it is to retain its power to judge American culture and save us from its seductions.

Oddly enough, this conception of religion, as something that stands over against the public world and imagines itself to be free of its defilements, is almost a perfect reflection of the way religion is viewed by many of its contemporary cultured despisers. According to them, too much of American religion represents a realm of the "Holier-Than-Thou" that regards itself as transcendent to, and in opposition with, a secular world committed, at least at its best, to principles of theological as well as political tolerance. This can create an odd paradox where the defenders of religion in the US often promote separation and withdrawal from society in the name of an inflated sense of self-righteousness while its critics undercut their own liberalism by deriding religion's predisposition to narrow-mindedness and bigotry.[8] If neither stance is entirely accurate or fair, both are being swamped by the astonishing success with which religion in the US has turned contemporary culture to account. Far from renouncing or rejecting that culture, religion in the US in all its variety has displayed extraordinary creativity in appropriating elements of it for its own purposes. Thus evangelicals find little difficulty reconciling Christianity with consumer-driven materialism and often celebrate it as a sign of divine favor, whether "in the ostentatious lifestyles of the televangelist, the success-oriented preaching of a Robert Schuller, or the explicitly procapitalist prosperity theology of the Kenneth Hagin Ministries of Tulsa, Oklahoma."[9]

But what of the multitudes referred to in the Beatitudes, one might ask? What place is reserved among such marriages of spiritual convenience for the meek in spirit, the broken in heart, those who hunger for justice or suffer persecution for justice's sake, not to mention the poor, the infirm, the despised, or the forgotten? Where do those who are abject or lost find succor and direction in such a religious economy? No problem, as religious historian Randall Balmer authoritatively summarizes the evangelical claim: "Jesus will save your soul and your marriage, make you happy, heal your body, and even make you rich. Who wouldn't look twice at that offer?"[10]

Whether or not Balmer's summary represents one of those offers that no one can possibly refuse, this is scarcely the first time that American Protestantism has presented the faithful with a deal almost too good to be true. It all began with the Federal theologians of the seventeenth century who set out to soften the harsh demands of the Covenant that God had made with the members of the New Israel by redescribing it as a kind of contract or transaction in which both parties would be obliged, as in business, to hold up their end of the arrangement—"divine grace," Perry Miller dryly observed, "conceived as an opportunity to strike a bargain, a chance to make an important move"[11]—but some such bargain has always been on offer in virtually every subsequent generation of American religious history. Selling religion by appealing to peoples' self-interest is in fact perfectly consistent with what Alexis de Tocqueville found so distinctive, if not strange, about American individualism itself. Far from being an ideology for non-conformists who seek genuine independence and autonomy, individualism in America, Tocqueville argued, is a credo designed by and for those who prefer to identify and mix only with their own kind. And what better way, in an expanding market economy, to mix with your kind than to join them in your common recognition of what constitutes a good buy?

This genial narcissistic strain in American individualism becomes truly problematic only at a secondary level where, if frustrated or rejected, self-love can then turn back against the self as hatred and then, in defense against the guilt and anxiety thus produced, compel the self to seek protection by incorporating within itself grandiose object images. The secondary character disorder thus established leads to the sort of commodity fetishism that Thomas Pynchon examines in *The Crying of Lot 49*, where people put their passions into things and organize their wounded feelings around idealized cultural figures like celebrities who are known chiefly for being known.

Little wonder, then, that the US has struck so many observers as, in G. K. Chesterton's phrase, "a nation with the soul of a church." Just as its earliest religious identity was formed around a theocratic experiment to create a new civil and ecclesiastical society organized according to Biblical warrants, so it's more recent religious identity has in no small measure been shaped by an individualist credo that has taken one of two forms, neither incompatible with the other. While it has provided many adherents with the incentive, as well as the rationale, to cut their faith, as Lillian Hellman might have said, to the cloth of contemporary fashion,[12] it has encouraged others to take refuge in "the politics of sin."[13]

"The politics of sin" refers to something more than H. L. Mencken's famous complaint about Puritanism's fear that someone, somewhere, might be happy, and represents something different from Nathaniel Hawthorne's earlier speculation in "The Maypole of Merry-mount" that American history might be reduced to a tale of "jollity and gloom contending for an empire." It suggests rather that the history of American empire was created in considerable part out of the conflict between fears of iniquity and struggles for redemption. "The politics of sin" thus offered American believers a spiritual alternative that amounted neither to adapting their faith to the public realm, nor of rejecting the public realm for the sake of preserving their faith, but rather of using their faith to change that public realm into something more congenial with their beliefs. Thus the politicization of morality transformed religion itself into a formidable instrument not only of character-building but also of state-building. While the morality in question has inevitably shifted from age to age, from crisis to crisis, from revival to revival, the end result has remained strangely the same. Whether the threats to virtue have been perceived to come from Indians, immigrants, slaves, women, wealth, other countries, fifth columns, or simple lust, the boundaries they have established between "us" and "them," the upright and the reprobate, the saved and the fallen, the sanctified and the damned, have always been "rewritten as the boundaries between good and evil."[14]

This is not, however, the way the story of American history is usually told. According to the standard liberal narrative, the new American state was born in reaction to old world tyrannies, not old world iniquities, and the way to prevent them from recurring was to draw a sharp line between the private sphere and the public. Religion plainly needed to be confined to the first of these spheres, but the task of keeping them separate, which was given to the First Amendment, has not been terribly effective. If to some the First Amendment's "no establishment" clause has encouraged a secularism at variance with America's founding religious myths, to others its "free exercise" clause has lent support to religion in a way that conflicts with the constitutional tradition of partition. To still others, the First Amendment has produced a religious and social pluralism that they regard as the spiritual essence of the American Way, while yet other Americans have deemed such pluralism a blasphemy against the religious character of the Constitution itself whose First Amendment guarantees to serve to protect the theological beliefs on which it is founded.

These conflicts of interpretation reflect a further contradiction between what Americans have always said they believed about the relation between church and state and how they have acted. If most Americans have until recently given their ideological support to the existence of the wall that divides the public sphere from the private, they have in practice happily confused them. Thus while courts and state legislatures have spent much time and energy seeking to prevent any religious group from achieving civil preference, American money carries the message of "In God We Trust," the work of the United States Congress is supported by a chaplain, American presidents and other officials routinely seek, when they do not claim, divine support for public policies, and Supreme Court Justice William O. Douglas, reflecting the feelings of many of his fellow citizens, concluded that Americans are a religious people who live under a system of government that presupposes the existence of a Divine Being.

These discrepancies between Constitution principles and social and political practices are hardly surprising. They result from the wide latitude of interpretation to which the provisions of the First Amendment have always been susceptible, and point to the fact that the place of religion in American life, as students of jurisprudence have often remarked, has consistently proved resistant to legal adjudication. As a result, the relation between the First Amendment's protections against civil involvement in religious affairs has been confounded by religion's omnivorous reach into the public realm. Americans have always lived in a religiously inflected public world where social and political progress has been measured less from crisis to reform than from revival to revival.[15]

If one asks what has made this religious collaboration in the US between the private and the public realm structurally possible, one of the answers must surely be found in the history of religious pluralism. That history has been anything but simple or direct, but it has managed to move slowly but steadily during the last two centuries in an ever more inclusive direction. In this case, however, one must distinguish between diversity, which from the colonial period on has always been a condition or fact of American religious life, and pluralism, which defines an ideal that has been achieved only intermittently and has frequently changed. Following the American religious historian Sidney E. Ahlstrom, who shocked his peers as late as 1972 by remarking that religious pluralism has remained stillborn throughout much American history, William Hutchison argues that the pluralist impulse has taken several distinct forms in the last two centuries. In its first appearance, religious pluralism was restricted to a mode of toleration, primarily legal and social, which was often honored, if at all, merely in the breach. In its second, which developed toward the end of the nineteenth century and the beginning of the twentieth, this ideology of acceptance slowly but fitfully gave way to a somewhat less restrictive and arbitrarily practiced but still circumscribed notion of inclusion, which reserved the rights of participation only to those on the inside of the social and political world but not the outside. It was only during the latter half of the twentieth century that pluralism moved into its third phase when, under extreme pressure from the movements for Civil Rights and Women's Rights, it was reconstructed as a mandate permitting, at least theoretically, all groups and individuals, and not just those who were dominant, to participate in establishing and implementing the American social agenda.[16]

This is not to deny that America's religious establishment, overwhelmingly Christian and Protestant even as it eventually became less and less Calvinist, was busy regulating the practice of diversity in all periods of American history. Nor is this to forget that the practice of diversity was frequently thwarted by waves of anti-immigrant nativism and also by less xenophobic forms of exclusion or conditional recognition. Yet even in the face of such obstructions, pluralism advanced to the point where now many Americans find themselves asking for different reasons—and not only in self-defense—whose country is it, anyway.

But this raises an important secondary question about what the right to participate may mean if the terms of participation have already been defined in advance by someone else. This, of course, is the predicament that has confronted so many members of minority groups in the US who have felt excluded by contemporary formulations of the meaning of pluralism and have accordingly been left with the task of defining for themselves the opportunities for full participation. The other side of the question is what pluralism means if some groups elect not to participate at all. Though hardly a frequent occurrence in American history, this is the recommendation of those on the Religious Right whose orthodoxy now compels them to withdraw from the public sphere altogether or at least renounce all forms of it not consistent, as they understand it, with Christian doctrine.

Hence the liberal narrative has frequently found itself in competition, James Morone contends, with two others.[17] The first is more communal in nature since it has long conceived the nation to be composed not of a collection of individuals, as in the liberal narrative, but of a collectivity of citizens. This community of citizens might well vary from Jefferson's rural units of small landowners to Lincoln's Union bound by the mystic chords of memory, but it has been recurrently understood as the source of American civic virtue and the vessel of American consensus. If this communitarian story has always had its many supporters (and still does), it has also had its persistent critics who have reminded us of the issues of inclusion, recognition, and participation that the story has glossed and the distinctive identities it has often blurred, occluded, or erased. The dream has so often been deferred indefinitely because of slave ships and their like that have always shadowed American Mayflowers.

Thus the communitarian narrative, like the liberal, has given way time and again to the moral narrative. This story conceives of the US as a redeemer nation whose mission has always been to convert itself, it not the entire world, to its own vision of the good, whether that good be defined as virtue, liberty, equality, democracy, diversity, free markets, or whatever. In this third narrative, the nascent capitalism of the first narrative and the social utopianism of the second narrative are folded into the militant imperialism of the third, which seeks to construct nothing short of a "righteous empire" founded on the wages of sin whose mission continuously oscillates between reforming "them" and regenerating "us."[18] The evils that menace "us" and infect "them" are various in form but surprisingly limited in kind, running the gamut from laziness and sloth through intemperance and addiction to violence and aggression and on to lust and promiscuity. All of these vices attest to a problem of self-control, and in a society still prudish after all these years, they generally refer back to the issue of sexuality, which becomes ever more complicated as it is linked to gender, family, children, marriage, ethnicity, and, of course, race.

But why, one might ask, does this third narrative of origin possess so much more credibility than the other two? What is it about "moral values" that allows them to displace individualism and community? One could explain part of their appeal by reference to the anxiety produced by a society where individualism breeds social indifference, competition often becomes rapacious, and the state does less and less to protect the security and wellbeing of its citizens. But social explanations alone do not seem to account for the paranoid style of our politics, a paranoia which permits the United States government to incarcerate more than two million of its citizens, mostly non-white, and to place an additional four million under the control of the prison system. These practices, which also display the oppositional character of American morality, can only be understood in terms of the way the politics of sin work to the benefit of the state itself.

Though each moral crusade is different, they all seem to fall into what Morone describes as the same general pattern. The first phase begins when people become convinced that they face a form of iniquity in others or themselves that needs to be identified and purged or reformed. The second phase commences when efforts to purify the sinner and expunge the sin prove less than fully successful and then the attack is shifted, if the nation and not just the self is to be saved, to the underlying causes of pollution themselves. Over the years various candidates have presented themselves, from witches, slaves, Native Americans, the British, slaveholding, abolitionism, women's suffrage, alcohol, foreigners, poverty, Catholics, trusts, communism, drugs, segregation, anarchism, illegals, gay marriage, to Muslims, but the strategy for combating them remains essentially the same. These abominations can be overcome only as the moral reforms they inspire begin in the third phase to actually revise governmental policies and create enduring legacies. Hence laws are rewritten, political culture refashioned, public agencies created, the Constitution amended, all on behalf of permanently altering the structure of society and transforming the attitudes of the public.

Had this phenomenon been better understood during and after the last several American presidential elections, there might not have been quite as much surprise and dismay that moral values played the role that they did. But this, of course, cuts in more than one direction. Just as moral politics can serve regressive ends, so they can serve progressive ones. Indeed, if hellfire politics witnessed the success of Victorian purity laws and a host of other reactionary measures in the latter part of the nineteenth century and the early years of the twentieth, the next half century from 1932, with the beginning of the New Deal, to 1973, when Roe v. Wade was passed, frequently witnessed the opposite, as barriers once erected to keep "others" in their place—Prohibition, Jim Crow laws, voting rights regulations, immigration restrictions, abortion laws—were to disappear. But this legacy of the Social Gospel movement was again to be challenged by the rise of Richard Nixon's Silent Majority and Jerry Falwell's Moral Majority, both of which not only swept away many of its reforms but resurrected the redeemer nation in a form more righteous and imperialistic than ever. Much of the nation went back to acting like a church and the office of the presidency, particularly under the administration of George W. Bush, was again converted into its pulpit.

However, it is well worth remembering that the modern faith-based presidency was not the invention of George W. Bush, or even of Ronald Reagan, or for that matter of Jimmy Carter. Its author was rather Dwight David Eisenhower, who famously declared in an extemporaneous speech a month before his inauguration in December 1952 that "our government makes no sense unless it is founded on a deeply held religious faith—and I don't care what it is." No one, as it happens, exploited this conviction more effectively than William Jefferson Clinton, though it was George W. Bush who then added for the first time to this tradition the caveat that the world, and not just the United States government or the Oval Office, should now be based not on reality but on faith.

The meaning of this conviction was clarified for the *New York Times*'s Ron Suskind when one of President Bush's senior advisors informed him that politics would no longer be answerable to the world as we know it but only to religion. As the advisor went on to explain, there is "the reality-based community," which assumes that "solutions emerge" from the "judicious study of discernible reality," and then there is a faith-based community, which has all the power. To amplify the point, the advisor went on to point out that accounting for, and seeking to be accountable to, the real "is not the way the world really works any more. ... We're an empire now, and when we act, we create our own reality. And while you're studying reality—judiciously, as you will—we'll act again, creating other new realities, which you can study too. ... We're history's actors [in the faith-based community] ... and you, all of you [in the reality-based community], will be left to study what we do."[19]

What was startling about this revelation, whether or not it exactly reflected the views of the President himself, was not only that it mimicked the language of the US's then-stated enemies, the fear of whom helped put and keep Mr. Bush in office in the first place, but that it took its imperial mandate from the same theological pretensions that inspired them. Faith swallows the entire cosmos of the actual and the practicable and taunts them with their own impotence. But one can go further: this was not a case of belief simply prevailing in the face of all evidence; it is rather a case of belief subsuming all evidence for the sake of securing its own sovereignty.

As a self-confessed, born-again Christian, Mr. Bush assumed, and was assumed by many others, to stand in a direct spiritual line with the US's Protestant past, but there had been slippage over the years and it was significant. The Puritans, as is well known, were under no illusions about the particular requirements placed on them by Holy Scripture. Their faith was specific and detailed, both as to its content and its obligations. Just as they shuddered at the thought of confusing their own utterances with the Divine Word, so they regarded certitude in matters of faith as an expression of pride, which for them was the most heinous of sins. In the strictest Puritan circles, it was even forbidden to talk about the attributes of God, much less of God's mind or intent. But not so, apparently, in the new religious dispensation created by the forty-third President, where his own beliefs could generate such wide appeal not just because of their vagueness and generality but because, as he informed an audience of the Amish before his first term, his ideas came from God himself.

One of his former speechwriters opened a further window onto the meaning of such claims by suggesting that the best index as to what President Bush believed could be found in what he said about a personal God who answers prayers by offering people judgment and wisdom without telling them explicitly what to do. Yet President Bush was soon to contradict himself when he was widely quoted as having said that God did in fact tell him to declare a war on terror, just as God told him (as we now know, eight months before President Bush informed the rest of us!) to invade Iraq. No wonder the President thought of his as a God who can not only improve one's life but save one, and "not just in the theological sense but in this world."[20]

How sharp the contrast between Bush's evangelical confessionalism and the Protestant political realism found in the neo-orthodox writings of Reinhold Niebuhr and Paul Tillich. In contrast to Mr. Bush and those who speak in the same terms about religion, they assumed that human beings are essentially imperfect and corrupt, that the only hope of redemption lies in the unmerited love of a merciful God, and that this redemption will only be completed beyond history rather than within it. While this did not deter either of them from turning their attention to the world around them—Niebuhr's great themes were not inherited doctrines like Creation, Atonement, and Eschatology, or spiritual technologies of divine assistance and personal salvation, but practical concerns such as the problematics of freedom, the immorality of society, the dangers of national pride, and the dialectical relations between love and justice—Niebuhr and Tillich were not interested in remaking reality as vindication of their faith but of using their faith to grapple with the great burdens and inequities of the real. And they believed that the only way to do this was by refusing to confuse the words of human beings with the truths of scripture. In his famous book *The Courage to Be*, Tillich in fact argued for the theological necessity of positing the existence of "the God beyond God" who, in contrast to the God of classical theism, is not to be mistaken for any of the structures of being or power, human or otherwise, except as their unconditional and unassimilable depth and ground.[21]

One can be grateful that President Bush did not share the penchant among many of America's religiously reborn to conceive of the Second Person of the Trinity either as a friend or, as many automobile bumper stickers across the nation imply, a kind of pal or chum. This is the religious practice that is mocked in the Matt Damon and Ben Affleck movie *Dogma*, where the Archbishop, played by George Carlin, decides that the image of Christ crucified has proven too difficult for many Christians to embrace and so proposes, in an act of charity, to substitute in its place the less forbidding image of Jesus as the "buddy Christ." What is, of course, so remarkable about this recurrent, public familiarization of the Second Person of the Trinity is, as with Mr. Bush's God, just how user-friendly he is, how few real demands he seems to make. Jesus in the one case, God in the other, is known not for the exactions he imposes or the sacrifices he demands so much as for the availability he offers. Little judgment, or self-examination, or need for forgiveness, or repentance is found in much of the popular discourse about Jesus or presidential discourse about God, just what, in the politics of the Beltway and of Hollywood, is called "access."

Such observations sometimes leave one wondering if there is not something incommensurable about various of the faiths that people claim for their own as Christian. Perhaps some of the believers have got it wrong, or the historian of American religion William Clebsch was right all along when he posited the existence of multiple Christianities.[22] Either way, what is meant by "access" may be more intelligible by analogy not with politics alone but by certain features of what some call the Post-Information Age, where the future that beckons, thanks to distributed computing, embedded processors, and a myriad of iPods, BlackBerries, iPads, Kindles, Droids, and other inventions, is information on demand, getting personal by reducing the audience to one, becoming assynchronic by communicating in convenient time, and possessing zero tolerance for delay. "Welcome to the desert of the real," Morpheus says to Neo in *The Matrix*, only this time reality has not only been hijacked by a semblance of itself but, as Slavoj Žižek notes in his book by that title, rendered less a likeness than an apparition because of the lie built into the simulations by which we normally keep life at a distance. The issue is not whether these simulations go all the way down, but the fact that they are currently shadowed by an anxiety that those same images could be both copy and counterfeit, fabrication and forgery, and there is no easy way to tell the difference.

Žižek's chief exhibit is the horrific attack on the Twin Towers and the Pentagon, where the US's addiction to make-believe, or rather to the cinematic world of illusion that we have created to resemble life and at the same time hold it at bay, suddenly took, as so many have pointed out, terrible revenge. On 9/11, it is often said, life was rendered as spectacle, as theater, as cinema, as horror film, indeed as the movie *The Towering Inferno*, but this gets less than half of it. The larger truth is that this simulation of the real was actually shadowed by the reality of which it was only a copy, a specter of which we were in denial, and by which we assuaged our fear of the real by fictionalizing it. Here, of course, that specter turned corporeal, malevolent, personal, deadly, and almost, but not quite, inconceivable. Yet perilous as it is to mistake fiction for reality, it is still more hazardous to view reality simply as fiction, for this misses Jacques Lacan's point "that, while animals can deceive by presenting what is false as true, only human beings … can deceive by presenting the true as false."[23]

What was the great recession of 2008, when the financial markets nearly took down the entire global economy, if not viewing, and more importantly treating, reality as fiction, which hid the fact that the true could be presented as false? Built around instruments like derivatives that were constructed around wagers concerning price movements of real economic assets, or the reference rate to which they were linked, traders and banks not only disguised the values they were attempting to manage and control but often purposely rendered the risks involved less apparent, if not invisible. In all this, the actual economy was haunted by a phantom specter of itself erected out of computerized algorithms and blind diversification that placed the former in threat of complete collapse by techniques seeming to protect and expand it but that were actually devouring it.

So what, then, is wrong with faith as access, with God on demand? Chiefly that it encourages people anywhere to remake reality as an expression of their own power and to view their faith in this fiction as beyond criticism, much less doubt, which turns faith into a caricature of itself. Employing the contemporary discourse through which power often masks its true aim, Christianity or any other religion becomes a monstrosity: faith so powerful that in its own estimation it can take the place of God himself by doing with reality, including the reality of its own fallibility, what it will. No need to acknowledge, much less respond, to the "Downing Street memo"; no obligation to face the facts on the ground in Iraq or Afghanistan; no reluctance to falsify the relation between religion and the political rather than confront the religious grievances that lie behind militant jihad. Deceit and dissimulation define the discourse of the day.

While such beliefs are by seventeenth-century standards innocuous if not heretical enough to constitute a serious theological problem, their chief difficulty in the twenty-first is that they provide shelter, intentionally or not, for so many different kinds of creedal affirmations, from the identification of Jesus as Liberator among African American evangelicals who vote Democratic, forgive their oppressors, eschew violence, and possess conservative social values, to the views of Christian extremists like Randall Terry, founder of the anti-abortion group Operation Rescue, who feels "called by God to conquer this country" and urges his followers "to let a wave of hatred wash over you" because "those who love God must hate sin."[24]

Though Terry and his like are clearly the exception rather than the rule, the Christian Right has for the present consolidated its control over the American moral debate and displays less tolerance for deviance the more certain it becomes of the infallibility of its own cause. Its energies having first been awakened during the Carter years of the late 1970s, then gathered strength and sophistication through the two Reagan presidencies in the 1980s, were eventually consolidated during the midterm elections of 1994, and finally swept the whole field before them during George W. Bush's two terms and the Tea Party movement that has succeeded them. As a result of these developments, Christian conservatives and their many fellow travelers, from Pentecostals and Seventh-day Adventists to Mormons, have put Liberalism and its Social Gospel tradition in retreat, and the cost to moral politics of the sort that, for example once characterized the Civil Rights Movement, has been deeply debilitating. Whether this retreat can be reversed, and Liberalism again recover its balance and reassume its place in a genuine debate about which values should define American politics, will depend on its ability, among other things, to recover its own ethical story. But this will also require it to come to terms with the religious roots of its own progressivism.

The ethicist Jeffrey Stout thinks that this is to misconstrue the problem. Without discounting the fact that religion can be misused to justify any kind of politics, he is less worried about the public sphere being recreated in the image of the president's, or for that matter anyone else's faith, than of the public sphere prohibiting the discussion of contending faiths because they do not belong there. If the public sphere is to remain open, it must learn to accommodate, he insists, both to the concerns of religious conservatives who see modern secularism as inimical to religious perspectives and morals, and to secular liberals who view religion as incompatible with the need to base political discourse on assumptions that no reasonable person can reject. Stout's position, grounded in some of the writings of Emerson, Whitman, and Dewey, centers around the discursive practice of holding ourselves accountable to each other for the reasons we give for our convictions, the choices we make with our lives, the kinds of people we are or seek to become.

This democratic tradition of moral reasoning is based neither on assent to certain propositions, nor on allegiance to a transcendent source of authority, but rather on the ethical responsibilities that fellow citizens bear to one another. It sees itself as an alternative both to the kind of secular liberalism that sees all theological reasons as potential rationalizations and to the traditional orthodoxies which hold that a common life based on anything but Christian, Jewish, Muslim, or some other principle is theologically and ethically empty. Hence to anti-democratic religious traditionalists like Father Richard John Neuhaus, who want to place a sacred canopy over "the naked public sphere," as well as to liberal secularists like John Rawls, and particularly Richard Rorty, who initially contended that religion should be kept out of public debate because political behavior must be governed by assumptions from which all citizens can reason in common, Stout maintains that democracy is not hostile to religion but merely to the belief that anyone's views, including the president's, are beyond explanation or challenge. Democracy should not rule out the justification of positions on religious grounds; it should merely insist that citizens have a right to adopt any intellectual position they wish so long as they do not treat it as wholly privileged or use it to inhibit exchange with others.

Such practices as these may not produce the kind of consensus that communitarians look for, any more than they can enforce the acceptance of certain standards of reasonableness, but Stout is convinced that no single hierarchy of commitments can hold a country like the United States together. What unites its citizens is neither a single creed on which all can agree, nor a normative model for thinking that all can practice, but rather an ethical obligation that all should honor. Democracy is not created by an independent conception of justice or a uniform conception of faith but rather by what people in fact do to make it work. In this pragmatist conception, what matters is not what people accept as true so much as how they act in constituting themselves as a political community. The proof that Americans are committed to democratic norms is found in how they behave: "If we were not committed to continuing a discussion that perfects and honors our democratic norms, we would happily accept more restrictive and exclusionary ways of conducting political deliberation."[25]

But who can any longer assume that Americans are committed to democratic practices of political debate and ethical deliberation when in the present moment such procedures are everywhere under siege or in a state of collapse? When a majority of the members of the United States Congress use power as a lever to gain advantage over the other side, security issues since 9/11 have consistently overwhelmed rights issues, the general populace, under the sway of the media, has difficulty focusing on anything other than sound-bites or the next spectacle, and the White House is more interested in the next election than the country's wellbeing, what hope is there that this kind of pragmatic, democratic traditionalism can be believed, much less prevail?

Stout knows as well as anyone that we can no more trust our own rulers to respect such moral and discursive virtues than we can anyone else's, but his confidence in the strength of such virtues, especially when now they must be used, he believes, to negotiate our relations not only with strangers and but also with enemies, rings hollow. How do you hold—and what does it mean to hold—militant suicidal jihadists accountable, as he thinks we should, when the United States government itself refuses to discuss with anyone its new legal authority, secretly obtained by President Bush, to undertake wars abroad without public knowledge or Congressional oversight, and when President Obama has extended that authority to conduct military operations in the sovereign territory of other states, to use drone technology for the purpose of targeted assassinations, and to perpetuate use of torture for the sake of combating terror? With power now so strongly centralized in the White House, the military so thoroughly politicized, Congress so completely polarized, public opinion so easily manipulated, and the Supreme Court supporting the corporate control of presidential and other elections, when it is not actively deciding them, this is an unrealistic scenario.[26]

But perhaps this represents a misreading of the moral and spiritual legacy of American pragmatism and thus of its availability for democratic reflection on the relation between religious traditionalism and secular pluralism. Jackson Lears has developed a very different historical narrative of contending American faiths and their relevance to the Manicheanizing and absolutization of American politics. The first of those faiths derives from the Protestant Reformation and owes its allegiance to the Calvinist God of Providence, who lent his support to the initial creation of a religious culture of control and self-discipline that has now merged with, or at least sanctioned, the later evolution of a more secularized culture of management and progress. The second of those faiths owes its origins to the rather different god or gods of risk, chance, luck, and the practices of divining, conjuring, and hazarding by which they are solicited, and it assumes by contrast that worldly success, like spiritual fulfillment, depends as much or more on fortuitous accidents as it does on divine election. Just as the tradition of the entrepreneur borrows from both these veins of religious practice, so these two traditions have always been intertwined in America from the earliest Puritan period on—what was conversion, after all, if not in some sense a wager?—but they have generated two very different character types and two predictably apposite moral cultures. If the ideal type of the first is the self-made man who lives by discipline, hard work, and the postponement of gratification, that of the second celebrates the confidence man who places his trust in happenstance, serendipity, and inexplicable good fortune.

While there is no doubt that the self-made man has prevailed over the confidence man in the US's public morality, the cultural link between them is secured on two different levels. On the first, the two are doubles since the ideal of the self-made man was largely created to offset the social chaos threatened by the confidence man. On the second, they both rely on the operations of something they call grace, which reminds the gambler no less than the communicant that salvation is a gift from God and the dream of mastery and domination in life ultimately illusory as well as selfish. For the pious no less than the irreverent, grace is a gift that confounds the cultures of control just as much as those of coincidence by opening the self to possibilities undreamt of in ordinary experience. Likening its operations to the work of beauty, where the unevenness of the world's surfaces sometimes, for no ostensible reason, cracks or splits and we are then pulled through these fissures "into some vaster space,"[27] Lears defines grace as "what happens when openness to chance yields a deeper awareness of the cosmos or one's place in it—when luck leads to spiritual insight."[28]

While Lears does not deny that gambling has ruined far more lives than it has enhanced, he believes that its deepest appeal is no less admirable than that offered by more traditional faiths. The gambler, after all, seeks that moment where money no longer matters, where prudentiality, utilitarianism, instrumentalism, and, above all, self-regard falls away in a hope, however groundless but still sustaining, that for once the coordinates of life will be in perfect alliance, that dreams of felicity can be matched by life's realization of them. Support for this argument can be found in no less an authority that Johan Huizinga's masterful *Homo Ludens*, which shows how the modern obsession with systematic work has never been able to obliterate entirely the spirit of serious play that inhabits such endeavors as religion, law, philosophy, war, medicine, and business. This same spirit of receptivity to accident, unpredictability, spontaneity, improvisation, and transformation can also be found, Lears maintains, in the work of some of the US's greatest modern artists, from Ralph Ellison, Joseph Cornell, Alan Ginsburg, and Louise Nevelson to Robert Motherwell, John Cage, and Frank Gehry.

But it was the pragmatist William James who became America's "greatest philosopher of chance" and therefore presented the Protestant culture of control and its successors with their strongest competition. Arguing that experience is much too vital, irregular, incorrigible, and decentering to fit within most of our conventional categories of reflection and theological templates, James held that life involves risks, that thought is like taking a chance, that feeling contains a large element of the uncertain. Experience, said James, is fluid and unfinished, rationality no more than a sentiment, reality a thing defined as much by the affective as by the material relations among its component elements. Pleasure like aesthetics, James went on to argue, is not an incidental embellishment of life but among its very constituents, part of the *res*, as Wallace Stevens might have said, and not about it. Therefore the trick intellectually was not to confuse the stopping places of reflection, sometimes called ideas, with the movements between and among and beyond them. Life, James insisted, is in the transitions, and all our conclusions merely provisional and in need of correction. In life's unfinished trajectory, we learn where we are and what we should be about only by betting that the consequences of our, and others', actions can in some sense be measured, can to some degree be assessed, chiefly by, as in a democracy, imaginatively putting ourselves in the place of those who might be most effected by them.[29]

Stout would rightly say that such consequentialism requires considerable refining and needs to be applied most specifically to the practices by which we do, or do not, attend to one another. Lears would not dispute this, but would add that there is a good deal more guessing, conjecture, speculation, supposition, and downright art in figuring out who the other actually is and how she or he might be taken seriously. Taking others with the kind of seriousness Stout associates with democracy involves for Lear more than holding one another responsible to each other's arguments. It depends as well, as Emmanuel Levinas has pointed out, on gratuitous acts of generosity where we put aside the requirement that others attend to us and simply confront their claims, particularly those of the powerless, for what, insofar as we can comprehend them at all, they are. This is more than the exercise of responsibility; it is a game, as Lears calls it, in which, as Levinas says, "someone plays without winning. ... Something that one does gratuitously, that is grace."[30] It is itself an act of grace, "not unlike those tears in the curtain of the everyday where the light of less imperfect possibilities shine through."[31] For Lears as well as for Levinas, this is the essence of morality, and its graciousness confounds the dreams of mastery, domination, and manipulation implicit in our cultures of control in the same way that it enables democracy to mean more than being responsible to each other's positions. While it may lack an elaborate theology, it does not want for a religious basis, which is found in the yearning for a sense of completion, in effect of consummation, that can neither be bought nor earned but merely hazarded with the coin of one's own life.

This pragmatic deference to experiment, risk, pluralism, and self-correction, which lies at the heart of American traditions of reform, would have struck a thinker like the political scientist Samuel P. Huntington as beside the point. Stout's assumption that democracy requires us to take the positions of our opponents as seriously as we would have them take our own, much less Lears's contention that it involves a hospitality that asks nothing in return, are simply sentimental because any conflicts that derive from differences in religious worldviews are likely to be non-negotiable. This is the position he is famous for taking in his well-known book *The Clash of Civilizations and the Making of World Order*, which laid the responsibility for global violence at the door of the incompatibility of religious ideologies, but he later extended this perspective to the study of American national identity. In *Who Are We?* Huntington argues that the chief threat to the US comes not only from Muslims bringing their militancy to the American mainland or, somewhat earlier, from deconstructionism bringing its cultural relativism from the Continent, but now, primarily, from Latinos bringing their alien way of life and thought to America's Anglo-Protestant culture.

Anglo-Protestant culture is, in Huntington's estimation, based on a unitary set of core values that America's earliest founding settlers carried with them to the New World and eventually used in the eighteenth and nineteenth centuries to establish what Gunnar Myrdal was the first to call the "American Creed," with its "principles of liberty, equality, individualism, representative government, and private property."[32] Central to those values were the Christian religion, Protestant morality and the work ethic, the English language, and a series of British traditions "of law, justice, and the limits of government power," along with a European legacy of art and thought.[33] Derived from England's early modern "Tudor Constitution," the religio-cultural and political components embodied in the American Creed have enabled the US, Huntington asserts, to be a cohesive society chiefly because of agreement on the ranking of its values. But now that social cohesion, and the identity on which it is based, has been imperiled. The dangers come from several directions, but the chief one originates from south of the border and has been augmented, first, by the arrival of deconstruction from the Continent and, more recently, by militant jihad from the Middle East.

One can obtain some sense of the cast of Huntington's argument from what he says about deconstruction. Constantly blurring the lines between its function as an intellectual strategy and method and its effects as now a cultural, even a period, style, Huntington claims that deconstruction is chiefly responsible for legitimating the multicultural move to redefine the US as many people created out of one, rather than one people created out of many. Insisting that America was originally composed of many races, ethnicities, and sub-national cultures that eventually became one people sharing common convictions, he believes that the recent deconstruction *of* America, not the arrival of deconstruction *in* America, has licensed the development of a host of minority identities that have eroded the idea of American citizenship itself. By the same logic, he argues that all forms of cosmopolitanism risk "merging America," in the language of one of his chapter titles, "with the world." Denationalized elites in business, the media, and the academy are referred to in this book as "dead souls"; diasporan identities are viewed as inescapably weakening the national sense of self; and the blurring and fading of race produced by intermarriage constitute a genuine threat to the ethnicity of white Americans.

No doubt such prejudices are shared by many white Americans, but what can these allegations mean in a study that also makes a point of noting that 75 percent of American blacks have white ancestors, 22 percent of whites are in fact non-white, and marrying out now ranges from 12 percent for black Americans to as high as 51 to 55 percent for Asian Americans, at least between the ages of 25 and 34? Huntington's blizzard of statistics provides impressive evidence of the increasing diversification of the American population, much greater in fact than most citizens are prepared to acknowledge, while he maintains, often with no substantiation, that this blurring of race and ethnicity is eroding the sense of American nationhood.

What Huntington most fears, however, is not the intermixing of peoples in the US, much as this may dilute the sense of whiteness, but their bifurcation, and here Latino resistance to assimilation represents what he clearly perceives as the gravest internal peril to American identity. Even if by itself the American Creed does not constitute the nation, the nation has been placed in jeopardy by policies and practices that support the infusion of Hispanics. Moreover, this internal danger is now exacerbated, Huntington believes, by the external threat posed by a resurgent, hostile Islam, which leaves Christian America with only three options: cosmopolitanism, imperialism, or nationalism. In the first, the US is reshaped by the world, despite the fact that it possesses strong cosmopolitan traditions of its own (as Huntington seems to forget) deriving from those same Enlightenment beliefs and ideals that he assumes to be essential cornerstones of the American Creed. In the second, the world is supposedly reshaped by the US itself, even though, as Huntington acknowledges, the world contains other powers and superpowers whose cooperation the US requires to fulfill its global ambitions. This leaves the third option as his only viable alternative. The US needs to play its nationalist card because this is the only alternative that prevents it from being swallowed up either by the universalism implicit in cosmopolitanism or by the illusory sense of strength implicit in any unilateral imperialism—and, at the same time, it justifies the US's exceptionalism in terms of its historic religiosity.

Huntington's views would not deserve this much attention if their biases were not so widely shared by a significant number of Americans. While he acknowledges that American Protestantism is, or at least was, a dissenting tradition, he treats it in its current evangelical form as almost exclusively an instrument of moral and theological consensus. Never acknowledging that elements of the American Creed have often been in conflict with one another, he ignores, in addition, the evidence that it has only been imperfectly realized at selective times and places in American history. He frequently associates multiculturalism only with elites, as though minority populations could not, and have not, often at great cost, spoken for themselves or not been emphatic that as US citizens what they wanted mainly was the right, wholly consistent with democratic principles, to participate with others in determining the American future. Huntington's belief that white ethnicity, which he wants to preserve, is somehow more American than other kinds sounds for all the world like nativism redivivus—Alan Wolfe in fact charged him with this, which led to spirited defenses of Huntington by a number of centrist and conservative policy intellectuals.[34] Still more troubling, Huntington frequently gives a spin to the statistical information he has gathered, which leads to the stereotyping of 40 million Americans of Hispanic descent who clearly do not all think, much less believe, alike but are, in various ways, seeking to join what can only be called the American mainstream.

But among all the other difficulties posed by Huntington's book, perhaps the most ironic is his shaky grasp of American religious history. Anglo-Protestant culture in the United States, even during the years of its formation and heyday between 1730 and 1860, was by no means as unified or coherent as Huntington makes it out to be. Moreover, it was dealt a heavy blow in the Civil War from which it never entirely recovered. Composed of an uneasy but productive synthesis of Protestant Christianity, Republican political ideology, and Common-Sense moralism that was greatly facilitated by the expansion of market economics from the Revolution to the War Between the States, this composite culture not only influenced the Americanization of Christian, and essentially Protestant, theology but also promoted and, more significantly, shaped the rapid Christianization of the United States.[35]

Yet even as this synthesis helped form a sense of American nationhood during its most crucial phase of development, it was eventually to founder over disputes between the North and South about the scriptural basis of slavery. Christians on both sides of the Mason-Dixon Line used the Bible to justify their positions, but this only produced a crisis that shattered the synthesis of religion, morality, and rationality to which they both appealed. Only in Lincoln's Second Inaugural Address was this shattered synthesis temporarily restored, but there in a form that neither side could use to defend their own positions. Combining Calvinist, Enlightened, and Republican insights, Lincoln warned a divided and embittered nation against the danger of claiming divine favor or sanction for either side. Lincoln reminded all who held that they were acting in accordance with God's will that the Almighty has his own purposes, which are beyond human comprehension. While it was natural for partisans on both sides to read God's hand in their own cause and to invoke God's aid against their enemies, scripture, moral humility, and ordinary reason all conveyed the truth that events are finally disposed by God alone and that no one can read their true intent. Though Lincoln's theological contemporaries would continue to believe that the War not only confirmed the chosenness of the American people but God's blessing on their own side, Lincoln retained a firmer hold on the central Protestant principle of God's sovereignty by cautioning all against the presumption to know the mind of the Almighty, much less to speak for it, as too many in the US still think they can.

The emergence of this intellectual synthesis of Protestant evangelicalism, republican ideology, and common sense, first initiated by Edwards and later brought to a kind of completion and fulfillment by Lincoln, was largely unforeseen in colonial American history before the Revolution and had no parallel before or after in the Atlantic world, according to Mark Noll.[36] As profoundly as this synthesis eventually became woven into the fabric of national life, it differed significantly, as a matter of fact, from Protestant developments both in the British Isles and on the Continent. The construction of this synthesis thus did not amount to a simple transfer of Tudor culture to the American Strand but rather involved a complex adaptation and extension of elements from Reformation Christianity, early modern traditions of civic humanism, and the European and English Enlightenments to American conditions. What was without precedent, then, was how the spheres of religious and secular discourse were connected over time during this period and the way their connections reshaped the central doctrines of the Christian faith in the process of helping to fashion the sense and limits of American nationhood.

That notion of nationhood, however, was dependent on far more than the influence of Protestant, and especially English, culture in the US. The religious development of what was to become American society did not conclude with the transplantation of European peoples to the New World. It involved from the beginning the transit of peoples from the entire Atlantic, or rather circum-Atlantic, world interacting with indigenous populations from North and South America. This process may have left America "awash in a sea of faith," to quote a famous title,[37] but that faith is now understood to have been of multiple derivations— Spanish, African, Amerindian, eventually Eastern European, South Asian, and East Asian—which have been responsible for the creation of a plurality of different, if also interlinked, religious narratives driven by attachment mechanisms such as revitalization movements that had nothing to do with religion as such.

Thanks to the work of many scholars, the focus has now rightly shifted from religion in the US to the religions of the US, and the place once reserved for English Protestantism has been significantly rethought in relation to Protestantism's contacts, interactions, and exchanges with a multitude of other religious and non-religious perspectives and practices. Indeed, during the 1970s and 1980s, Protestantism itself, and its Anglo-Puritan variants, was reconceived as a religious formation that developed in various stages, displayed regional variations, suffered internal fractures, and was always bounded by an emergent popular culture to which it was continuously, as we have seen earlier in this chapter, adapting. Thus the old Protestant synthesis quickly took on a more multicultural appearance in the historical writing of the last quarter of the twentieth century and began to present new challenges to the possibility of writing any cohesive narrative of American religion at all.

What saved the study of American religion from falling victim to incoherence was the discovery, also originating in the 1960s with the publication of Will Herberg's *Protestant-Catholic-Jew*, that the great diversity of religious belief and behavior in the American experience might be based on an underlying faith in something Herberg called "the American Way of Life."[38] Herberg took this to be a sign of the superficiality of the three largest religious formations in the US, but within less than a decade the sociologist Robert Bellah had discovered this civil religion to be a new source of cultural renewal best expressed, perhaps, in the inaugural addresses of various American presidents, not least of them John F. Kennedy.[39]

Bellah's proposition that there might well be a religion of the US as well as a distinctive kind of religion or religiousness within the US, had precedents both theoretical and historical. Émile Durkheim had first expressed the view that religion furnishes societies with mirrors by which to see and valorize themselves, and Walt Whitman had even earlier articulated the idea that the US needed to construct a "New World metaphysics" to underpin its "New World democracy."[40] In part, Bellah was merely conflating these ideas for the sake of explaining how American religion could encourage diversity without being inconsistent with itself. But the religious historian John Wilson believes that this new attempt to turn the US itself into an object worthy of religious worship has given rise to a third way of writing the history of American religion, epitomized by Harold Bloom's *The American Religion*.[41] Wilson concedes that Bloom's Gnostic predisposition to center this faith on an ecstatic egocentrism that conceives of the individual self as "a spark of God floating in a sea of space" needs to be complemented by a more dialectic sense of the role that community also plays in this newest form of the American religious sensibility.[42]

But there are still other problems with Bloom's formulation and Wilson's appropriation of it. If Bloom never manages to explain how this radical individualism can be squared with the religious identity of his chief religious exhibits, Southern Baptists and Mormons, let alone with the communal faith and religious practices of African Americans, Jews, and others, Wilson fails to explain how a version of faith so potentially solipsistic can simultaneously find expression in the sense of solidarity that attends collective experiences of grief and mourning associated with events like 9/11 and the leisure-time activity, albeit often undertaken in deadly earnest, of hanging out at the mall. Where the Puritan tradition and its successor faiths in America had available to them certain possibilities of self-criticism (Calvinism in its doctrine of God's sovereignty, other faiths in their proximity to and competition with divergent modes of belief and action), the particular form of market globalization that Wilson holds up at the end of his book, coterminous with American imperialism and exemplary of the way we live now, offers nothing by way of self-revision but its own power to browse for pretty much exactly what it wishes. Desire, even if not always consummated, has become just another sign of election, and the saints can now be recognized by their money, style, yearning, and, yes, access.

This is not a comforting prospect when it is reinforced by a view like Huntington's that we are confronted in the United States and elsewhere with a clash of fundamentalisms. Paradoxically, the only position that Huntington's discourse normalizes is the talk of such Christian warriors as the aforementioned Randall Terry, who headed the rescue effort to prevent Terri Shiavo from being taken off life support, and James Dobson, founder of Focus on the Family and still one of the most powerful religious lobbyists in the United States today, who believe that if we cannot, in Huntington's language, shore up the Christian West against the rest, then it may become necessary, in the idiom of the second Bush administration, which has been reinforced in the continuing practices of the Obama administration, simply to take some of them out. And now we have drones.

6

WAR NARRATIVES AND AMERICAN EXCEPTIONALISM

> One is left with the horrible feeling now that war settles nothing; that to win a war is as disastrous as to lose one.
>
> Agatha Christie, "An Autobiography," 1977, p. 503

War is a venerable practice in America, just as venerable, some may be surprised to learn, as imperialism, and the glue that so often holds them together is religion. They first found triangular expression, as has been previously noted, among the early colonists in tidewater Virginia, who were more than prepared to use conquest to aid conversion for the sake of creating their "righteous empire." Well over three centuries later in *The Bigelow Papers*, James Russell Lowell discerned the same imperial thematic without condoning it in his panegyric to "O strange New World":

> thet yit wast never young,
> Whose youth from thee by gripin' need was wrung,
> Brown foundlin' o' the woods, whose baby-bed
> Was prowled roun' by the Injun's cracklin' tread,
> An' who grew'st strong thru shifts an' wants an' pains,
> Nussed by stern men with empires in their brains.[1]

Physical domination, then, both economic and political, along with ideological control, would henceforth tend to be yoked together as the two components most indispensable for fashioning America's religiously imperial project, a project that a majority of its citizens and no small number of its presidents and other elected representatives view as their international imaginary. War and the other operations of a security state conducted in the name of that imaginary is what makes the United States exceptional.

Thus it should come as little surprise that the United States has spent roughly 20 percent of its history in wars intended not simply to protect its people and ensure its safety but to extend its sacred legacy. However, this tells only half the story. The other half is that since the end of World War II, the United States has entered the permanent condition of what Secretary of Defense, James Forrestal, was the first to call "semiwar" where, in the face of perpetual threat, the nation must be ready to launch continous war.[2] Since 1945 and the cessation of hostilities with the Axis Powers, the United States has initiated combat actions throughout the world, from the Caribbean to East Africa, Latin America, the Balkans, Asia Minor, and the Middle East. It has intervened or gone to war in Korea, Cuba, Vietnam, Grenada, Panama, the Persian Gulf, Somalia, Bosnia and Herzegovina, Serbia, and Sudan. In Afghanistan it is now in the longest war of its history, and it has only recently, after seven years of the third longest war in its history, removed the last of its combat forces, but by no means all of its military personnel, from Iraq. To support these forces it has constructed a military empire that includes more than 716 bases around the world (somewhat less than the highest Cold War number of 1,014), some of them larger than entire states, which are serviced by over a half million men and women in arms and their dependents, ten naval task forces built around aircraft carriers, more than 50,000 locally hired foreigners, and tens of thousands of private contractors. The Defense Department's Base Structure Report estimated in 2009 that it would require nearly $125 billion just to replace foreign bases (there are another 4,863 in the United States and its territories) and $720 billion to replace them all.[3]

These developments have conspired for decades to create a situation where no sitting president can afford to lose a war without risk of losing office, despite the fact that continuous warfare is bankrupting the American economy and slowly but inevitably pauperizing the American middle class.[4] Even at the risk of jeopardizing their financial wellbeing, not to say international security, the American people would rather support an all-volunteer military and its mercenaries to fight foreign wars than question their religious sense of nationalist global entitlement. Many of America's best critics, both within the country and outside, view this behavior as a form of international, or at least imperialist, suicide, but nothing short of complete financial collapse or international catastrophe seems capable of shaking most Americans or their leaders from the conviction that it is America's responsibility to shape world order according to its own designs and to safeguard that right by its willingness to maintain a global military presence which is prepared to be projected and deployed anywhere. Over the last six, now going on seven, decades, Andrew J. Bacevich is convinced that this Washington consensus, broadly but somewhat blithely shared by the entire national security establishment, has created a "path to permanent war."[5]

That path has in effect created what John Dower has described so brilliantly as "cultures of war" that link in the most intimate fashion momentous events as dispersed as Pearl Harbor, Hiroshima and Nagasaki, the response to 9/11, and the wars in Iraq and Afghanistan. These events share a number of features, not restricted to

Americans but rather binding them to their enemies, which include everything from failures of imagination to delusions of innocence, wars of choice to strategic imbecilities, Manichean mindsets to the rhetorics of cosmic war, faith-based policies and secular priesthoods to the capacity for radical evil. Central to them all as a matter of holy writ is a fundamentalist conviction that the state can go to any lengths, no matter how violent, to insure its own security and interests, but this has closed such faith-based thinking off from any critical appraisal either of its own advocates or of others. "This seems counterintuitive where policy making affecting war and peace is concerned, since the essence of strategic planning presumably is to know the enemy while also knowing and acknowledging one's own flaws and vulnerabilities."[6] Moreover, the assumption that reality is, or should be, a creation of faith, that dogma trumps reason and reflection, has permitted the justification of atrocities and slaughter of unimaginable proportions throughout the postwar period. Cultures of war normalized mass destruction and gave new allure to technologies of devastation.

Against this background, I would like to take up a group of what might be called new global war narratives. Strictly speaking, the first might be more fairly described as a counter-war narrative, the second a potential-war narrative, the third an anti-war narrative. One is organized around a sequence of events in the past that goes back to the end of World War II and relates to the development of the international human rights movement. The second is organized around a sequence of events in the future associated with lowering the nuclear threshold and could well inaugurate, if it hasn't begun already, the first phase of World War III. The third may well have been stimulated by social activist movements in Latin America and Central Europe in the 1970s and 1980s dedicated to curbing the power of states, but it is now better known, because of the explosive growth of INGOs (International Non-Governmental Organizations) in the 1990s, as the development of a new global civil society.

In the first war narrative, American exceptionalism has very nearly written the nation out of world history in the name of claiming to represent its future. In the second war narrative, American exceptionalism has permitted the nation to write itself back into history but only at the risk of annihilating history altogether. This leaves a the third narrative, where the only possibility of any reasonable, any historical, future at all may depend on America's ability to curb, if not entirely renegotiate, its exceptionalist pretensions and ambitions.

Describing as "narratives" sets of events whose sequentiality does not necessarily conform to the logic of conditional contrary-to-fact statements, or whose form doesn't represent plausibility structures, may risk stretching the term a bit too thin. But if this terminological maneuver presents problems, one could just as easily instead call these fictive constructs, variously organized under the signs of human rights, nuclear war, and civic society, symbolic actions. In the well-known formula described by Kenneth Burke, they all constitute responses to the problematics of particular situations and seek not only to size up those situations, and delineate their component parts, but also develop a strategy for metaphorically, if not materially, encompassing them by projecting an appropriate attitude or stance to take with respect to them.[7]

Yet none of these global war narratives would warrant our attention if it were not for the disturbing role that American exceptionalism tends to plays in each. They take on particular interest because of their capacity to reveal several of the more significant ways that the United States has defined, expressed, and defended its primacy as well as uniqueness within the community of nations. Stated more explictly, they each reflect the new authority that the national imaginary has assumed for itself in a world where American power is so often tempted to act unilaterally, or at least without due consideration of the interests of others, and international protocols and constraints are viewed mainly as impediments to policy.[8]

Such exhibitions of exceptionalism may not be new to American self-conceptions, but neither should they be confused with a variety of other well-known forms that American entitlement has taken that have been associated with being, in David Halberstrom's phrase, "the brightest and the best" and codified in the "Washington rules."[9] Still less should they be restricted to changes that occurred to the national psyche after World War II, when the United States emerged from total war as the most economically powerful and politically stable nation on the planet. America's sense of exceptionalism was already deeply rooted in America's political unconscious when President McKinley justified the acquisition of the Philippine Islands by arguing that "we could not leave them to themselves—they were unfit for self-government—and would soon have anarchy and misrule over there worse than Spain's was."[10] Describing his critics as those who "have no confidence in the virtue or capacity or high purpose or good faith of this free people as a civilizing agency," McKinley spoke for a great majority of his countrymen when he stated "that the century of free government which the American people have enjoyed has not rendered them irresolute and faithless, but has fitted them for the great task of lifting up and assisting to better conditions and larger liberty those distant peoples who, through the issue of battle, have become our wards."[11] This presumption allowed the Philippines to become an American colonial possession that was not relinquished until 1946. But the Philippine Islands were only one of many territorial acquisitions after the Spanish-American War, which in the Pacific included Guam, the Hawaiian islands, Wake Island, American Samoa, and the Northern Marianas, and in the Caribbean Cuba, Puerto Rico, the Panama Canal Zone, and the Virgin Islands.

It is generally assumed that the roots of this exceptionalism go back to the nation's Judeo-Christian myths of origin, which were initially given their most famous expression in John Winthrop's well-known call to his fellow passengers, arriving in Massachusetts Bay on the flagship *Arabella*, to become a "City upon a Hill" that might light the way back to the truth of the Christian gospel. By representing the Puritans to themselves as a people set apart to assist in the regeneration of the world, Winthrop was planting the seeds of a predisposition that would subsequently flower into an axiom of belief for many future Americans. Just as Winthrop saw himself as a latter-day Moses leading his people out of darkness to a New World of truth and righteousness, so America's continuing responsibility was to lead the world itself forward to a future of democratic prosperity.

But Winthrop's eschatological hopes were for a time seriously threatened by Oliver Cromwell, when the English Puritan Revolution shifted attention away from the theocratic experiment the American Puritans were fashioning in the New World and thus very nearly succeeded in reading them out of history altogether. Yet by the time the Stuarts had found their way back into power in England, the American Puritans had discovered a way to read themselves back into history. The key to this new hermeneutic lay in reinterpreting the trope by which Puritan New Englanders saw themselves as the "New Israel" called upon to help fulfill God's plan for history as a whole. While this trope permitted them to view their "errand into the wilderness" as an illustration, an exemplification, a realization of Biblical patterns, what was to keep them from arguing that the New World was, or could become, an authentification, even a legitimation, of them? Never mind that for many of the faithful, as could be seen in the antinomian controversy or Roger Williams's schism, consensus on matters of belief was far from assured; or that the disappointments and hazards of life in the New World settlements tested the convictions of even the most steadfast, like journalist Mary Rowlandson and the poet Anne Bradstreet; or that the great majority of people who followed the pilgrims (even some who accompanied the Massachusetts Bay colonists) came for reasons other than religion; or that at least one-third of the colonists who emigrated during the first century of European settlement soon returned home—never mind any of these and other facts, a significant number of religious Americans not only managed to re-inscribe themselves back into history but reconceived themselves—and the emergent country along with them—as history's potential, and often martial, savior. Theologically, it was essentially a problem of figuring out how their own history could be transmuted into scriptural history, could in effect become, a version of the Holy Scriptures. What was required was ultimately no more than a series of textual mutations—scripture into history, history into nation, nation back into scripture—and suddenly the coordinates of consecrated election would fall into place and be etched into the American imaginary. America's religious world mission not only set it apart from, and above, all other nations but dictated the terms in which it could be achieved. American exceptionalism could become the instrument of history's deliverance and also its fulfillment—in the first war narrative I want to examine, emboldening the nation very nearly to write itself out of world history in the name of claiming to represent its future; in the second war narrative I wish to take up, permitting the nation to write itself back into history but only at the risk of terminating history itself.

If these claims sound exaggerated, merely consider the fact that while the United States has, from the Constitutional period on, affirmed the general importance of human rights as an integral component of its national traditions, often employing them as a central instrument of foreign policy, the American Congress has for the better part of the last half century been reluctant to ratify many international rights conventions on the grounds that American citizens should not be held accountable to juridical standards that lack the political legitimacy conferred only by the nation's own laws. Insisting that American citizens, alone among the world's people, derive their rights as individuals not from international compacts but from the US Constitution, the United States actively promotes and, where expedient, attempts to enforce human rights norms around the world that it does not believe, or at any rate does not act as though it believes, apply to its own citizens.

This is not to assert that the United States is the only country in the world that has tried to exempt itself and its own citizens from honoring international human rights covenants; it is merely to note the paradox that the United States continually confronts when, with other European and Asian nations, it has invoked the rights tradition again and again to justify humanitarian intervention in places like Haiti, Somalia, Iraq, Bosnia, Kosovo, Iraq, and Afghanistan. Such interventions have often occurred in response to violations that the United States and other nations have found to be humanly intolerable, and there is no question but that these interventions have sometimes helped reduce cruelty and relieve suffering. Yet the moral authority of such otherwise ethically significant and legally acceptable acts is immediately placed in question when, in the face of other circumstances, the United States is prepared to disregard such obligations when it suits its own convenience. From the beginning, the United States was a reluctant signatory to the Universal Declaration of Human Rights itself, refused to ratify the Convention against Genocide until it was shamed into doing so 40 years after it was first drafted, recurrently vacillates in its support of the United Nations, actively weakens and manipulates the powers of the International Criminal Tribunal, refuses to accept various legal rights enshrined in the U.N. Convention on the Rights of the Child, and has now taken the unprecedented step of voiding its signature, in the *Nuclear Posture Review*, on the treaty, signed by 136 nations and ratified by 66, that established the International Criminal Court.

This last decision to disavow a binding international treaty could well have large implications for the whole edifice of international law and may indeed be a sign that we have entered the age of what Antonio Negri and Michael Hardt call "Empire."[12] Negri and Hardt mean by the term "Empire" a new concept of world governance that replaces the old notion of state sovereignty with a form of rule which, by becoming decentered and deterritorializing, is able to incorporate more and more of the entire global realm within its open and expanding frontiers. The utility of this new concept of global governance is that it suggests how sovereignty can exert still more hegemonic power when it is permitted to circulate in a world without the usual limitations provided by international covenants, a world where a country like the United States is free to place the structure of international law at risk through arbitrary acts that nullify some of its chief components and mechanisms.

One might well wonder if any practice, however imperialistically arrogant, actually conforms to the new world of global governance that Negri and Hardt have in mind, a world which, by their own admission, cannot be adequately described or anywhere specified as fully instantiated. But they might well claim that the system they call "Empire" is never completely realized because, in an effort to subsume or resolve all conflict within its juridical processes of constitution, it opens new conflicts in the very process of closing others. If this is partly a fault of the system itself, "Empire" at the same time confronts what, in the title of their next book, Hardt and Negri have identified as *Multitude*. "Multitude" refers to the plurality of "productive, creative subjectivities of globalization that have learned how to sail on this enormous sea." Forming "constellations of singularities and events that impose continual global reconfigurations on the system," the multitude, in this radically postmodern diagnosis of our political malady, is the one creative force that can, at least temporarily, destabilize the system.[13] However unequal their power and authority, the revolutionary potential of the "multitude" rests on the form taken by its claim to global citizenship. "Multitude" constitutes the perfect counter to "Empire" by asserting "the general right to control its own movement."[14]

The problem with this oppositional way of recasting the relationship between hegemony and resistance is that it requires, as Hardt and Negri maintain, that the multitude adopt a posture of perpetual political militancy in order to avoid capture by the imperial apparatus that lives off its vitality—"as Marx would say, a vampire regime of accumulated dead labor that survives only by sucking off the blood of the living."[15]

Such political heroics sound more romantic and utopian than radical if Empire is as totalizing in its ambitions and operations as Hardt and Negri claim it to be, but there is no doubt that their asseverations have been given a certain measure of credence by the way human rights have, since 9/11, been eclipsed by national security. And nowhere has this development been more obvious than in the second war narrative I wish to examine.

I describe this second narrative as a potential, if not possible, war narrative because I associate it with a text like the *Nuclear Posture Review*, though one could just as easily have chosen *The National Security Strategy of the United States of America* (1999) or the *Patriot Act* (2001) and its revision (2006). The *Nuclear Posture Review* is a formerly secret report prepared by the Department of Defense at the direction of the United States Congress to develop a strategic posture for the twenty-first century. First leaked to the *Los Angeles Times* and then the *New York Times*, the *Nuclear Posture Review* argues that its distinctive recommendations derive from a new security environment that was created long before September 11 and was initially introduced to the American public in the "First Phase" of the *Report of the U.S. Commission on National Security/21st Century*, chaired by former Senators Warren Rudman and Gary Hart and released in 1999.

The most comprehensive review of American security since the National Security Act of 1947, the First Phase *Report of the U.S. Commission on National Security/21st Century*, sometimes called the Hart-Rudman Commission, outlined a series of threats to the international security environment emerging in the first quarter of the twenty-first century.[16] These threats included the following: increasing exposure of the United States to hostile attack; new vulnerabilities created by advances in information and biotechnologies and an evolving global infrastructure that would in turn both divide and unite the world; the continuing strategic significance of energy; the new porousness of state borders which, in some cases, threaten state sovereignty and, in others, allow failing or fragmenting states to destabilize neighboring states; escalations of violence that include increased atrocities and the terrorizing of civilians; further militarization of space; the resort, or the threat of the resort, to weapons of mass destruction; the inability of intelligence agencies to prevent, or even predict, all attacks; the need to intervene militarily around the world with less support from allies and over-strained troop reserves; and, finally, the need to devise different military and other capabilities for the twenty-first century. Nowhere, however, does the *Report*, even in its second phase (released in 2000), which developed a strategy for dealing with these threats, or in its third phase (issued in 2001), which recommended comprehensive changes, both institutional and procedural, necessary to meet these challenges, consider the radical possibility of altering nuclear policy, much less altering it unilaterally, and with an eye to its preemptive use.

In response to the new security challenges outlined in *Report of the U.S. Commission on National Security/21st Century*, the *Nuclear Posture Review* (2002) by the Bush administration, however, assumed that the United States now faced a different security environment requiring a major alteration in capabilities.[17] The new threats represented by 9/11 clearly demanded a dramatically revised set of options for defense and response, which now included the possible offensive use of nuclear power, either in some combination with conventional weapons systems or as an independent strike force. In fairness it must be noted that the *Nuclear Posture Review* steadfastly maintained that its recommendations were designed to deter or avert the scenarios about which it fantasized, but it also maintained that these scenarios may not only require first strike capabilities but also involve a great many contingencies that we have never before considered. While the *Nuclear Posture Review* claimed that deterrence and not aggression remained the fundamental basis of American military nuclear planning, it asserted that the New Triad of forces on which this new policy was based—nuclear and non-nuclear offensive strike systems, active and passive nuclear and non-nuclear defense systems, and a revitalized defense infrastructure— would draw down the arsenal of operationally deployed strategic nuclear warheads by fully one-half. It also insisted that planning for every conceivable contingency in which the president might wish to employ nuclear weapons was the only prudent way to help prevent their eventual use.

What Bush's *Nuclear Posture Review* sought, without saying so, was to initiate a radical break with a tradition that had been honored since the very commencement of the Atomic Age. This tradition held that if nuclear armaments were considered weapons of last resort, they would nevertheless be used only if the existence of the nation itself was at stake. While the United States had always reserved to itself the right of first use, it never assumed, until the publication of the 2002 *Review*, that first use of weapons of mass destruction might be justified as a credible, legitimate, and necessary option in the face of any number of less catastrophic situations, situations that might include anything from attack by biological or chemical weapons, to the presence of targets capable of withstanding a non-nuclear attack, to the emergence of what it simply could not foresee. Thinking of these and other possibilities, the *Nuclear Posture Review* called for a "a new mix" or "boutique" approach, where nuclear weapons, possibly in combination with non-nuclear but much advanced armaments and expanded technological capabilities, can be used against enemy facilities difficult to attack, or particular groups that are well concealed, or other weapons of mass destruction that need to be neutralized.

Throughout the *Nuclear Posture Review*, which contemplated the possibility of crossing the nuclear threshold without any psychic shock to the international order if "collateral damage," as it is euphemistically termed, is contained and presumably large numbers of civilians, perhaps in the millions, are not contaminated or simply incinerated, there is emphasis on a rhetoric of "adaptability," "flexibility," "timeliness," and "proportionality" that belies the gravity of the actions they are meant to describe. Such language, emphasizing America's measured reasonableness and prudence, is employed to assure friend and foe alike of the United States's resolve never to use such weapons unless circumstances, now bearing on "national security" rather than "national survival," leave it with no other alternative but to invoke the threat of catastrophic destruction to discourage others from provoking it.

The revised version of the *Nuclear Posture Review* published by the Obama administration in 2010 addresses some, but by no means all, of the controversial elements of the Bush document. In an effort to moderate rather than heighten the importance of nuclear weapons to national security, which it claims has already been going on for some time, the 2010 *Nuclear Posture Review* reaffirms that the fundamental role of nuclear weapons is deterrence, not aggression, but goes on to point out that this deterrence encompasses nuclear attacks not only on the United States itself but also on its allies and partners. Moreover, it asserts that the United States will never use nuclear weapons against states that are signatories to the Nuclear Nonproliferation Treaty and in compliance with its nuclear regulations, President Obama's version of the *Review* does not rule out the possibility of a change in US policy if any non-nuclear state develops weapons, whether chemical, biological, or even conventional, that constitute a direct threat to the United States or its friends. What the 2010 version of the *Nuclear Posture Review* does repudiate is the Bush administration's "boutique" approach to the use of nuclear weapons in certain combinations with highly advanced conventional weapons. In addition, it promises to end further nuclear testing on the grounds that the present stockpile of weapons can be maintained without it.

These are not insignificant revisions to a set of policies that, when first published by the George W. Bush administration, radically altered past understandings. But how much reassurance do these revisions provide any states, nuclear or otherwise, if they carry with them the implication that "first use" is still an option should states develop weapons that can be construed as a direct threat either to the United States or to partners or allies. What constitutes a "direct" threat? How narrow or specific is the definition of "ally" or "partner"? Once nuclear weapons are employed by a nation that prides itself on still being the world's only military superpower, no hostile parties with the ability to defend themselves or seek revenge will hold back from considering the employment of similar weapons for their own security, and thus the door will be opened, if all doors are not destroyed, for the normalization of such policies. It is hardly farfetched to imagine that at least one of the reasons that Iran could be seeking to develop a nuclear weapon would be in part to protect from what occurred to its neighbor in Iraq, especially when the invasion of Iraq was justified by the argument, spurious as it turned out, that Iraq was developing weapons of mass destruction itself, even as the United States held back from directly challenging a potentially belligerent state like North Korea armed with nuclear weapons and the systems to deliver them. The inference is obvious. Those who can threaten the use of such weapons for their own strategic purposes will be left alone; those who lack them will have all the more incentive to acquire them.

Nothing said here is meant to discount the danger to which the United States and its people and friends are exposed because of the spread of these weapons that are now possessed by at least eight states (the United States, Russia, the UK, France, India, Pakistan, Israel, and North Korea) and are being sought by other powers, state and non-state, some of which have indicated they would have no compunction about using them against the US or its allies or their citizens. This new peril to America and the world was undoubtedly signaled by the events of September 11 but it was by no means first introduced then. Nor will this level of peril be reduced, as the Obama version of the *Nuclear Posture Review* still maintains, by assurances that the United States is now prepared to use these same weapons in the face of a variety of nuclear *and* non-nuclear threats. That the United States believes itself entitled to revise so radically the rules of engagement with nuclear weapons without consulting, through the usual channels, the world's opinion about such matters, much less considering how their use under any circumstances or in any theater might affect the good of the world, is not only a sign of the lengths to which the authors and defenders of the several editions of the *Nuclear Posture Review* are prepared to carry American exceptionalism; it also indicates how thoroughly naturalized nuclear warfare has potentially become in a continuing narrative where the enemy to be engaged can include anything from another sovereign state to a jihadist group like Al Qaeda or one of its imitators. This is an improvement from the willingness of George W. Bush's administration to target any of the nations belonging to the so-called "axis of evil," or any nation that harbors or supports terrorists, or any battlefield where the use of such weapons would allow us to prevail. But the narrative itself still remains determinedly open-ended and could very quickly become dangerously, indeed tragically, complicated if certain states with which the United States is mutually, if also somewhat differently, allied, such as Pakistan and India, were to go to war.

The alternative to such a calamity has been imagined as the fulfillment of a third narrative, which could only have developed under the conditions we now recognize as global but which is more naturally disposed to resist rather than advocate war. While this anti-war narrative possesses clear and direct relations with the counter-war narrative associated with the international human rights revolution and its advocacy initiatives, its origins possess a more direct connection with social movements of the 1970s and 1980s, particularly in Latin America and Eastern Europe, which were concerned to develop legal instruments capable of limiting the power of states and eventually creating "islands of engagement" where humanitarian norms and other issues could be debated, promoted, and critiqued.[18] By whichever route and in whatever forms (social activist, neoliberal, or postmodern), these political-ethical concerns led during the last quarter of the twentieth century and the first decade of the twenty-first to the reinvention of what we now recognize as an international civil society committed to the establishment and enforcement of a system of global rules designed to address the needs of security and dignity for all the world's people.

This is not to suggest that the plethora of agencies, institutions, associations, and actors who are participating in this new attempt to reshape global governance in more humane ways always agree with one another or act independently of state interests. It is only to assert that together they comprise a transnational effort to restrict the amount and level of violence employed by state and non-state players against their own and other people's citizens and to relieve, as well as attempt to repair, the wounds created by global conflicts. In this sense, the global emergence of a new civil society operating both above and below state control served then, as it still does now, as "an answer to war." It is anti-war because it does not believe that killing is as effective a way to resolve differences as dialogue and debate. Nonetheless, it recognizes that violence cannot be reduced without the creation of a security system based on international law and supported by adequate juridical instruments. In this system, states will need to retain their sovereignty even as the basis of that sovereignty will have to shift from what Mary Kaldor describes as "unilateral war-making institutions" to "multilateral law-making institutions."[19] This is why she can claim that global civil society is, as she puts it in her subtitle, "an answer to war."

Though it has sometimes been assumed that global civil society cannot fully be established without the creation of a world government, Kaldor maintains that certain of its newest features, such as the linkage of human rights laws and humanitarian interventions, the establishment of the international criminal court, and the broadening of international peacekeeping as a result of the Enforcement Revolution, are already producing a framework for de facto global governance. But this is to assume that such elements are working in coordination, which is very far from being true except in rare instances.

Indeed, humanitarianism has itself been long under siege not because international NGOs have lacked real successes but because those successes have too often been tied directly or indirectly to the specific policies of given states. Humanitarianism may have made modest improvements to the overall moral imagination, say, of the West, but that advance has not diminished the fact that humanitarianism functions so often as little more than a "containment" system for the developed world, which uses "relief" to soothe its own conscience. The "international community" to which humanitarianism's proponents and defenders appeal as the global source of its civil ideals is in a very real sense no more than a kind of fiction both related to a community less actual than imagined and existing more on paper than in fact. And even where international community does exist as a sphere of social action, it remains painfully clear that it has done nothing to shrink the widening gap between rich and poor or to explain why there are so few cures for the ills it creates.[20] Mary B. Anderson is less cynical but no less sensible of the ambiguities of aid:

> We know that aid provided in conflict settings can feed into and exacerbate the conflicts that cause the suffering it is meant to alleviate. And we know that aid too often does nothing to alter—and very often reinforces—the fundamental circumstances that produced the needs it temporarily meets.[21]

Alberto Navarro, former Director of the European Commission Humanitarian Aid Office, is more pessimistic: "Mankind is slowly, but in a very determined way, going back to barbarism."[22]

Bleak as these conclusions are about what can be learned, much less done, about other people's suffering, they are shared widely enough to carry with them a warning about whether the moral universalism on which humanitarianism in effect depends actually makes the world safer or more dangerous for victims of the world's injustice. Raising false hopes, Rieff points out, may be riskier than trying to dispel them and causes one to wonder whether the world is "really more interdependent or only more connected."[23]

Kaldor insists that it is both, which is why she believes that it is possible to develop new forms of cosmopolitan politics to counter the politics of conflict, exclusion, and indifference. Doing something to alleviate suffering is better than doing nothing, many people believe, but for Kaldor this is not enough, especially when the problem is violence and conflict. In the face of recurrent aggression, savagery, and suffering, it is more effective to identify zones of civility that can be expanded rather than to define oppositions in the hope of eventually reconciling them. But this requires a respect for international law, including the Laws of War and Human Rights Law that applies to individuals rather than to states, and a willingness to apply force to protect those rights when violations to them are gross, systematic, and pervasive. Techniques such as these, she reminds us, are already a part of the new global social contract that has been developing for a number of decades and already exists in several defining events, such as the founding of the United Nations in 1945, the establishment of the two Covenants on Political and Human Rights and on Social, Economic, and Cultural Rights in 1966, and the Helsinki Accords in 1975. The question is whether such rights as these can be implemented if people are not prepared to risk their lives for something larger than the state or nation. This kind of sacrifice is, of course, practiced every day by those who put their lives on the line as medical and relief workers, experts in conflict mediation, soldiers working for the United Nations, and countless others. Kaldor calls these citizens who are willing to risk their life for the good of the planet and its people "cosmopolitans" who may provide the moral basis for a new kind of humane global governance. The other possibility is that such prospects for heroic service have already been foreclosed by the events of 9/11 and its global aftermath.

Do the new rules of nuclear engagement, which permit first use when national survival is not at stake—together with such concepts as "Forward Deterrence," which allow the United States to project the defense of its cities, friends, allies, deployed forces, space assets, and computer networks—represent strategies for containing the use of weapons of mass destruction or for sanctioning their use when other options have been exhausted? In the new *National Security Strategy* published May 27, 2010, President Obama wisely distanced himself from the Doctrine of Pre-emption enunciated by the Bush administration, which authorized the use of force, including possible nuclear force, against threats before they were fully formed, and he de-escalated the rhetoric, but not necessarily the assumption, behind the equally dangerous Bush Doctrine of Pre-eminence. But President Obama still reserves in this document the right to defend US interests unilaterally if he believes that they are at risk, while at the same time promising to respect the standards that govern the use of force.

Bob Woodward maintains that President Obama is clearly interested in weighing the costs and benefits of every option less than war before choosing force itself, and he notes that Obama overrode the objection of most of his military advisors in devising a strategy for eventual withdrawal in Afghanistan by 2014. However, despite these gestures of reassurance, which carried him to the point of offering to engage with any hostile parties or powers in the region of conflict, the question is not whether President Obama can prevail over the opposition of his advisors but whether his credibility can survive what is perceived by the public as the loss of a war.[24] And given many of the other military responses he has made since taking office—keeping Guantanamo open, drawing down the disastrous Iraq War without removing a residual force that has in effect militarized the State Department in Baghdad, vastly expanding the use of drone attacks for the purpose of targeted assassinations in foreign countries, inserting Special Operations forces into the sovereign territories of other nations—it would seem as though he harbors some doubts of his own.

Gordon M. Goldstein has extracted from America's defeat in Vietnam many of the lessons yielded by presidential decisions and has drawn from them several that seem to apply at present in Afghanistan.[25] They include the realization that "counselors advise but presidents decide"; "politics is the enemy of strategy"; "generals must be commanded rather than followed"; and "military means" should never be deployed "in pursuit of indeterminate ends."[26] But lessons such as these are difficult to apply in a country like the United States that has already been at war for more than 47 of its 230 years, or 20 percent of its history, and supports a national security bureaucracy that includes 1,200 government agencies, utilizes another 1,900 private companies that work on homeland security, counterterrorism, and intelligence at 10,000 sites across the country, and employs something like 854,000 people with top-security clearances.[27] And, furthermore they seem not to have deterred the opposition, even as support for the war in Afghanistan has sharply declined. They have instead succeeded in reviving some of the most reckless policies and bullying of the most recent Bush era while retaining at times a conciliatory style. American posturing about pre-eminence and exceptionalism is particularly appealing to a badly confused and misinformed electorate during presidential campaigns and for a period thereafter, but what happens if prospective enemies like North Korea and Iran or someday, perhaps, China, or presumed allies such as India, Pakistan, or Israel decide to hedge their bets by embracing the Doctrine of Pre-emption themselves? And how will they or others, such as Russia, respond to the inevitable decline, in the long run if not the short, of America's power and influence?

In the face of such imponderables, with their sometimes, as it used to be called, "unthinkable" prospects, all one can hope for is that in this case life does not imitate art, that America's Biblically informed penchant for perceiving itself as history's savior will not inadvertently provide the rationale for encouraging it to become something closer to history's potential executioner. "The end of history" is no longer a glib phrase trumpeting the benefits of capitalism. In this second global war narrative reflected in and created by the Bush administration's *Nuclear Posture Review* and still latent, though considerably more circumscribed, in the Obama administration's version of the same document, it is now one of the possible outcomes foreshadowed by the text of America itself. If the exceptionalist claims of America's text cannot be rewritten in light of the global narrative of a new civil society forming around and within it, and informed by more empathetic and less imperialist cosmopolitan principles, the story, at least any global story we can think of composing, could conceivably come to an end.

7

THE TRANSCIVILIZATIONAL, THE INTERCIVILIZATIONAL, AND THE HUMAN

> It doesn't make me blush
> that right now
> I'm this weak,
> this selfish,
> this *human* simply.
>
> Nazim Hikmet, from "Letters from a Man in Solitary"
> (tr. Randy Blasing and Motlu Konuk), 1993, p.498

In a world where war narratives have become endemic, Yasuaki Onuma has been arguing for more than a quarter of a century that global conflicts cannot be addressed and reduced, or world order preserved, so long as political thinking is based on perspectives that are merely "international" or even "transnational."[1] International perspectives are subject to the Westphalian system's reliance on regimes of law within and between states to adjudicate and resolve humanitarian crises, and they eventually fall victim to the iron rule of self-interest. Transnational perspectives hold out better prospects for escaping the hold of the national imaginary, but while their chief non-state expressions, such as multinational corporations and international NGOs, have global pretensions, they still reflect a West-centric bias. As long as the "national" remains the default term to be utilized in confronting outrages to our sense of the human, state-based notions of sovereignty and the hegemonic interests they trail in their wake will inevitably trump all others.

The alternative is to develop a perspective that encompasses the international and transnational but goes beyond them by refusing to restrict itself to boundaries that are national, social, cultural, or even civilizational. Onuma calls this perspective "transcivilizational" because it is based on a recognition of the plurality of civilizations that have existed over time, and is therefore responsive not only to the multiple perspectives of various people but also to the fact that diverse people can sometimes agree on the legitimacy of certain values and virtues.[2] This is a theoretical and evaluative but also functional construct premised on the assumption that human beings are not products of only one civilization, any more than all civilizations are products only of themselves. And just as civilizations are not fated or predestined to develop in only one direction, neither are the human beings whose convictions, identities, and solidarities are formed and experienced within their frames of meaning. As an instrument for engaging all transboundary problems in an increasingly global world, the transcivilizational perspective, Onuma believes, offers itself as ultimately the only ethically and politically viable source of normative authority in a world marked by humanitarian catastrophes of intolerable violence, cruelty, and devastation.

My specific intent in this chapter is to examine this proposition further before putting it under some degree of critical pressure. I propose to do so by exploring the link, at once necessary but somewhat unacknowledged, between the transcivilizational and the human. I assume that these two conceptual orientations are connected by way of the idea of rights, which is now routinely invoked to designate that which transcends the nation and also that which defines the human. I will begin by assessing how well the notion of the "transcivilizational" holds up in its own terms, so to speak, as a necessary complement, if not supplement, to the ideas of the "international" and "transnational." This will lead me to propose that the better term for the kind of perspective Onuma is looking for may be instead the one he began with, the "intercivilizational," but I will go on to argue that the "intercivilizational" may provide inadequate grounds to suggest or support any concept of the normative if it is not backed up with an acceptable concept of the human. It is no coincidence that the idea of the human is again being rethought as a result of the international failure to extend human rights to all. Rehabilitating this notion may thus hold the key to developing a non-sectarian, and convincingly universal, framework for normative thinking beyond the law. Before developing this argument, however, I will circle back to retrieve further elements of Onuma's conception of the "transcivilizational" itself and place them in perspective.

Onuma is suspicious of all perspectival constructs that are less than transcivilizational—and employed to regulate global order and render it legitimate—not only because of their typically West-centric origins and predictable bias but because they thereby dismiss, overlook, or neglect the traditions, norms, and customs of up to 80 percent of humanity. Rather than aiding inter- and cross-cultural understanding, they delimit and frequently over-shape it. But the difficulty with invoking—as a corrective to such blindness—a still politically and intellectually broader, and historically deeper, perspective than the international or the transnational is that it implies for many people, as Onuma fully appreciates, the indefensible assumption that civilizations are self-contained, stable, and unified. If opinions like these derive from historical and cultural ignorance, as Onuma believes, they have nonetheless enabled Samuel P. Huntington and others like him to claim that civilizations are so different from one another as to, in effect, be incommensurable as well as incompatible. Such views, to which the clash of civilizations thesis is allied, are at a minimum uninformed and at a maximum essentialist and incipiently racist. They rest on Huntington's belief that civilizations are anchored in religions whose boundaries are clear and comparatively stable.

But this is to confuse the beliefs of their adherents with the behavior of such systems. Religions have always suffered from heterodoxy because they have so often been constructed out of components of other faiths and practices. Religions, like the civilizations with which they are only loosely allied, are clearly, except perhaps in their "official" versions of themselves, more fluid, diverse, fractured, inconsistent, and, above all, porous within themselves, not to say between themselves, than the "clash thesis" allows. Yet these same totalizing prejudices about religions and civilizations also resurface in a more benign but still simplistic and offensive form in much talk about "Asian values," "Muslim practices," "Latino beliefs," or "African customs."

What gives the lie to these prejudices is that a great majority of the world's people belong to more than one so-called civilization, and often by choice; that most civilizations are deeply influenced by, and thus the creatures of, contributions from other civilizations; that all civilizations are in processes of rapid change and of even more rapid redescription; that the structures of relation and tension between and among civilizations are arranged at all sorts of oblique angles and cross-hatched with diverse lines of pressure, fracture, hierarchy, and power.[3] Indeed, it is precisely because of this historicity, mobility, and adaptability that even in times of crisis, when their back, as it were, is up against the wall, civilizations can be repositories of ideas and values that are capable—at least potentially—of being widely shared even when variously expressed. Onuma's purpose in elaborating what might be called the conditions of possibility for such a transcivilizational perspective, then, centers around the hope that we can either extrapolate or fashion from it (I'm not quite sure which) certain norms based on mutual goals and needs that can more constructively inform the work of law as it addresses humanitarian and other problems in the global sphere. For Onuma, this seems all the more plausible because the work of law, as he usefully points out, is not confined to responsibilities of control and adjudication but extends also to the guidance of life, so to speak, "out of court."

Despite the appeal of such an argument—what perspective can provide a normative basis for the notion of "legitimacy" except one that takes account of the situation of all humankind?—I am troubled by what it may simplify. Talk of the transcivilizational possesses its own legitimacy problem in an age when so many unities and large coherences have already been shattered and we are now compelled to root some of our thinking, as even the "clash thesis" reminds us, in what Clifford Geertz refers to as "the world in pieces."[4] Even as civilizational differences make themselves available for explaining, and also for justifying or rationalizing redistributions of power and reconceptualizations of ideas of order and governance, there is abundant evidence of as much decentering going on in the global sphere as of recentering, of deconstruction as of reconstruction, of deterritorialization as of reterritorialization. The civilizational, as we are calling it, is continually being threatened, on the one hand, by the so-called "global" or "worldwide" and, on the other, by the so-called "regional" or "local," and while both the local and the global are in fact relative terms, the opposition between them is not so much between the "local" and the "worldwide" or "global" as between one kind of "local" that is more "regional" and specific and another kind of "local" that is more "global" and dispersed.

But this leads to a second issue that Onuma's notion of the transcivilizational may undervalue, which has to do with just how difficult it is to acquire or achieve such a perspective and what might be seen because of or through it.[5] As no one needs to be reminded, cultures are by themselves—forget about civilizations—extraordinarily complex organisms whose components at any given point or moment are difficult to disassemble and whose internal logic and power cannot to be reduced to, or simply identified with, any one of them. As a vast ensemble of complex, interrelated, interactive forms in which parts inform wholes and wholes inform parts without managing to subsume or be subsumed by the other, culture has been likened to a game and its interpretation, as Geertz once pointed out in a famous series of comparisons, to the process of getting a joke, grasping a pun, fathoming a proverb, reading a poem, or even comprehending baseball. To follow a baseball game, Geertz observed, one must not only understand what a bat, a hit, an inning, a left fielder, a squeeze play, a hanging curve, and a tightened infield are but also, and most crucially, "what the game in which these 'things' are elements is all about."[6] To get the game, then, requires knowing what is at stake when the play conforms to an accepted structure of rules. The principle or point of the game, and the structure of rules defining it, go together: the principle or point at stake in the play exhibits some of the "truth" or "insight" embodied in the structure, while the structure grounds the meaning and significance embodied in the principle.

As I have pointed out elsewhere, this comparison is true as far as it goes but it falls short exactly where the thing to be known and the character of the knowable change in those games, whether cultural or civilizational, that are not completely rule-governed.[7] Cultures, not to say civilizations, are rife with such forms, and they, rather than the games whose rules are clear and discrete, often give both to cultures and to civilizations their distinctive styles and signatures. One set of such forms would be those considered aesthetic, another, those that are deemed religious, and still a third those, perhaps, viewed as legal. In figurative formations like these that are not, like rule-driven games, necessarily formulaic, and which make up a not inconsiderable amount of the content of any culture or civilization, complete knowledge—understanding "what the game in which these 'things' are elements is all about"—is inherently unattainable. Here the point of interpretation, indeed much of the purpose of the play, is to learn how to use the structure of rules to change or, at any rate, to complicate the game by exploiting what is not actually fully knowable or predictable and can frequently only be inferred. These are the meanings and significances that are not fully represented by the structure, or by any of its elements, but are simply potential to it. To be sure, such meanings are not easily defined or categorized in any given culture or civilization, but they are nonetheless indispensable to the kind of work that cultures and civilizations perform, by constituting the horizon of possibility within which the relations between the known, the unknown, and unknowable are cast. Representing elements in any culture or civilization that are indefinite, even undecidable, but still determinative and consequential, they point to yet another dimension in their composition that makes them so difficult to disassemble or reconfigure.

Thus, by suggesting that it may be more difficult than it looks to extract from various cultures or civilizations elements that on some meta level can be rearranged and recombined into a pattern of shared values and beliefs, I do not mean to imply that such extrapolations never go on—they are of course going on all the time—but merely to point out that the hermeneutical processes by which the wisdom of one cultural or civilizational tradition can be rendered correspondent with those of another entails several discrete and rather arduous steps. The first involves an act of deciphering, of reading, of interpretation itself, which depends less on the identification of one mind or culture with another than on the determination by one mind or culture of what the other's is up to or seeks. The problem is that such determinations often depend on more than just the ability to solve a puzzle, get a joke, or figure out a poem. To fathom representative forms, elements, practices of cultures or civilizations other than one's own on the pulses, in what William Butler Yeats once called "the fury and mire of human veins," is like entering another *lebenswelt*, or felt world, in which one must learn to breathe in a different atmosphere or calculate in an alien mathematics.

The second step in the process that leads to cross-cultural understanding entails an act of translation in which we must convert the practices, performances, or purposes of one mind, culture, or civilization back into the purported idioms of another that is our own. This step actually holds out more possibilities for misreading than the first, but we can only grasp what to some degree we can analogize, even if that operation only succeeds in defamiliarizing what we think we already know. What we cannot know, unless through some Barthian act of radical divine revelation, is the *totaliter aliter*;[8] all we can ever know, Emmanuel Levinas notwithstanding, is that which is not completely and absolutely different.[9]

Yet the fullest possible understanding of whatever it is that we seek to comprehend from across cultural or civilizational divides remains incomplete without a third and final step. This is the interpretive step known as appropriation where one attempts, with the techniques at one's disposal, to gauge the difference such translations make to one's previous self-understanding and the internal adjustments they exact as a consequence. Without this final step, interpretation is left hanging and the possibility of achieving new understanding permanently thwarted.

The third issue I wish to raise with regard to Onuma's attempt to delineate a perspective that would complement or supplement the international and the transnational, has to do with whether it is more useful to think in transcivilizational terms or rather, to return to his earlier description of his project, in intercivilizational terms. Whatever Onuma may have meant by this term in his previous work, the aforementioned question begs to be raised due to one of the critiques that Huntington's clash thesis has consistently attracted. Edward Said may only have been the best known of Huntington's doubters when he described the latter's thesis as a "clash of ignorance" and reminded us that warring civilizations often share more affinities than we would like to believe and experience many of the same inner divisions.[10] This point has recently been made in a different way by Martha Nussbaum, who argues that most civilizations are now roiled by a similar struggle in which those who demand certainty and uniformity of belief are pitted against those who prefer a world of variety and change. In all modern nations, she writes, the real clash is to be found "within—between people who are prepared to live with others who are different on terms of equal respect, and those who seek the ... domination of a single religious and ethnic tradition."[11]

There is nevertheless a risk to conceiving the conflict in these terms because it may make it sound as though the clash within civilizations is essentially a replay of the battle between religious and ethnic absolutism and secular modernism. Part of what is misleading about this is that religion and secularity have, in many parts of the world, worked hand-in-glove for millennia, and this relationship was perpetuated in the West, once the Westphalian system was more or less in place, merely by a shift of religious focus from the church to the secular state legitimated by nationalism.[12] But a deeper source of misunderstanding lies in the way the cultural nature of this relationship has been minimized in Western scholarship and what this obscures about the civilizational basis of the distinction itself. On the one hand, the distinction seems to treat as almost ontological a set of terms that since well before the Early Modern era can only be understood in specific historical and inter- as opposed to transcivilizational contexts. On the other, it views these same terms as oppositional when they have rarely functioned historically, or for that matter theologically, as a simple binary. The so-called secular has often been created in no small measure out of elements of the religious—the history of the novel in the West provides such an example—that emerge as much from a relaxation of its constraints as from an outright repudiation of them. Thus what to some may appear in actual processes of secularization to be a dismissal or negation of the religious—according to conventional wisdom, the secular refers to a realm of thought and experience from which all traces of the supernatural or the transcendent have been rejected in favor of embracing more pragmatic solutions to perennial problems—often presents itself to cultural and religious historians to be more than not a reconstruction of the world out of some of those same interpretive and imaginative activities that religion itself set free, and that must now be brought into play if some alternative vision of life, experience, or the really real is to take its place.

Robert Bellah has articulated what needs to be perceived about this process in *Religion in Human Evolution* where he insists repeatedly that the history of this process, both from one human stage to another—the mimetic, to the mythic, to the theoretic—and from one religious formation to another—the archaic, to the tribal, to the axial—reveals that each stage or phase succeeds what proceeded it not by supplanting or superseding it but by reorganizing and readapting it in new ways. Axial religion does not destroy tribal or archaic religion but makes itself out of elements of the former two that it reconfigures for its own purposes. Hence the emergence of new forms does not require, and cannot take place, by their simple disembedding from older ones. Earlier stages of religious development, as in all evolutionary schemes, are "not lost," as Bellah argues with the assistance of Merlin Donald, "but only restructured under new conditions."[13]

This point would not be worth belaboring if confusion surrounding the civilizational basis of the distinction between religion, secularism, and modernity were not so central to contemporary discussion.[14] Its centrality has been given new prominence in Charles Taylor's magisterial *A Secular Age*, which attempts to dispel it. While Taylor acknowledges that the terms "secular," "religious," and "modern" have very different meanings in different traditions and eras, his principle contention that from the seventeenth century onward the term "secular" became associated with a domain understood to be inhospitable to any claim made in the name of transcendence, "that the lower, immanent or secular, order is all that there is and that the higher, or transcendent, is a human invention," is in some ways deeply problematic.[15] Yet before spelling out what I find troubling about Taylor's account of the relation between the religious and the secular in Western spirituality, it is necessary to describe the coming-of-age narrative that Taylor is seeking in important ways to correct.

That narrative has most recently been expressed in one of two ways. In the first, which is found in the work of the late American pragmatist philosopher Richard Rorty, the secular is the result of a process of de-divinization that began with metaphysical idealism's attempt to relocate the sphere of ultimate reality within rather than beyond human experience; then led to Romanticism's claim that whether ultimate reality is now immanent or transcendent, its meanings can in any case be described in more than one vocabulary; and eventually wound up with pragmatism's assertion that these different vocabularies are finally no more than different ways of expressing what we need but only sometimes get. In the second narrative, really genealogy, of the secular, this sequence of historical transformations follows the course charted by Hans Blumenberg, where the love of God initially gave way, in the seventeenth century, to the love of truth, the love of truth was then replaced, by the end of the eighteenth century, with the quasi-divinity of the self, and the Romantic love of self then succumbed, toward the end of nineteenth century and the beginning of the twentieth, to the realization that now nothing can be worshipped as divine since everything, as Nietzsche, Marx, and Freud demonstrated, is a product of contingencies and has been emptied of intrinsic significance.[16]

Taylor challenges this narrative by seeking to complicate it, showing that the move from a transcendentalist spiritual perspective associated with late medieval Latin Christianity to an immanentist spiritual perspective clearly in evidence by the seventeenth century was made possible because of the development of a new disposition to view religion itself as but one option or choice among others in a now wholly immanent sphere of possibilities. Here a new religious perspective is being partially remade out of components of the old, but for Taylor the process is one of irremediable loss rather than gain. The chief casualty of this transition or diminishment was the experience of "enchantment" which, like Max Weber, Taylor takes to be the differentiating essence of Western Christian spirituality before it began its long advance to secularism.

The problem with Taylor's treatment of enchantment is that it is exceptionalist and, at least in the metaphor he uses here, too unidirectional, homogenous, and degenerative. By exceptionalist I mean that Taylor treats enchantment, or the experience of living in what he thinks of as a magical world, as something limited primarily to Christians alone and dependent on the kind of theological transcendentalism that Taylor posits as its precondition. But it is comparatively easy to argue, as Bellah has, that if the meaning of enchantment is identified with the experience of inhabiting a universe suffused with a sense of divine presence, it can be found as perfectly expressed in one of Vaclav Havel's remarkable letters from prison before he became leader of the Velvet Revolution and eventually president of the Czech Republic as it can be in a well-known passage about the fullness of Being from Jonathan Edwards's "Personal Narrative,"[17] as richly evoked in some of the most abstract natural landscapes of the nineteenth-century English painter John Constable as by certain of the southwestern canvases of Georgia O'Keefe. The sense of living as a porous self open to the infinite above is, by personal testimony, as easily accessible to astro-physicists (or anyone else capable of reckoning on this scale) who can contemplate a universe composed of up to 500 billion galaxies like our own Milky Way, which is itself composed of hundreds of billions of stars such as our own Sun, as it can be by ancient Christians, Zoroastrians, or other cosmologists.

Taylor might reply that these representations and experiences of enchantment are, at best, intermittent and do not derive from habitation in a spirit- or Being-filled world, but surely no one, including saints in the thirteenth or fourteenth centuries, lived in a continuously enchanted world open to a sense of the divine effulgence except at moments, and they needed all the trappings of ritual, symbols, music, and the visual to do so. Indeed, one of the explicit purposes of Christian art in the late Middle Ages was to assist communicants in developing and preserving a religious sense that they were always in danger, even the most pious, of losing. Take, for example, the relationship between Quattrocento painting and Early Modern Roman Catholicism in fifteenth-century Italy. Such painting existed not only, or even mainly, to reflect spiritual concerns but also, as Michael Baxendall has demonstrated, to enrich and augment, and thus change, them however subtly.[18] The artist was interested in doing more than depicting religious material on canvas; he was committed to encouraging the beholder to reflect on it in a specifically religious manner. In other words, the artist's aim was not merely illustrative or even exegetical but evocative. His public did not need what it already possessed; what it needed, in Clifford Geertz's words, "was an object rich enough to see it in, rich enough, even, in seeking it, to deepen it."[19]

Geertz is here drawing on a view of culture, and particularly of the role of the imagination in culture, which assumes that culture in its more creative dimensions is not additive but generative, not merely transcriptive but provocative, that it changes the thing it engages and in ways that are very difficult to map or narrate in linear or sequential form. Despite Taylor's abundant qualifications, his account of the transformations in the relations between religion and the secular is too episodic and successive, as if the break between the transcendental and immanent was sharp, successive, and final. Taylor would—and does—reply that German and English Romantics sought to recover a sense of unmediated Being but were doomed from the start because they were already working within what Taylor calls "the immanent frame."[20] But just how religiously immanent was the frame assumed by Romantics in the West if it could best be described, in the title of M. H. Abrams's definitive book on Romantic cosmology, "natural supernaturalism"? A cosmology that has lived a vigorous afterlife in the modern poetry of everyone from Rainer Marie Rilke, Paul Verlaine, and Wallace Stevens to A. R. Ammons, it suggests that transcendence can be experienced through immanence.

Second, his presentation of Latin Christianity is too uniform and, for want of a better term, sanitary. What of the masses of people who lived on the edges of this system, or perhaps within its center, often in utterly wretched conditions, but clung to earlier forms of archaic, tribal, and clannish religion that were vernacular, profane, folk, or improvised? Part of what has been too often left out of more traditional histories of Christianity were the irregular metaphysics, the disruptive logics, the unruly heterodoxies, and the powerful paganisms of people who may have been subjected to the theological and institutional governance of Latin Christendom but who at the same time worshipped their own, as the Anglican prayer refers to them, "ghoulies, ghosties and goblins." Even more likely, as well as distracting and clearly divisive, was the presence of the carnivalesque, the parodistic, the perverse, the subversive, the sacrilegious, the scatological—indeed, the entire realm of Gargantua and Pantagruel, of Rabelaisian, Bakhtian excess—that was always threatening to disturb the noise of solemn assemblies and crack the dome of the sacred canopy.

Third and finally, Taylor's argument conforms to the subtraction theory he purportedly disavows—secularism is not only different from religion but decidedly less. Where secularism emerges in Taylor's narrative, religion not only changes but is fatefully, or at least emotionally and existentially, reduced and impoverished. But that, I would suggest, is not exactly how it happened. The religious and the secular have not only coexisted in their modern formations—Taylor would not disagree—but actually adjusted to, and profited from, the rearrangements and adjustments required for their coexistence. Such was clearly the case with the United States, which is why America was not the exception to the rule but rather proof that far from displacing religion, "secularization and religion ... were deeply entangled at the outset of the modern state system and have remained so ever since."[21]

The problem is that these entanglements will not be fully understood until we revise our understanding, actually our models, of how, in considerable part, such matters are determined by civilizational processes. But these processes cannot be comprehended unless we give up the tendency to hypostatize them, as though civilizations could be understood apart from their effects on human beings, and reconceive them along the lines of Randall Collins's useful notion of zones of prestige that radiate outward to create networks of attraction and repulsion. They are sets of relationships and activities that exert magnetism because of the dialogues, debates, and disagreements at their center, which attract admirers, challenge uniformity, and stimulate creativity and change. Hence the differences and conflicts around which they organize collective life can become at least as determinative and influential as the structures of assent and consent by which they govern their relations. Emulation and rejection of particular zones of prestige—religion, science, the public sphere, aesthetics, sports—within or between civilizational systems can be deeply entwined, which creates the possibility of cultural commensurabilities being created across civilizational formations that are otherwise quite different. This creates what Peter Katzenstein calls a "polymorphic globalism" in which "various intersections of secularisms and religions are created through never-ending processes of mutual cooperation, adaptation, coordination, and conflict."[22]

Does this mean that the polymorphic globalism of which Katzenstein writes will be more secular than religious? Hardly. Think merely of the liberal, democratic sentiments that were expressed in Cairo's Tahrir Square (along with a good deal of collective feeling about just being "fed up") and the Islamist political sentiments that replaced them. Or, better, consider the reasons why the civilization of Latin Christendom was first able to unite and then fated, according to Karl Deutsch, to split. Deutsch's argument, which couldn't be more different than Taylor's explanation of spiritual disenchantment, is that the spiritual, political, and cultural unity of medieval Christendom—defined by a common Latin language, papal spiritual authority, governance by the Holy Roman Empire, the military and missionary effects of the Crusades, and Romanesque and Gothic styles of art and architecture—was a transitory rather than seminal stage in history and was destroyed by the very forces that gave rise to it. Drawing on a model of cultural commensurabilities and overlaps that function as networks of prestige, attraction, and coordination, Deutsch maintains that the international civilization of Latin Christendom was based on an economy of scarcity affecting goods, services, and personnel that enabled the growth of a thin web of supranational, intercivilizational trading companies that shared language, customs, laws, traditions, family connections, and religion.[23] Capable of traversing long distances, these trading companies eventually created a superficial internationalism knit together by commerce, intellectual life, politics, and faith. Initially composed of three distinct civilizations and two trading peoples, Latin Christianity had, by the thirteenth century, prevailed over the challenges represented both by Byzantium and by Islam, as well as by the Jewish diaspora and Viking conquests, but was then faced with decline as increasing contacts among village, manor, town, and sect enabled the rate of sectarian division, and then regional migration, to outpace the rate of international assimilation. What followed was the loss of the thin internationalism provided by Latin Christianity in favor of a more polymorphous regional and creedal differentiation to which modern state nationalism subsequently gave rise. But this only occurred because the nation and its imperial aspirations could as easily become a vessel for religious enchantments and manipulation as the seemingly more religion-based and ecclesiastically-centered civilization it replaced. In this complex historical process, the religious and the secular were not the engines of change so much as its products, and their relations were controlled less by spiritual revolutions than by tectonic shifts and clashes in the plates of civilization. This does not mean that change failed to occur but merely that it is less accurately described as an abrupt break or rupture with the past than as a repossession and rearrangement of it under new circumstances.

Arjun Appadurai defines the clash within civilizations in still other terms as a struggle between geopolitical systems that are vertebrate and those that are cellular. Vertebrate systems are organized around a large body of institutions, treaties, agreements, and protocols, and are symbolized by global bodies like the United Nations and the World Trade Organization, which attempt to "ensure that all nations operate on symmetrical principles in relation to their conduct with one another, whatever their hierarchies of power and wealth."[24] Cellular systems are associated with non-state actors and epitomized by al-Qaeda and its many imitators, operating outside the official international network of organizations and bureaucracies and organized less hierarchically through semi-independent units that rely on secrecy, loose coordination, offshore havens, and stealth. Appadurai is convinced that the post-9/11 conflict between these two systems has deeply threatened the Westphalian model of world order, producing a "crisis of circulation" that may only be resolved through the development of a new global civil society that operates altogether outside the control of nation states.

Yet another formulation of the clash thesis within rather than between civilizations has been offered by *New York Times* columnist David Brooks, who has drawn attention to the quarrel between those in America (and elsewhere) who favor integration and those who prefer separatism.[25] The civil rights movement, women's liberation, demographic shifts in population, the communications revolution, and the end of the Cold War, even globalization itself, all spoke to the possibility, indeed the hope, that people were coming together, even if only slowly and fitfully, across divides of all kinds. But now, just as recent Supreme Court decisions serve to remind Americans that racial integration may be beyond achievement, so the threat of terror, the globalization of trade and commerce, and the self-interest at play in the geopolitical sphere may attest that in the long run people find it possible to trust only their own kind.

However, as much as this version of the clash within may, under some circumstances, bring those who wish to give credence and space to others into conflict with those who wish to force everyone to live within the shelter of a single identity or outlook, the clash within civilizations provides the best argument for an intercivilizational rather than a transcivilizational perspective. It also helps illumine the divide between the global South and the global North, in which the greatest challenge in overcoming its inequalities has little to do with boiling down different civilizational values and synthesizing them in some encompassing formulation but rather with acknowledging, as Ashis Nandy contends, "that while each civilization must find its own authentic vision of the future and its own authenticity in [the] future ... , neither is conceivable without admitting the experience of co-suffering which has now brought some of the major civilizations closer together."[26]

Nandy's specific concern is the problem of human-made suffering: how to assess responsibility for it and help guide the struggle against it by reshaping social consciousness with the assistance of allegories of the future. This possibility, already reflected, perhaps, in the creation of the World Social Forum, and capable of being extended by what Richard Falk calls a "Global Peoples Parliament" and Ulrich Beck describes as a "global (citizens') parliament,"[27] is premised on the necessity of creating a form of what Nandy terms "intercultural communion."[28] A communion or dialogue between and within rather than across cultures and, by extension, civilizations, which depends on an acknowledgement that no culture or civilization possesses a monopoly on core values, this communion possesses two fundamental coordinates. The first entails a recognition, often overlooked in an era of more diversity than real pluralism, that the genuine values of different civilizations are not in need of synthesis because in many instances they are already congruent enough to enable us to rise above many of the barriers of exclusivist policies. A recognition as difficult for people on the Left to achieve as those on the Right, it is essential if we are to move beyond the soporifics of clash thinking. The second coordinate is an acknowledgement that the search for what is truly authentic in any culture or civilization is always a search for its "other face," either as hope or as caution. To discover the "other face" of any civilization depends, for Nandy, on the ability both to interpret one's own traditions for oneself and to incorporate the often recessive aspects of other civilizations as allies in one's own struggles for cultural self-realization. The object of both recognitions is to create an intercivilizational discourse that permits different parts of the world to learn from the experience of one another without pretending that norms can be derived that are similarly applicable in every situation to all. What is needed is not an agreement on norms per se, as though such accord would allow them to be applied uniformly across the board, but on which norms will encourage us to learn and assimilate what other civilizations can teach us. The goal is not, in other words, a new normative consensus, cosmopolitan or transcivilizational, but an "other" humanism that transforms the wisdom of different civilizations and cultures into resources for the potential reconstitution and self-development of each.

But this entails a methodological adjustment. In order to create an intercultural or intercivilizational discourse that permits different parts of the world to learn from the experience of one another, we must overcome, Nandy believes, the prejudice that the psyche is epiphenomenal, that psychological interpretation has no place in political and global thinking. To determine how the often recessive aspects of other cultures and civilizations can serve the self-fulfilment of one's own, we must abandon what Nandy terms the "Cartesian sickness" that dissociates thought from feeling and address the way consciousness is itself a datum of history. To accomplish this, however, we will have to overcome a second prejudice that Nandy overlooks. This is the belief that consciousness cannot be historically objectified, it cannot play more than a peripheral role in the affairs of states and the relations of nations. Yet this flies in the face of what we already know about nations as "imagined communities" whose identity is based on consciousness and whose influence, not to say their role, in international affairs is so often a function of perception, imagined or otherwise, that often has no basis in fact.

One place where it would be fair to say that an intercivilizational as opposed to transcivilizational consciousness has been evolving in recent years is the international human rights movement. Yet despite real successes, no one would deny that the movement has fallen far short of its goals. Such failures have convinced Judith Butler that part of the task of the international human rights movement is now to rethink what being human really means. The answer lies in considerable measure not so much in the idea that the human subject is constituted by certain inalienable rights, an idea deriving from natural law theory and influenced by early Christianity and Roman law, but in how those rights are recognized and adjudicated both by and in the world's various civil orders.[29] Even as the Universal Declaration of Human Rights refers to "the inherent dignity" and "the equal and inalienable rights of all members of the human family," it tacitly recognizes "that the universal character of the rights-bearing person is made the responsibility of sovereign states, each of which has exclusive jurisdiction of a limited group within the human family."[30] Given the scope of that jurisdiction, the universality of the rights that human beings are supposed to possess suffers a disturbing contraction. Suddenly "the self-owning, sovereign individual of the philosophers," who was always already a kind of socially and politically disembodied fiction, now becomes further de-realized. In a world where the decision about who is human and what it might mean to realize its promise is determined to a very considerable extent by the global market, "human rights become floating signifiers that can be attached to or detached from various subjects and classes constituted by the market principle and designated by the most powerful nation-states."[31]

But the situation is even more complex because neoliberalism has created a new culture whose features cannot simply be thought of as a replication, on the level of individual experience, of the operations of the market itself.[32] The culture produced by the market's neoliberal emphasis on deregulation, privatization, liberation, and freedom is by no means identical with those values. Moreover, the institution of these values at the global level has seriously destabilized social life by dismantling so many of the formerly fixed state and corporate practices that once lent structure to individual experience. Government, it will be remembered, has long established a compact with many of its citizens; corporations stood by their employees and became recipients, as a result, of their trust and loyalty. But now things are clearly different. The individual idealized by the new economy currently faces daunting challenges caused by the implementation of values that are in fact almost the reverse of their projected image. For one thing, time becomes hazardous as almost never before because the disruption of careers and the increased mobility of business life demands constant movement from job to job and task to task, and this threatens the possibility of developing any consistent or sustainable life-narrative. For a second, the acquisition of skills and the management of talent have become far more problematic because the velocity of technological and other changes has shifted so much of the emphasis from past achievements to future potential. For a third, the pace of change has eroded the illusion of permanence by encouraging the individual who models her- or himself on the consumer eager to make new purchases and discard still serviceable ones to forget the past and simply move on.

The world this evokes is the one most congenial to the talents of the consultant whose virtues are bankable so long as they stay ahead of the downsizing, resizing, outsourcing, and reinventing of jobs. Yet like all but a small minority of very successful players in the neoliberal economy, the consultant, like most everyone else, is threatened by "the spectre of uselessness."[33] This is the phantom that haunts and frightens so many people in the new capitalism precisely because people are actually so unsuited to such a work environment: "they need a sustaining life narrative, they take pride in being good at something specific, and they value the experiences they've lived through."[34] Hence it is not merely that the cultural ideals associated with the new neoliberal institutions damage so many of the people forced to accommodate to them; those institutions damage these people in some rather particular, and not always recognized, ways that radically diminish their autonomy and agency. Ignacio Ramonet, the chief editor of *Le Monde Diplomatique*, has accurately identified the dilemma that neoliberalism's culture of new capitalism has created by observing that "we have to formulate the problems it invents in the words it offers."[35]

One of those invented problems, to return to the earlier discussion, has to do with whether rights language has been so corrupted by the neoliberal framework of national and global discourse within which it operates that, as Asad implies, we can no longer employ it to identify the human at all. A second, somewhat different from the first, is whether at this late date we can think any longer about the human at all without recourse to the language of rights. These conundrums have elicited various answers that circle around the issue of whether we can reverse the usual procedure by deriving a sense of rights from a conception of the human rather than a sense of the human from a conception of rights. Suspending for the moment the actual history of these deliberations, which are in any case beyond the scope of this chapter, we can discern at least several different, though often related, positions.

The first might be called the sustainability argument, which is organized around the attempt to define what is needed in the most minimal terms to live a recognizably human life. The nineteenth-century American writer Henry David Thoreau called such essentials "the grossest groceries" and came up with a list that was far from trivial, including food, shelter, clothing, and fuel, but to such basics as these have usually been added other elements, such as security of person, equal recognition and treatment before the law, protection from servitude or cruel and inhuman treatment, rights to marry and found a family, own property, assemble with others, express opinions freely—and the list goes on.[36] The second argument, recently reprised by Martha Nussbaum and Amartya Sen, might be called the capabilities argument and stresses what is absolutely indispensable to make a recognizable human life functional.[37] This argument focuses on the capacities that all human beings presumably possess by virtue of their innate endowment, which include the ability to feel, think, reason, and imagine in ways that, through adequate education, permit self-expression and a measure of free choice. Then there is the moral argument, often linked to the sustainability argument, which takes up the definition of the human from the point of view of what all members of the human community deserve by way of recognition and response from their peers, or, conversely, what obligations we owe to all others.[38]

A plea for equal moral consideration for all human beings, this argument is often reinforced by two additional ones: first, the pragmatic claim that treating people with equal moral consideration has beneficial effects in reducing cruelty and relieving suffering;[39] second, an economic claim that the basic nature of the human is revealed most starkly in those systematic processes of de-humanization where it is most at risk of being lost. Such "crimes against humanity," as they have come to be termed,[40] are for good reason usually identified with the Holocaust and other genocidal atrocities of the century just past. But from a more historical perspective, the origin of such practices reaches back much farther to the institution of various forms of human slavery and severe incidents of collective punishment inflicted on enemies. Sociologist Orlando Patterson first defined slavery famously as "social death"—"the permanent, violent and personal domination of natally alienated and generally dishonored persons"[41]—but historian David Brion Davis has more recently argued that in its most vicious New World incarnations slavery deserves to be viewed as "inhuman bondage" because its intention was literally to negate the human.[42]

Each of these arguments seeks to identify the human without necessary recourse to the language of rights, though all of them, in the process, presuppose a basis for defining the human from which a notion of rights might be derived. In addition, it could be said that none of these arguments would have proved so durable had it not been for the creation of the international rights regime, despite the fact that all of them remain susceptible to co-optation by the neoliberal language of exchange and advantage. This is a language that has grown still more discordant and grotesque in a world where loss and aggression seem to reign and what Butler calls "the powers of mourning and violence" vie for the control of political life at the expense of human rights.[43] If grief and hostility, which seem to feed off each other, can no more be accepted as norms for political life than commerce and leverage, are there any other grounds on which to found a new global political community that is at once protective and supportive of the human?

Butler's cautious answer is that such grounds are created by the relation between violence or aggression, human complicity, vulnerability to loss, and the need to mourn. Her question is whether such conditions provide the basis for human community, but this only provokes a different question about who matters as human. Butler is convinced that this is different from the question as to whether there is a universal human condition but, rather than speculate about the latter, uses the former to conclude that all human beings experience loss, though not in equal ways, and are thus in part constituted politically by the vulnerability of their bodies. But if no one can escape loss—it is, after all, a product of change—how are people compensated for it? Butler's reply is the process of mourning, which cannot replace what is lost but can transform the experience of accepting it. Thus her project is to show how the process of mourning provides a new basis for a politics of non-violent solidarity.

Butler is particularly sensitive to the phenomenology of loss which not only produces grief but makes the sufferer inscrutable to him- or herself. In losing another, she says wisely, the self in effect goes missing because part of itself is lost as well. Loss is thus like an amputation of sorts, but also something more because what in addition vanishes, and for which one has no words, is, the relationality of self to other. Grief, then, is an expression of how the self is, or can be, literally undone by loss; we are created and, at the same time, dispossessed by our relations. Our vulnerability to others—what she at other times calls our "injurability"[44]—therefore comprises no small part of our relationality to them and thus remains the primary source of our sociality, but that vulnerability is unequally distributed in the world and thus brings up again the earlier issue about those who seemingly do not count, who are de-realized. Adopting some of the language of Emmanuel Levinas, she describes the perception of another's violability as the recognition that ethically calls each of us into being. Finding ourselves confronted by the vulnerability of others in ways we cannot deny or dismiss, we come to exist in a new manner: "this impingement by the other's address constitutes us first and foremost against our will, or, perhaps put more appropriately, prior to the formation of our will." Moral identity has little do with taking a stand and everything to do with "the demand that comes from elsewhere, sometimes a nameless elsewhere, by which our obligations are articulated and pressed upon us."[45]

Butler's human is therefore no mere agent. Something both active and acted upon, the human is constituted instead by the linkage between the two, which provides the grounds of its responsibility and the possibility of creating an ethics that is non-violent. Such an ethics would not be completely purged of violence but would presumably be capable of providing an appropriate motivation for opposing violence. Nonetheless, just how this is to be accomplished is less clear than by what. Butler locates the source of this moral motivation in Levinas's well-known evocation of the face of the other. The face of the other reveals to us both the fragility and instability of the other's life and the conditions of our engagement with it. It is this latter point that presents the greatest difficulty. That face, mediating to us the unconditional appeal of human vulnerability and fragility, is at the same time assumed to be strong enough to overcome all the more dominant, seductive forms of representation that seek to obscure or erase it anywhere that it is presumably in peril. But what, beyond self-interest, motivates us to do this? If we ask how this occurs, Butler merely returns to the subject of mourning which, though not a substitute for politics, nonetheless enables us to recognize in the face of the other both the precariousness that constitutes our own humanity and the reason to resist all that threatens to violate it worldwide.

There is much to admire in this argument, along with a few things that deserve fuller examination. Before noting several difficulties that attend her use of Levinas,

I want to examine more closely, from the point of view of its normative implications, Butler's view of loss and her association of loss primarily with the body. As Freud noted about melancholy—it took him much longer to apply this insight to mourning—the experience of loss to which melancholy and mourning are both responses (the first Freud thought of as pathological, the second as curative) is ordinarily associated with far more than the loss of the body alone. What is grievable—and in a global register is often as, or more, grievous—are losses that are not only physical but also symbolic, material but equally ideological, axiological, spiritual—losses, in other words, not just of other selves but of any object of value, from traditions and institutions to narratives and meanings. To many people in the world, the loss of individual life is in fact far less unacceptable than the loss of status, or of authority, or of recognition, or of dignity, or of community, or of agency.

Butler certainly knows all this but still fails to make of it as much as I believe it deserves, and this lapse in an otherwise unusually sensitive discussion of grief and mourning helps explain why she downplays the element that so fatefully links the experience of loss with the outbreak of anger and the resolution of anger with a process of mourning that eventually decouples the self or community from its experience of trauma and opens up the possibility for remaking the self or community in relation to the energies that mourning enables. Loss not only produces grief but also anger, what the anthropologist Renato Rosaldo described as "the rage in grief" that leads Ilongot men in the Philippines to want to cut off human heads[46] and emboldens and inspires, and sometimes even compels, other mourners to take up paramilitarism, espionage, and terrorism. Far from being a mere byproduct of grief, rage is an integral aspect of it that derives, as Freud observed, from the inability of the ego or self to represent loss as anything other than an impoverishment of itself, an impoverishment that frequently, and understandably, turns the ego or self vengeful.[47]

Hence the potentially symbiotic relationship between bereavement and aggression, sorrow and violence. And if the loss is widely shared, the rage it provokes can quickly be socialized and politicized into forms of violence intimately linked with rites of sacrifice, where the shedding of blood is associated with the preservation of the social or political bond.[48] This shedding of blood does more than preserve the social world from destruction; it binds the sacrificers into a community of ritual cleansers, which can be related, often through religion, to larger structures of life through the mediatorial role played by the sacrificial victim. At the extreme, this scenario can lead to "cosmic war" if victims, like enemies in battle, are discovered to be "out of place" and therefore representative of a form of disorder that further endangers the community, which must then, to protect itself from destruction, renarrativize its history as a redemptive story of persecution, resistance, liberation, and renewal.[49] Short of this, the community can be saved through the ritual practice of scapegoating, where the social fabric is preserved by allowing the community to realign itself around the common repudiation of a victim. That victim is held responsible for aggression against the community but the community can be preserved because a surrogate has been found to divert and absorb its violence.[50]

From this perspective, scapegoating and the sacrifice it ritualistically promotes is, if not an antidote to violence, then a means of containing it, which is why Rene Girard maintains that religions have traditionally functioned not to inflame anger and hostility but to redirect and ultimately restrict it. But this may underestimate the therapeutics of scapegoating, which are not simply vivisectionist but purgative.[51] As a ritual technology that allows one to project onto others what one potentially fears or despises in oneself, scapegoating both protects the community from the threat of pollution and also cleanses it, thereby making it indispensable to social and political health. Ritual sacrifice, for some even perpetual war, is the key to community development and renewal.

The challenge for mourning as a political and not just a personal project is therefore to reverse the process of scapegoating, which involves decoupling the community from its experience of loss. This requires "working through" the painful memories of the loss suffered *by* and *to* the self, and in very significant part, as Butler says so beautifully, *of* the self, until one can find the only thing that can at least partially compensate for it. That compensation comes in the form of understanding how the life of the self or community has been changed by the passage through it of what is now otherwise lost to it. What the self or community must eventually relinquish is a sense of themselves as defined chiefly in terms of their experience of loss. What they may in time acquire is a new sense of themselves based in considerable part on the interpretive and imaginative energies that this process of mourning has released. If the mourner can never find an adequate substitute for what has gone missing, she or he can at least gain the possibility of an altered relation to the experience that in mourning defined them. Working through memories of what has been lost introduces or reintroduces new symbolic forms that draw off some of the rage in grief. At the same time, these forms and, more important, the interpretive and imaginative energies necessary to contemplate them, help redescribe grief by translating the loss suffered by and to the self into something other than diminishment or impoverishment. Those energies slowly empower the self or community to transform the source of bereavement into an opportunity to more deeply comprehend and memorialize what the passage through the mourner's world of the life lost can now mean in its absence, what Jacques Lacan calls "the unique value/valor of the dead's being."[52] This turns loss from something that needs to be avenged into something that can be born, even shared.

But what role, to return to Levinas, does the face of the other play in enabling this transformation that comprises the act of mourning? And who exactly is that other to whose face we are called to respond? Is it, as can be inferred from the way Butler uses Levinas, some aspect of ourselves associated with our own elemental precariousness, or is it something radically different and unlike ourselves, a kind of radical alterity? This is in part a rehearsal of the old argument that Levinas had with Derrida about whether the Other who summons us into ethical being is radically and irreducibly Different or part of the Same. Derrida took the position that if the other were not part of the Same, we would not be capable of recognizing it and could thus not be held to be accountable to it.[53]

But this, then, leads us back to the fundamental issue about how we know ourselves as human and what that process has to do with mourning and the possibility of developing the basis of a new politics of non-violent solidarity. The initial answer, on which I agree with Butler and with Levinas, and which goes back to Mikhail Bakhtin and George Herbert Mead, is that we begin to know ourselves exotopically: by imaginatively constructing ourselves in relation to someone or something outside ourselves by which we feel ourselves confronted or addressed. Epistemologically and morally, this amounts to saying no more than that selves, like cultures and civilizations, develop only in relation to other selves, other cultures, other civilizations or, more exactly, only in relation to the symbolic materials by which those others (selves, cultures, civilizations) represent themselves both to themselves and to us. In this formulation, "self" and "other" are conceived neither as fundamental opposites of one another (here is one of the places where I differ with Levinas), nor as complements, counterparts, or corollaries of one another (here is where I differ with Butler), but as components, however varied their circumstances, conceptually and psychologically integral to each other's construction.[54] They are, even if they fail to acknowledge this, potential allies, as Nandy calls them, in each other's composition, but what they stand to gain from this relationship is not so much the call to be ethical as the terms in which that form of accountability might make sense. If neither self nor other is, in Wallace Stevens's great line, "the single artificer of the world in which she sang ... and, singing, made,"[55] so neither one is constituted merely by their reference to or address by the other. What each offers the other is what their own "other" face hides or obscures or denies: a knowledge that can only begin to be liberated and actualized through exchanges, interactions, and communions that are, at the level of the individual, inter- as opposed to transpersonal and that are, at the level of the cultural and beyond, inter- as opposed to transcivilizational.

Being human, then, refers to a particular kind of process or action rather than to a specific condition or state. While Butler is correct that the human is often found where we least expect to discover it, "in its frailty and at the limits of its capacity to make sense,"[56] what is disclosed at such boundaries is not simply that it is precious because it is vulnerable, frail, and perishable, but that, despite these limitations, the human, as with no other creature on the planet, is dependent on learning, even at the cost of its own existence, from its exposure to others. What is learned from exposure to the otherness in, as well as the otherness of, others is not how human experience is ultimately and everywhere the same, or yields similar lessons, but rather how, in its difference, it can nonetheless yield insights that are indispensable to cultural and civilizational, not to say individual, self-actualization.

In sum, the human is that creature for whom all experience, including that of another civilization, is potentially instructive. This not only sets the terms of its dependency but suggests the terms of its accountability. Its accountability is less to a set of values, beliefs, or perspectives that may or could exist at some supra-civilizational level than to how the impingement of the other's life on its own at whatever level, local or global, renders it both educable and responsible. This involves a double lesson. The first, most eloquently enunciated by Levinas, is that the self is rendered ethically significant not by anything it does for itself but rather by the impingement on it of the other to whom the self is, in effect, neighbored. The second lesson, which is almost a corollary of the first and most recently articulated by Butler, is that "the source of my ethical connection with others" is not my similarity to them but rather "my own foreignness to myself."[57] Butler means that we are unfamiliar to ourselves partially because of "the enigmatic traces of others" in us.[58] This is not inconsistent with, but somewhat different from, the claim I have formerly made that the other's importance to the self derives in considerable part from its ability to serve as a reflexive mirror that refracts back to the self things it did not know about itself.[59] Such an assertion is also consistent with a pragmatist notion of the intersubjective nature of the formation of selfhood as well as of cultures, which develops in response to others precisely because of their ability to see themselves at least partially from the perspective of those others.

Putting these several lessons together helps to bring out an important distinction between Jewish and Christian interpretations of the great moral injunction they share and that Butler, like Levinas, is attempting to develop. It is the injunction about our responsibility to the neighbor, or, in Levinas's vocabulary, the other by whose "face" we are addressed and to which we are "called" to be accountable.[60] This is the neighbor we are twice commanded to love in the nineteenth chapter of Leviticus: "You shall love your neighbour as yourself" (Leviticus 19:18) and "You shall love the alien as yourself, for you were aliens in the land of Egypt" (Leviticus 19:34). The neighbor is, in other words, the stranger who is not to be killed but treated as one of your native-born. This is not the neighbor we are enjoined to become, as in the Christian tradition,[61] but the neighbor we already owe and must acknowledge, as in the Jewish.[62] In Christian texts, the neighbor is "a category of being into which we may enter"; St. Paul goes even further by shifting the focus from the state of being a neighbor to and for others to the love that supports such a state or condition and thus fulfils the law by in effect replacing it.[63] In Jewish texts, the neighbor is that which one is by virtue of being confronted, even against one's will, by others like oneself who deserve recognition in terms of their injurability.

The ethical commandment to love one's neighbor as oneself thus works rather differently in these two religious traditions. In the Christian, the relationship of neighbor to oneself is interpreted as a challenge to recognize, despite obvious and inevitable differences, one's similarity with others, whether selves or civilizations, and thus create by means of this sympathetic identification a more universal human community. In the Jewish, the relationship of neighbor to oneself is construed instead as a challenge to recognize, despite potential or obvious affinities with another, one's vulnerability with others and thus create by means of this empathetic identification a more responsive human community. Hence the community of the human in the Christian tradition is composed of those who are regarded and treated as neighbors and opens toward perspectives that are shared or sharable by all but those excluded from this category. The community of the human in the Jewish tradition is, on the other hand, composed of those already neighbored by others and opens toward perspectives that allow one to consider others as potential allies rather than enemies in the self-realization of the entire human communion.

To summarize, then, I have argued that reliance on a conception of the transcivilizational is less clarifying or useful than is the concept of the intercivilizational when it is supported by a reconceived notion of the human and the neighbor. In addition to avoiding the hazards of either reductionism or totalism, the idea of the intercivilizational allows us to perceive others as potential partners or collaborators in our own self-actualization. To view others, whether personal or civilizational, in this light is to see them as neighbors whom we are ethically called upon, in the two great Western religious traditions, to love as ourselves. But it makes a world of difference whether that neighbor is viewed as, in Christianity, the self whose foreignness can be subsumed within our own ethical universality or is viewed instead as the self whose foreignness constitutes the ethical basis of our recognition both of them and of ourselves. The global reframing of the human and of the corollary study of the humanities depends on the latter and not the former.

8

GLOBALIZING THE HUMANITIES AND AN "OTHER" HUMANISM

> Whatever may be the ultimate ground of all possibility, the proper study of [humankind] is [our] tendency to misjudge reality as inspirited by the troublous genius of symbolism. But if we were trained, for generation after generation, from our first emergence out of infancy, and in ways ranging from the simplest to the most complex, depending upon our stage of development, to collaborate in spying upon ourselves with pious yet sportive fearfulness, and thus helping to free one another of the false ambitions that symbolism so readily encourages, we might yet contrive to keep from wholly ruining this handsome planet and its plentitude.
> Kenneth Burke, *Symbolic of Motives*, quoted in Rueckert, 1982, p. 162

As virtually no one else in literary and humanistic studies in America, Edward Said became, during the last decades of his life, something like the global conscience of the profession. By conscience I mean that scholars, teachers, and critics of literature and culture looked more often to him than to any other figure not only for how to reframe their subject but, still more significantly, for how to reconstrue their task—even when, on individual issues and questions, they may have disagreed with him sharply on various particulars or been unable to follow exactly where he led. The only other Anglo-American critic and scholar and public intellectual who in different ways served a comparable function for his own peers was Raymond Williams. Said's thinking not only reflected a deeper sense of the humanity we share with others, despite our differences, but also a deeper feeling for the ways to which we must become answerable to it.

To be more specific, Said argued that critical inquiry should take on global traction in at least three different but related ways. Politically, he did so by contending that the geographies of feeling, which in literature must be submitted to, expressed through, and realized in the disciplines of form, are nonetheless—and often in ways sometimes disguised even from their authors, when not purposely disguised by their authors—expressions of power, modes of manipulation, conceits of control. Said knew that there is nothing, strictly speaking, "innocent" either about the act of writing or the act of reading. These are both, as we now say, "situated" undertakings that require the utmost tact as well as cunning, learning as well as discernment, to detect what John Dewey would have called their "prejudices" and to mount a sufficiently informed critique of them.

Against all formalisms and formalists, Said asserted that literary and discursive texts are not so much embedded in history as sedimented with history. He also insisted, however, that the history with which texts are sedimented rarely fits within some rigid Foucauldian formula of subversion and containment. But this observation could cut in two different ways. Accepting the notion that there is "an irreducible subjective core to human experience" did not mean that this subjective fundament is inaccessible to "analysis and interpretation." It simply meant that this irreducible essence was "not exhausted by totalizing theories, not marked and limited by doctrinal or national lines, not confined once and for all to analytical constructs."[1]

The historicity of that experience is precisely what made it impossible, as Antonio Gramsci had taught him, to develop an analysis of it around "exclusions," as Said called them—the sort of exclusions "that stipulate, for instance, that only women can understand feminine experience, only Jews can understand Jewish suffering, only formerly colonial subjects can understand colonial experience."[2] While these were scarcely sentiments that would endear him to the politically correct, Said was convinced on empirical grounds that such exclusions "give rise to polarizations that absolve and forgive ignorance and demagogy more than they enable knowledge."[3] His predilection was therefore to see literary and other texts less as undecidable objects, in deconstructionist terms, or as ideological templates, in some variants of Marxist criticism, than as sites of effective action, scenes of forceful or fateful statement, with "consequences," Said noted, voicing the pragmatist side to his temperament, "that criticism should make it its business to reveal."[4]

Critically, Said widened and complicated methodological horizons by refusing to define those same consequences in terms of the solecisms or soporifics of grand theory, reminding us again and again that reductionism, essentialism, totalism, and absolutism are all opiates of the intellectually indolent that can—and often do—lead to mental oppression. This is not to say that his criticism was hostile to theory or untheoretical but merely to contend that he was suspicious of, and impatient with, any theories that claimed more for themselves than the ability to isolate some problematic and then formulate its nature in general terms.[5] Said could thus "take pride," as he stated in one of his last books, "in playing a part in the [theoretical and critical] revision which has expressed itself in a critique of Eurocentrism, the display of the relative poverty of identity politics, the silliness of affirming the purity of an essential essence, and the utter falseness of ascribing to one tradition a kind of priority over all others."[6]

One very important key to the way he deployed these convictions was based on a distinction he made between the "religious" and the "secular" in his moving and important book *The World, the Text, and the Critic*. A differentiation that was already for many of his critical contemporaries in the American academy virtually canonical, Said meant by it something less tendentious if still in some ways problematic. By "religious criticism," he did not mean criticism that operates exclusively from within the shelter of some inflexible form of religious orthodoxy; he meant instead all criticism that defers normatively, if not also politically, "to the authority of the more-than-human, the supernatural, the other-worldly."[7] Evidence of the "religious" was therefore to be found not only in the eruption of religious fundamentalism all over the world (Christian, Jewish, Hindu, Sikh, and even Buddhist, as well as Muslim) but also in the increased role now played in contemporary intellectual life by what he called the "contemporary Manichean theologizing of 'the Other.'"[8] This theologization of "the Other" was clearly apparent in the tendency to convert such notions as the Orient, the Feminine, History, Terrorism, the West, Blackness, the Third World, Logocentricity, Communism, America, God, or Democracy into vague, semi-sacred, abstractions of contrast. But it could also be detected in the recurrent methodological recourse typical of so much contemporary criticism to, on the one side, forms of impassability, indecipherability, the unthinkable, the abyss of meaning, nothingness, and silence, or, on the other, to appeals to magic, mysticism, divine necessity, ultimacy, or the unconditional. Reflecting what he considered a terrible, almost unappeasable, need in our time for a kind of human assuagement that only the largest and crudest metaphysical generalizations can provide, he also felt that this "basically uncritical religiosity" shares with much other discourse making its appeal to a standard of ultimacy, an interest in premature closure, metanarrative, and subservience to the transcendent.[9]

Over against this deference to the metaphysics of cultural alterity, Said sought to establish a criticism that was by contrast worldly, skeptical, iconoclastic, and avowedly secular. The antithesis to what he called "organized dogma," "secular criticism" is suspicious of most universalizing moves, wary of all reifications, and discontent with all professional "guilds, special interests, imperialized fiefdoms, and orthodox habits of mind." Opposed to every form of intellectual and emotional manipulation and control, "secular criticism" should seek to advance what Said called, naming one of his own intellectual ideals, "non-coercive knowledge produced in the interests of human freedom."[10]

Such sentiments put Said at odds with those in the anti-humanist camp who were likely to dismiss such sentiments on the grounds that they had been rendered suspect as early as the Enlightenment when, as Foucault alleged, human beings turned themselves into a privileged subject of study. No matter that René Descartes had asserted that knowledge begins in doubt rather than certainty, or that Vico had provided what Said took to be the secular core of humanism by arguing "that we can really know only what we make or, to put it differently, we can know things according to the way they are made."[11] By humanism, then, Said referred to "all those things not amenable to adequate explanation in terms of general laws of natural processes, physical or biological, or in terms [only] of collective social conditions or forces. ... They are, in short, what we commonly speak of as human achievements."[12]

From this Said concluded that there are no realms of understanding reserved for a select few, no privileged sanctuaries where truth can be protected from public scrutiny. For the humanist, the domain of the knowable and the known are potentially common property and their continual critical revaluation a democratic art. This helps explain Said's resistance to regimes of criticism that either on the Right specialized in exercises of endless refinement or on the Left managed to confirm contemporary values in the process of challenging or revising them. If on the Right this produced a critical practice that turned the subject of "difficulty" into a kind of fetish or totem, it yielded on the Left a criticism so enamored of the anatomy of power that it forgot that authority "is a more interesting and various idea."[13]

Foucault's theory of power, with its corollary notions of discipline and containment, had in fact made it so ubiquitous as to turn its invocation for many of his American acolytes and disciples into a license for political quietism.[14] Said agreed with Raymond Williams "that however dominant a social system may be, the very meaning of its domination involves a limitation or selection of the activities it covers, so that by definition it cannot exhaust all social experience, which therefore always potentially contains space for alternative acts and alternative intentions which are not yet articulated as a social institution or even a project." This belief convinced Said that "criticism belongs in that potential space inside civil society, acting on behalf of those alternative acts and alternative intentions whose advancement is a fundamental human and intellectual obligation."[15]

However, Said risked forgetting this truth in his most famous book *Orientalism*. Referring to a practice more than a profession, the term "Orientalism," as Said selectively employed it, shifted attention away from methods and even subjects of inquiry to the modes by which cultures control and manipulate one another merely by virtue of the ways they represent and talk about each other. But the term itself possessed as well a much more specific provenance and range of governance. "Orientalism" referred explicitly to the special place that the Middle and Far East have held in the European (and, latterly, the American) imagination ever since they offered themselves to the West not simply as objects of formal study but also as sources of Western self-validation. The term "Orientalism" has thus now entered the critical lexicon, though not without contestation, in fields far distant from literary and cultural studies. It has become a blanket term to describe any and all instances when the "West" has constructed critical generalizations about the "East" for the sake of reinforcing its own self-image as superior.

Little wonder that the term "Orientalism" aroused considerable resistance in various quarters because of its critical unwieldiness, its potential for simplification and misrepresentation, and its tacit employment of the same binarist thinking that it wishes to put in question.[16] Still more troubling, it created the impression that all the major uses that Asia and the Middle East had for the West were self-serving. But this was to forget that Montesquieu employed his *Persian Letters* to cast a critical eye on the French Court, that Pierre Bayle and Voltaire used China's lack of organized religion to criticize French clericalism, and that Oliver Goldsmith's *The Citizen of the World* turned to ancient Chinese civilization as a measure of the inadequacies of European Christendom. And with the arrival of Sanskrit texts from India and the translation of the Upanishads, Indian thought became an important influence on the thinking of Continental philosophers from Schopenhauer and Herder and of Americans from Ralph Waldo Emerson and Henry David Thoreau to Lafcadio Hearn.

Yet *Orientalism* nevertheless managed to sensitize many to the cultural politics of knowledge and confirmed in others a belief shared by all but the willfully ignorant or the prejudicially indifferent that collective identities, no less than personal ones, are frequently constructed at the expense of those in contrast to whom they imagined. To put this more simply, Said's book, along with a great deal of other writing along similar lines, asserted that societies and civilizations, just like selves, are too often disposed—and not just in the West—to create themselves by means of the disparagement, inferiorization, and sometimes even demonization, of the culturally different.

Such insights may not have been new, but to see their effects played out in Western literary and cultural texts of the last several centuries, not only in *Orientalism* or the earlier *Beginnings* and the later *Culture and Imperialism* but in others like *Reflections of an Exile*, *Covering Islam*, *Representations of the Intellectual*, and *Freud and the Non-European*, afforded impressive witness to the moral difference between a political criticism that is essentially reductive and self-serving and one that is advocative, internationalist, self-reflexive, and oppositional. The function of such oppositional criticism was, at its narrowest, to challenge and, where possible, deconstruct all the forms in which literary and humanistic study, whether intentionally or not, has collaborated in the maintenance of cultural (which is to say, religio-humanistic) pieties. At its broadest, it risked turning comparative literary and cultural criticism into something more like a critique of religion, or, rather, a critique of the possible collusion between organized religion and the critical defense of the Western literary tradition that is implied by such titles as Frank Kermode's *The Genesis of Secrecy*, Northrop Frye's *The Great Code*, Harold Bloom's *Kaballah and Criticism*, and René Girard's *Violence and the Sacred*.[17]

Such suspicions sound exaggerated only if one discounts the kinds of arguments made by traditional humanists who were inclined to respond to threats to conventional humanistic values posed by poststructuralist and postmodern predispositions by steering criticism in the direction of a kind of spiritual apologetics. There is no more impassioned example of this than the later criticism of George Steiner, which not only urged a restoration of ethical standards in literary criticism but also proposed a revival of the notion of religious transcendence on which he thought they were formerly based.[18] Recovering the concept of transcendence would not only encourage an attitude of intellectual humility among literary and cultural critics, Steiner maintained, but hopefully induce in their readers an appropriate sense of reverence towards it. Steiner wrote as though the literary canon of Western humanism carried within itself a kind of religious warrant, as though its deepest spiritual intention had always been to bring those individuals critically capable of achieving a satisfactory appreciation of it into a new understanding of the divine, into a more intense and definitive relation with the presence of the sacred. In its most sublime expressions, then, literature was a form of sacred scripture and the humanities in general, like one half of T. S. Eliot's notion of tradition, at once invulnerable to time and perennially relevant.

To "religious" or transcendentalist critics like Steiner, then, the chief value of all interpretive or hermeneutic activity is to reveal that fundamental oneness of human identity that underlies all the otherwise superficial differences that separate human selves and societies. To "secular" or anti-transcendentalist critics like Said, on the other hand, any humanistic project that views literature and the other arts as, at their best, a medium of revealed truth risks effacing that "irreducible subjective core to human experience" that it is attempting to comprehend.

But there are problems with both these critical positions because of the way the difference between them was framed. While Steiner was surely justified in defending the linkage between the history of literary expression in the West, or anywhere else for that matter, and the striving for transcendence of what besets the human condition, he and other so-called "religious" critics like him were clearly mistaken in assuming that the humanities do, or necessarily should, valorize a specific view of the transcendent itself. And while Said was equally justified in believing that the deeper religious question posed by the humanities has to do with whether distinctive expressions of them can transcend various forms of cultural valorization, he was at the same time mistaken in concluding with other "secular" critics that every intellectual attempt to explore the lure of the transcendent, or what Said described in a more irenic mood as "the essential unmasterable presence that constitutes a large part of historical and social situations," is ethically questionable.[19] Both were in danger of forgetting that when religion, at least in the West, lost some of its priority of place in the modern period to the domain of art, what was formerly thought of as a problem of belief was simply transformed into a problem of values, and particularly into a question, as Nietzsche was the first to realize, of the value of life itself.

What both kinds of critics, both the "religious" and the "secular," failed to grasp is that in the present scene of crisis in the humanities the nature of the relationship between the literary and the religious is principally morphological and pragmatic rather than thematic or prescriptive. The issue is not one of essences so much as of homologies: the question at the center of their relationship has far more to do with the processes they serve than with the propositions they assert. Religion has less to do with deities, duties, or divinization than with how to make sense of experience when for a variety of reasons—because of the erosion of meaning, or the eruption of evil, or the breakdown of justice—experience becomes almost too agonizing to bear. One makes religious sense of such radically problematic experience by devising a mode of living *within it* that feels congruent with what seems to be the underlying or overarching structure *of it*.

To view religion in this way is to suggest that religion differs from other cultural formations not because it is made up of different materials—they, too, can presumably concern themselves with gods, codes, and rites—but because it possesses different aims and seeks to realize them through different alternative forms. Religious forms attempt to secure a measure of existential confidence in the face of circumstances that threaten to undermine them by constructing an image of the way the world is put together that possesses a structural, if not a formal, analogy to the way one is supposed to dispose her- or himself towards this understanding of the world. This morphological understanding of the distinctiveness of religion, and the basis of its comparison with other kinds of cultural forms, was captured by John Dewey when he observed that "the deepest problem in modern life" is how to restore integration and cooperation between [our] beliefs about the world in which [we] live and [our] beliefs about the values and purposes that should direct [our] conduct.[20]

The terms "religious" and "secular" thus turn out to be too unstable as well as imprecise to mark the critical distinction that was at issue for Said. If "religious" criticism, as too many traditional, not to say Western, humanists define it, amounts to little more than a technique for effacing otherness through Manichean idealizations of the Other, "secular criticism," as various anti-humanists construe it, too easily risks idealizing opposition by assuming that criticism can constitute itself solely through what Said calls "its difference from other cultural activities and from systems of thought [and] method."[21] Both could benefit from William James's reminder that "the only *real* guarantee we have against licentious thinking [in any field] is the circumpressure of experience itself, which gets us sick of concrete errors, whether there be a transempirical reality or not."[22]

To be more specific, the humanities need not, as Steiner everywhere wrote as though they should, induce in us a sense of piety toward their intellectual canonizations, nor need they direct the bulk of their critical energies, as Said assumed they must, toward the exposure of religion's complicit relation with them. In a number of textual instances, the humanities as a discipline, no less than humanism as a critical stance, enables the religious task to be seen as, contra Said, the deconstruction or reconstruction of the canonical truths of the classic literary heritage on behalf of a universal sense of the human, and in others the humanities as a discipline, and humanism as a critical stance, permits the literary task to be viewed as, contra Steiner and others like him, the revaluation, or even transvaluation, of religion itself.

Nowhere has this double truth been more eloquently expressed than in Erich Heller's neglected critical masterpiece *The Disinherited Mind*.[23] A book which from the outside appears to be the quintessential example of what a "secular" critic would call "religious" criticism—its orientation is Eurocentric, its bias anti-positivist, its view of culture metaphysical, its own discursive practice relentlessly ontological—it explains how the modern Western or European mind was decentered through the erosion of certain of its axial assumptions. If it tends to view culture metaphysically in terms of the beliefs by which culture is constituted, its interest is less in those overt beliefs on which people purportedly agree than on those covert beliefs that determine their sense of what is disputable. If it challenges the positivism of the scientific establishment on the grounds that such a mentality typically effaces important questions of value, it does so not on behalf of proposing another standard of value to take its place but only in the interest of showing how processes of valuation are an ingredient in all mental operations. Finally, if it assumes that axiological reflection inevitably leads to fundamental thinking about the nature of being itself, it treats ontological questions in anything but an essentialist manner. In each of these ways, *The Disinherited Mind* exposes itself to the strictures of "religious" and "secular" criticism alike, only to elude them both in an effort to clarify what was at stake, and still is, in the move toward a more worldly humanism.

A study of modern German literature and thought, *The Disinherited Mind* is everywhere characterized by the assumption Heller shares with Steiner but construes like Said. Modern writers and thinkers were confronted with a spiritual crisis that was historically unprecedented, but what made it exceptional was the fact that now one found oneself living in a world whose intellectual and symbolic constructs no longer housed or nourished one's deepest feelings. The superstructure of belief no longer bore any intimate relation to the substructure of feeling, and thus what Goethe once termed the "Age of Prose"—where people felt compelled "to drag into the vulgar light of day the ancient heritage of a noble past, and destroy not only the capacity for profound feeling and the beliefs of peoples and priests, but even that belief of reason which divines meaningful coherence behind the strangeness and seeming disorder"[24]—was still upon us. Moderns now live in the grip of what Heller calls a little grandly "the Creed of Ontological Invalidity," a creed that dismisses a priori all assertions about being as such and deprecates the faculty of mind that "grasping their intelligence, responds positively to questions about *what the world is.*"[25] In its place we have installed unquestioned faith in the supremacy of science, which not only reduces the question of truth to "a plebiscite of facts"[26] but evades Werner Heisenberg's warning that experimentation may only lead us further away from rather than toward truth, "for our complicated experiments have no longer anything to do with nature in her own right, but with nature changed and transformed by our own cognitive activity."[27] Much that had been discovered in the name of science is simply not worth knowing, and much of what science claims to determine depends on rarely acknowledged underlying assumptions about the nature of reality itself. As Goethe put it, "every scientific theory is merely the surface rationalization of a metaphysical substratum of beliefs, conscious or unconscious, about the nature of the world."[28]

But to Heller "the Creed of Ontological Invalidity" contained within it still greater difficulties. By dismissing all thought about the nature and meaning of being as an irrelevance, it had turned modern spirituality into a kind of invalid where the human capacity "to respond creatively to the ontological mystery had been stunted into something that produce[s] merely an irritated state of mystification."[29] In this diminished condition, human beings are thrown back on their own divided being where they find themselves precariously suspended between one of two convictions: either that they are nothing in the face of the vastness of all that is, or that they are all that is and the rest is nothing. In the first instance, as Pascal discerned in his *Pensées*, despair engulfs the self; in the second, as Conrad portrayed in *The Heart of Darkness*, the self engulfs the world.

Heller's response was to turn for guidance to those intellectuals and artists in the modern German tradition who attempted to think their way through this crisis from different directions—Goethe from the philosophy of science, Burckhardt and Spengler from the philosophy of history, Nietzsche from ethics and the theory of tragedy, Rilke and Yeats from the theory of poetry and poetics, Kafka and Karl Kraus from the theory and practice of prose. Cut off from the past, to paraphrase Heller, by their conviction that the framework of belief that once gave significance and order to human experience has now been shattered; alienated from the rest of the human community by their commitment to see through and beyond this crisis to implications following from it that have never been contemplated or willed before; subjected during the course of these reflections to the most terrible self-doubt and emotional agony by virtue of their awareness that in willing what they believe to be true but also know to be terrible they must somehow transmute the pain and sorrow of a world without God into a source of joy instead of despair, all in the very act of willing it; and, finally, racked with skepticism and guilt about whether it will ever be possible to create a new "idea of order" that is not achieved, as they are convinced all former spiritual orders have been achieved, at the expense of the fullness of life itself—these intellectuals and artists persevered to the end in the conviction that when the spiritual framework or thought-mold of one's world no longer springs from the deepest levels of personal experience, then the creative person must engage in a kind of fundamental thinking for him- or herself, must, in effect, do *all* the thinking.

Each of these thinkers and writers thus took it upon themselves to become, in Wallace Stevens's words, a kind of "metaphysician in the dark/ twanging/ An instrument ... that gives/ Sounds passing through sudden rightnesses, wholly/ Containing the mind, below which it cannot descend,/ Beyond which it has no will to rise."[30] For them the relationship between immanence and transcendence, between the profane and the sacred, had broken down under the weight of its own frustrated achievement, and every experience of immanence was bordered with the realization of a sphere of existence that seemed to invite, and yet simultaneously to discourage, any attempt to reach it. This sphere of existence represented to all of them what might be called a "truer order" of experience, even a transcendent order, precisely because it promised to match, in its profoundest emotional registers, the terms of their own need for it. Its pursuit was predicated on the assumption that there should be some congruence, however obscure, between the geology of human feeling and the architecture of human truth; that between our felt need as human beings to believe and the ultimate horizons of the believable, there should be some at least fragile structure of correspondence.

But history, as Said appreciated, offers hard lessons, and none more difficult than the paradoxical spectacle of many things once regarded as true now being discarded as such. Thus for some of the figures of Heller's study, such as Burckhardt and Schopenhauer, this search for a "truer order" precipitated a realization that while Christianity might still offer the best interpretation of human pathology, the Christian scheme of redemption—the fall from grace, the iniquity of sin, the need for repentance, and the promise of deliverance and new life—was incapable of earning their own personal credence. All they could do was admire the aptness of the diagnosis and reject the prescription. On the other hand, when the world refused to satisfy Nietzsche's rage for a similar sense of order, he was forced to conclude that the rage itself was to blame, that the desire for "true order" was the disease from which humankind must be delivered. Hence his creation of the concept of the Superman joyfully accepting the eternal recurrence of senselessness as the cure. Yet for still others—Rilke comes to mind and, with another side of himself, Nietzsche again—this quest for "true order" turned into what Heller describes as a kind of *religion intransitiva*. Though scarcely to be confused with a fixed faith, Heller thought that this religion "on the way" might one day be acknowledged as the most distinctive religious achievement of modern Europe, a Continental analogue to Stevens's more American-sounding invocation of a "dimension in which,/ We believe without belief, beyond belief."[31]

From this Heller eventually concluded that if the candidates for truth are always being displaced, the one thing that may remain constant is our uncertainty about just what the truth is—not simply because people keep discovering newer truths to take their place, but rather because, from time to time, they decide to experience differently, or at least to describe their experience of truth in different vocabularies. This left Heller believing that if Goethe, Nietzsche, Rilke, Burckhardt, and the others were religious, it had less to do with where they "came out" than with where they "got in," and with what tenacious logic they followed it through. Referring to Goethe in words that applied to them all, Heller insisted that "it is neither his opinions nor their inconsistencies that matter in this context. What matters is the level on which his convictions are formed, or the pressure of spiritual energy by which they are sustained."[32] Heller's witnesses were therefore united not only in their shared sense that "the great experiment of separating meaning from reality, and symbol from fact, had ended in failure" but in their refusal to take comfort in some new facile synthesis, some easy reconciliation.[33] The "true order" for which they sought, then, and to which Heller refers, was an order that is "transcendent" only in its resistance to all efforts to hypostatize the metaphysical quest, all attempts to reify foundations, all endeavors to subsume the transitive within the substantive. Essentialism, foundationalism, substantialism were scandalous not in themselves, to contradict the view most popular among their own contemporary critics as well as many today, but because they worked to restrict the sphere of the real.

Said would have agreed. Not the least among the contributions he made on behalf of his own generation's extended self-education centered on what he meant by the term "world" and how we must widen our sense of it by becoming more accountable to its own efforts at transcending lived contradictions. The world he tended to place before his readers more and more, thinking in particular of the last several decades, was one roiled by vast human migrations provoked by war, by colonialism and decolonization, by economic and political revolution, and by "such devastating occurrences as famine, ethnic cleansing, and great power machinations." It was a world that often caused him immense, almost visceral dismay and outrage, but it was a world in which he refused to be anything other than relentlessly engaged.

Said took some of his bearing for this commitment from William James, who insisted that the only place for a genuine thinker is at the center of a battle, but he was obliged to pay a very high price for this belief.[34] If it earned for him greater admiration than any other literary or humanistic intellectual, it also exposed him to greater personal dangers than many of his contemporaries. These dangers came most obviously from his responsibilities as the most prominent American advocate, as well as critic, of the Palestinian cause, and it led to his increasing feeling of exile in his own country. This feeling of exile helps explain why he felt so deeply drawn to New York City, the "capital of our time," as he termed it, because it was itself created by immigrants and displaced persons.[35] In giving him a sense of place in a world of dislocation, which included "the re-emergence of the Palestinian people as a political force, and my own engagement with that movement, ... New York made it possible," he wrote, "for me to live, despite the death threats, acts of vandalism, and verbal abuse directed at me and my family."[36] In addition, this site of exile, where he felt, as he titled his 1999 memoir, "out of place," furnished him with an evaluative criterion and agenda that he called "worldliness."

"Worldliness," when applied to critical responsibilities, referred to an obligation to link works together in order to "bring them out of the neglect and secondariness to which for all kinds of political and ideological reasons they had previously been condemned."[37] In other terms, "worldliness" constituted the recuperation and relocation of such works and their interpretations in what Said called their "global setting."[38] Jane Austen's *Mansfield Park* deserved to be read, as he insisted at the risk of outraging many, against the background of the shadow cast by the depredations of Empire. Tayeb Salih's great Sudanese novel *Season of Migration to the North* cried out for interpretation as a rewriting, like N'gugi wa Thiong'o's *The River Between* or Camera Laye's *The Radiance of the King*, no less than V. S. Naipaul's *A Bend in the River*, of Joseph Conrad's *Heart of Darkness*. Herman Melville's *Moby-Dick* demanded to be seen as, among other things, a denunciation—sometimes satirical, sometimes deadly earnest—of America's quest for global governance. Defining that setting in contrast to all forms of cultural separatism and exclusivism, he argued that the restoration sought by a global criticism could only be accomplished by appreciating that literary and cultural texts dwell not in "some tiny, defensively constituted corner of the world" but in "the large, many-windowed house of human culture as a whole."[39]

Yet if the nationalized historical frameworks by which we have traditionally studied literature and culture require drastic revision, increasing globalization had posed new challenges, issues, and problems for literary and cultural study that had yet to be worked out. Addressing the topic of "globalizing literary studies," Said noted three. The first had to do with the humanities' lack of any model of its own work that would enable it to mount an effective attack on globalization's most terrible excesses. The refocusing of much anti-imperialist and anti-colonial research on the ambiguities of the identity of the colonizer as opposed to the colonized, and the academicization of a celebratory multiculturalism, were two among many reasons why the humanities had been unable either to offer the more negative effects of globalization any but token resistance or to discern where the real sites of resistance most likely exist. Instead, he worried that we were in danger of enfranchising those practices even while diagnosing them. Second, he was concerned that as descendants of a Eurocentric world system, we had inherited a cultural bifurcation—whether it divides the world into science and the humanities, centers and peripheries, international English and languages marginal to it—that is basically consumerist and that can, perhaps, only be combatted by realizing its tension with, and alienation from, the realm of the aesthetic. Third, he believed that the study of identities, along with the academic subspecialties in which it is grounded, and where many in literary and cultural studies now situate their teaching and research, has eroded any sense of a history that is to some degree shared in common, and this has raised difficult questions about the relation between parts and whole, local and general, individual and collective.

In response to this issue, he turned to the image of the intellectual as one whose proper work in the academy is "connecting it with ongoing and actual processes of enlightenment and liberation in the world."[40] There are, he maintained, synoptic knowledges, universal (or at least perennial) questions, recurrent issues, persistent problems, and available methods to be explored, but he wanted to re-emphasize "the importance not of synthesis and the transcendence of opposites but of the role of geographic knowledge in keeping one grounded, literally, in the often tragic structure of social, historical, and epistemological contests over territory—this includes nationalism, identity, narrative, and ethnicity—so much of which informs the literature, thought, and culture of our time."[41]

What lay behind these convictions was, as Said knew, a literary transformation of long duration, as writing throughout the world began to aspire to an identity that was more than local. Indeed, that process occurred in several stages.[42] The first stage required decoupling the practice of writing itself from the service of ancient orthodoxies and the official languages by which they were previously defined and mediated. In the West this entailed the replacement of Latin by any one of a number of vernacular languages and the shift of literary focus from approved ecclesiastical and religious subjects to more secular, or at least heterodox, ones.

The second stage could not begin until those older formations of solidarity and their institutional languages of validation had weakened enough to permit literary practice to turn its energies instead to the building of institutions like the state designed to take their place and to help fashion the correspondent ideology of nationalism that would legitimate it. Here the challenge for writing was to enable the state to construct itself as the normative structure of collective belonging, and this required overwriting the record of what was formerly known as "local knowledge" and replacing it with a new narrative of nation-centric triumphalism.

The third stage in the growth of a literary perspective directed toward the translocal, transregional, and transnational commenced when literary nationalism began to be experienced as too narrow and distorted a lens to capture the contours of contemporary experience, and writing sought to establish a different justification of itself premised on new confidence in its own potential to serve as a medium of alternative self-realization and self-transcendence. Writing now beyond, if not also against, the nation and its imperial projects of colonialism, literary practice began to seek a fresh source of value in the imaginative energies released by its own modernist break with the nationalist and state-based paradigm of human experience and loyalty.

But this modernist break with literary regimes of formerly nationalist and colonialist imaginaries would ultimately need to give way to a fourth stage of development (some call it "postmodernism," others "postcolonialism," still others a "second modernity") where art's future could now be seen to lie in rendering the newly emergent global economy of values more representative of those who had been, purposely for the most part, left out of it. In this expanded global phase, literature was transformed from a medium chiefly presumed to reflect consciousness into an instrument for critically reshaping it through an exploration of the myriad ways that the local and the global are at once reflective and constitutive of one another.

It was this latest phase of literary development that most engaged Said, where literatures address not simply issues of a global nature—imperialist oppression, political aspiration, diasporic experience, climate change, human rights—but where verbal experience is drawn into networks of transnational interconnectivity and interdependence. This way of viewing literary and other forms of humanistic expression was to be differentiated both from the discipline known as Comparative Literature, in which Said was trained, as well as from the field referred to as "World Writing." That is, it was neither, as in the first instance, a disciplinary enterprise devoted to comparing and contrasting representative texts from the world's major literary traditions, mostly national, in order to come up with a generalized sense of their chief characteristics, nor was it committed, as in the second instance, to developing a more generalized, if not unified, model of writing itself. This more broadly humanistic and global criticism was rather a mode of reading that permits one to study the relations that particular kinds of literary production, consumption, and circulation possess with one another when they are seen within what might be called a global frame. A global frame is defined less by the contents that make it up than by the horizons within which it seeks to situate its subjects, horizons that allow us to read—and, almost more important, be read by—frameworks other than our own. Indeed, it is just because of the cross-lights provided by different cultural frames that we can read self-reflexively or critically at all—that we can discover in the stories, histories, and lives of others elements, features, and dimensions of ourselves, and of our own narratives that have been overlooked, denied, shunned, or undiscovered.[43]

This is how Said helped reframe the humanities under the sign of an "other" humanism. Repudiating any facile generalizations about globalization and its benefits, he nonetheless established as the aim of all criticism worthy of the name the resituation of the works of the imagination in the context of all the human struggles for meaning that inform, threaten, or thwart them. His concern was not in the remedial wisdom contained in such texts but in how the challenges to human self-realization that informed them, if projected onto a richer, denser, more ethically equitable sense of the worldwide, could be emancipatory, liberating.

Little wonder that Said found himself drawn back again and again to the words of Hugo of St. Victor: "The man who finds his homeland sweet is still a tender beginner; he to whom every soil is as his native one is already strong; but he is perfect to whom the entire world is as a foreign land."[44] Perfection in this case does not derive from the presumption that we can become familiar or intimate with the world as foreign but rather from the realization that the world in its foreignness is actually what is knowable about it. In the first case, worldliness is merely a form of knowingness, a presumption that the world is potentially accessible to the intelligence of the knower; in the second, worldliness gives way to a sense of worldedness, an appreciation of how our being bounded by others is ultimately the key not only to our understanding of, and relation to, it but also to ourselves, to being other-wise.

NOTES

Preface

1 This is borrowed from Jacques Derrida who used it on a number of different occasions.
2 S. Benhabib, *Another Cosmopolitanism*, New York: Oxford University Press, 2008.
3 O. Roy, *Holy Ignorance: When Religion and Culture Part Ways*, New York: Columbia University Press, 2010.
4 A. Appadurai, *Fear of Small Numbers: An Essay on the Geography of Anger*, Durham and London: Duke University Press, 2006, pp. 11, 82–5.
5 G. Borradori, *Philosophy in a Time of Terror: Dialogues with Jurgen Habermas and Jacques Derrida*, Chicago: University of Chicago Press, 2004, p. 98.
6 T. S. Eliot, "Gerontion," *The Complete Poems and Plays 1909–1950*, New York: Harcourt, Brace and Company, 1952, p. 22.
7 C. Rumford, *Cosmopolitan Spaces: Europe, Globalization, Theory*, London: Routledge, 2008; G. Delanty, *The Cosmopolitan Imagination: The Renewal of Critical Social Theory*, Cambridge: Cambridge University Press, 2009.
8 This statement owes its inspiration to J. V. Cunningham, *Tradition and Poetic Structure*, Denver: Alan Swallow, 1960, p. 141.

1 Introduction: mapping and remapping the global

1 Z. Bauman, *Globalization: The Human Consequences*, New York: Columbia University Press, 1998; J. Gray, *False Dawn: The Delusions of Global Capitalism*, London: Granta, 1998; F. Jameson and M. Miyoshi (eds.), *The Cultures of Globalization*, Durham: Duke University Press, 1998.
2 Several lines in this paragraph and elsewhere in the Introduction are drawn from G. Gunn, "Introduction: Globalizing Literary Studies," *PMLA*, 116, January 2001, 16–31.
3 For someone who favors the first view, see B. Axford, "Globalization," in G. Browning, A. Halcli, F. Webster (eds.), *Understanding Contemporary Society: Theories of the Present*, Thousand Oaks, CA: Sage Publications, 2000, pp. 238–51; I am more inclined to the second, in G. Gunn, *Beyond Solidarity: Pragmatism and Difference in a Globalized World*, Chicago: University of Chicago Press, 2001.
4 M. B. Steger, *Globalization: A Very Short Introduction*, Oxford: Oxford University Press, 2009, p. 15.

5 See J. Bhagwati, *In Defense of Globalization*, New York: Oxford University Press, 2004.
6 For a defender of the first opinion, see T. Friedman, *The Lexus and the Olive Tree*, New York: Farrar, Straus and Giroux, 1999; for an advocate of the second, see D. Harvey, *The Condition of Postmodernity: An Enquiry Into the Origins of Cultural Change*, New York: Blackwell, 1989.
7 This position is most often associated with A. Giddens, *The Consequences of Modernity*, London: Polity Press, 1990.
8 I. Wallerstein, *The Modern World System*, New York: Academic Press, 1974.
9 R. Robertson, *Globalization: Social Theory and Global Culture*, Thousand Oaks, CA: Sage Publications, 1992; M. Waters, *Globalization*, London: Routledge, 1995; A. Appadurai, *Modernity at Large: Cultural Dimensions of Globalization*, Minneapolis: University of Minnesota Press, 1996; F. Buell, *National Culture and the New Global System*, Baltimore; Johns Hopkins University Press, 1994; M. B. Steger, op. cit.
10 I. Wallerstein, *The End of the World as We Know It: Social Science for the Twenty-First Century*, Minneapolis: University of Minnesota Press, 1999.
11 J. Abu-Lughod, *Before European Hegemony: The World System A.D. 1250–1350*, New York: Oxford University Press, 1991.
12 A. Sen, "How to Judge Globalism," *American Prospect*, January 1, 2002, p. 1.
13 J. Needham, *Science in Traditional China*, Cambridge, MA: Harvard University Press, 1981.
14 W. H. McNeill, *The Rise of the West: A History of the Human Community*, Chicago: University of Chicago Press, 1963; M. G. S. Hodgson, *Rethinking World History: Essays on Europe, Islam, and World History*, Cambridge: Cambridge University Press, 1993.
15 See R. Robertson, op. cit.
16 W. H. McNeill, "Short History of Humanity," *The New York Review of Books*, XLVII/11, 29 June 2000, 9–11.
17 W. H. McNeill, "*The Rise of the West* after Twenty-five Years," *The Rise of the West*, Chicago: The University of Chicago Press, 1991, p. xvi.
18 C. Geertz, "Blurred Genres: The Refiguration of Social Thought," *Local Knowledge: Further Essays in Interpretive Anthropology*, New York: Basic Books, 1983, pp. 19–35.
19 R. Barthes, "From Work to Text," in Josue V. Harari (ed.), *Textual Strategies: Perspectives in Post-Structuralist Criticism*, Ithaca: Cornell University Press, 1979, p. 75.
20 C. Geertz, op. cit., p. 20.
21 A. Appadurai has most famously discussed these paradigm shifts, primarily in connection with the study of cultural formations, in *Modernity At Large: Cultural Dimensions of Globalization*, op. cit.
22 D. Harvey, *Cosmopolitanism and the Geographies of Freedom*, New York: Columbia University Press, 2009, p. 252.
23 A. Appadurai, op. cit.
24 B. Anderson, *Imagined Communities: Reflections on the Origin and Spread of Nationalism*, London, Verso, 1983.
25 C. Castoriadis, *The Imaginary Institution of Society*, (tr. K. Blamey), Cambridge, MA: MIT Press, 1998.
26 J. P. Arnason, *Civilizations in Dispute*, Leiden: Brill, 2003; R. Collins, *The Sociology of Philosophies: A Global Theory of Intellectual Change*, Cambridge, MA: Harvard University Press, 1998, and "Civilizations as Zones of Prestige and Social Contact" in S. A. Arjomand and E. A. Tiryakian (eds.), *Rethinking Civilizational Analysis*, Thousand Oaks, CA: Sage, 2004, pp. 132–47; C. Rumford, *Cosmopolitan Spaces: Europe, Globalization, Theory*, London: Routledge, 2008.
27 Even as we refer to cosmopolitanism as a general, if multi-dimensional, disposition toward what is assumed to be the world and its people, it is important to remember that there have been many versions of this way of regarding ourselves in relation to others. See C. Rumford, op. cit.
28 J. Dewey, *Art as Experience*, New York: Perigree Books (G. P. Putnam's Sons), 1980 [1934], p. 346.

29 The next several pages have been adapted from G. Gunn, *The Interpretation of Otherness: Literature, Religion, and the American Imagination*, New York: Oxford University Press, 1979, pp. 134–9.
30 G. Ryle, *Theory of Mind*, London: Hutchinson's University Library, 1949.
31 J. Dewey, op. cit., p. 264.
32 Ibid.
33 J. Dewey, *Experience and Nature* (1929; LaSalle, IL: Open Court Publishing Company, 1971), p. 247.
34 Ibid., p. 251.
35 Ibid., p. 248.
36 S. K. Langer, *Philosophy in a New Key*, Cambridge, MA: Harvard University Press, 1959, p. 42.
37 Ibid., p. 21.
38 P. Sorokin, quoted in C. Geertz, *The Interpretation of Cultures*, New York, Basic Books, 1973, p. 145.

2 Being other-wise: cosmopolitanism and its discontents

1 S. Vertovec and R. Cohen (eds.), *Conceiving Cosmopolitanism: Theory, Context, Practice*, Oxford: Oxford University Press, 2002; Giles Gunn, *Beyond Solidarity: Pragmatism and Difference in a Globalized World* Chicago: University of Chicago Press, 2001.
2 D. A. Hollinger, *Cosmopolitanism and Solidarity: Studies in Ethnoracial, Religious, and Professional Affiliation in the United States*, Madison, WI: University of Wisconsin Press, 2006, p. xviii.
3 The notion that the "thematization" of subjects like humanity and human rights is one of the ways we imagine the world was first introduced in Roland Robertson's path-breaking *Globalization: Social Theory and Global Culture*, Thousand Oaks, CA: Sage Publications, 1992. It was given earlier expression in slightly different terms by Robert Wuthnow, who described "the production and reproduction of 'the world' as the most salient plausibility structure of our time," in "Religious Movements and the Transition in World Order," in J Needleman and G. Baker (ed.), *Understanding the New Religions*, New York: Seabury Press, 1978, p. 65.
4 C. Calhoun, "The Class Consciousness of Frequent Travelers: Toward a Critique of Actually Existing Cosmopolitanism," in S. Vertovec and R. Cohen (eds.), *Conceiving Cosmopolitanism: Theory, Context, and Practice*, pp. 86–109.
5 Ibid., p. 108.
6 D. Harvey, *Cosmopolitanism and the Geographies of Freedom*, New York: Columbia University Press, 2009, p. 79
7 T. Brennan, *At Home in the World: Cosmopolitanism Now*, Cambridge: Harvard University Press, 1997, p. 55.
8 C. Mouffe, *On the Political*, London: Routledge, 2005, pp. 2, 9. For this citation and several others in this chapter, I am indebted to the splendid article by G. H. Lenz, "Toward a Politics of American Transcultural Studies: Discourses of Diaspora and Cosmopolitanism," in W. Fluck, D. E. Pease, J. C. Rowe (eds.), *Re-Framing the Transnational Turn in American Studies*, Hanover, NH: Dartmouth College Press, 2011, pp. 391–425.
9 E. Balibar, *Masses, Classes, Ideas*, (tr.) J. Swenson, New York and London: Routledge, 1994, p. 56.
10 P. Gilroy, *Postcolonial Melancholy*, New York: Columbia University Press, 2005, p. xv.
11 Ibid., p. 142.
12 Ibid., p. 143.
13 Ibid.
14 Ibid., p. 71.
15 Ibid., p. 75.

16 P. Cheah and B. Robbins (eds.), *Cosmopolitics: Thinking and Feeling Beyond the Nation*, Minneapolis: University of Minnesota Press, p. 38.
17 J. Nederveen Pieterse, *Globalization and Culture: Global Melange* (2nd ed.), Lanham, MD; Rowan and Littlefield, 2009.
18 D. Held, *Global Covenant: The Social Democratic Alternative to the Washington Consensus*, Cambridge: Polity Press, 2004, pp. 170–8.
19 S. White, *The Ethos of a Late-Modern Citizen*, Cambridge, MA: Harvard University Press, 2009, p. 9. White's affirmation of these core values is qualified by his belief that they are to be understood not from the perspective of our capaciousness as creatures but rather from the perspective of our mortality and finitude. In other words, if these values reflect anything about the human bond, it has to do not with its strength and flexibility but with its tenuousness and fragility.
20 D. Held, op. cit., pp. 164–5.
21 S. Benhabib, *Another Cosmopolitanism*, New York: Oxford University Press, 2008, p. 177.
22 U. Beck, "Cosmopolitan Manifesto," *The New Statesman*, March 20, 1998, 28–30.
23 U. Beck, *The Cosmopolitan Vision*, Cambridge: Polity, 2005, p. 2.
24 U. Beck, "The Cosmopolitan Society and Its Enemies," *Theory, Culture, and Society*, 19, 2002, pp. 35–7.
25 Beck, *The Cosmopolitan Vision*, op. cit., p. 7.
26 Ulrich Beck, "Cosmopolitization Without Cosmopolitanism: Towards a Cosmopolitan Sociology," Unpublished paper presented at 17th ISA Congress of Sociology, Gothenburg, Sweden, July 2010.
27 K. A. Appiah, *Cosmopolitanism: Ethics in a World of Strangers*, New York: Norton, 2006, p. xiii.
28 Sheldon Pollock has developed this argument in *The Language of the Gods in the World of Men: Sanskrit, Culture, and Power in Premodern India*, Berkeley: University of California Press, 2006.
29 G. Delanty, *The Cosmopolitan Imagination: The Renewal of Critical Social Theory*, Cambridge: Cambridge University Press, 2009, p. 256.
30 Hannah Arendt, *The Human Condition*, Chicago: University of Chicago Press, 1958, pp. 9–10.
31 R. Fine and R. Cohen, "Four Cosmopolitan Moments," in S. Vertovec and R. Cohen (eds.), *Conceiving Cosmopolitanism*, pp. 137–62.
32 J. Derrida, and G. Anidjar, *Acts of Religion*, London: Routledge, 2001.
33 C. Geertz, *Available Light: Anthropological Reflections on Philosophical Topics*, Princeton: Princeton University Press, 2000, p. 260.
34 J. Derrida in G. Borradori, *Philosophy in a Time of Terror: Dialogues with Jurgen Habermas and Jacques Derrida*, Chicago: University of Chicago Press, 2004, p. 115.
35 Yet unconditional hospitality, as Derrida defines it, may in one particular represent an impossibility of another kind. Could anyone ever become completely open to an other if that other isn't, and never can be, "wholly other," and, for that matter, is utter openness to anything even possible if the self must be reflexive, even in the act of lowering its guard?
36 Michael Walzer, quoted in *The Hedgehog Review*, 11/3, Fall 2009, 61.
37 D. A. Hollinger, *Cosmopolitanism and Solidarity: Studies in Ethnoracial, Religious, and Professional Affiliation in the United States*, Madison, WI: University of Wisconsin Press, 2006 p. xv.
38 Ibid., p. xvi.
39 Ibid., p. xxii.
40 C. Geertz, "The Uses of Diversity," *Michigan Quarterly Review*, 25, Winter 1986, 121.
41 J. Rawls, *Political Liberalism*, New York: Columbia University Press, 1993, pp. 10–11, 54–60.
42 J. Rawls, "#15 and #16 of The Law of Peoples," in T. Pogge and K. Horton (eds.), *Global Ethics, Seminal Essays*, Vol. 2, St. Paul, MN: Paragon House, 2008, p. 443.

43 A. Sen, *The Idea of Justice*, Cambridge, MA: The Belknap Press of Harvard University Press, 2009, p. vii.
44 Quoted in ibid.
45 Quoted in A. Margalit, *On Compromise and Rotten Compromises*, Princeton: Princeton University Press, 2009, p. 7.
46 A. Margalit, *On Compromise and Rotten Compromises*, Princeton: Princeton University Press, 2009.
47 C. Taylor, "Conditions of an Unforced Consensus on Human Rights," in T. Pogge and K. Horton (eds.), *Global Ethics, Seminal Essays*, Vol. 2, pp. 10, 426.
48 A. Appadurai, *Fear of Small Numbers: An Essay on the Geography of Anger*, Durham and London: Duke University Press, 2006, pp. 113–14. See also Faisal Devji, *Landscapes of the Jihad*, Ithaca: Cornell University Press, 2005.
49 Though Benedict Anderson made this argument on behalf of an understanding of nationalism, certain of its features can also be applied to the other constructs discussed here. See *Imagined Communities: Reflections on the Origin and Spread of Nationalism*, London: Verso, 1991.
50 See J. Haidt and C. Joseph, "Intuitive Ethics: How Innately Prepared Intuitions Generate Culturally Variable Virtues," *Daedalus*, 133/4, 2004, pp. 55–66; and J. Haidt and F. Bjoklund, "Social Intuitionists Answer Six Questions about Moral Psychology," in W. Sinnott-Armstrong, (ed.), *Moral Psychology*, Vol. 3: *The Neuroscience of Morality: Emotion, Brain Disorders, and Development*, Cambridge, MA: MIT Press, 2008.
51 K. A. Appiah, *Experiments in Ethics*, Cambridge, MA: Harvard University Press, 2008, p. 149.
52 J. Derrida, "Avowing—The Impossible: 'Returns,' Repentance and Reconciliation, A Lesson," in E. Weber (ed.), G. Anidjar (tr.), *Living Together: Jacques Derrida's Communities of Violence and Peace*, New York: Fordham University Press, 2012, pp. 18–41, esp. p. 23.
53 R. Falk, "How to Live Together Well: Interrogating the Israel/Palestine Conflict," in E. Weber (ed.), *Living Together*, p. 281.
54 Ibid., p. 286.
55 Ibid., p. 291.
56 S. Khalifeh, *Wild Thorns*, (tr.) LeGassick and E. Fernea, New York: Olive Branch Press, 1985, pp. 177–8.
57 Ibid., pp. 171–2.
58 A. Sen, *The Idea of Justice*, p. 172.
59 S. Khalifeh, *Wild Thorns*, op. cit., p. 204.

3 Pragmatist alternatives to absolutist options

1 Quoted in E. Siskel, "The Business of Reflection," *University of Chicago Magazine*, August 2002, p. 29.
2 W. B. Michaels and S. Knapp, "Against Theory," in W. J. T. Mitchell (ed.) *Against Theory: Literary Studies and the New Pragmatism*, Chicago: University of Chicago Press, 1985, pp. 11–30; S. Fish, "Consequences," in Mitchell, ibid., pp. 106–12.
3 L. Menand, *The Metaphysical Club*, New York: Farrar, Straus and Giroux, 2001, p. 375.
4 L. Menand quoted in Leon Wieseltier, "Washington Diarist: 'Aspidistra,' " *The New Republic* 228/6, February 17, 2003, 42.
5 Menand quoted in ibid.
6 L. Menand, *The Metaphysical Club*, op. cit., p. xii.
7 K. Burke, "Literature as Equipment for Living," *The Philosophy of Literary Form*, (rev. ed.), New York: Vintage Books, 1957, pp. 253–62.
8 This Henry James's description, which he employed in a letter about the club to his friend W. E. Norton, is quoted in L. Menand, *The Metaphysical Club*, op. cit., p. 203.
9 R. B. Perry, *The Thought and Character of William James*, Boston: Little, Brown and Company, 1935; J. T. Kloppenberg, *Uncertain Victory: Social Democracy and Progressivism in European and American Thought, 1870–1920*, New York: Oxford University Press, 1986.

10 Quoted in G. Gunn, *Thinking Across the American Grain: Ideology, Intellect, and the New Pragmatism*, Chicago: University of Chicago Press, 1992, pp. 80–1.
11 Quoted in F. O. Matthiessen, *The James Family*, New York: Alfred A. Knopf, 1961, p. 343.
12 Quoted in ibid., p. 345.
13 R. Poirier, *The Renewal of Literature: Emersonian Reflections*, New York: Random House, 1987; R. Poirier, *Poetry and Pragmatism*, Cambridge, MA: Harvard University Press, 1992; A. Douglas, *Terrible Honesty: Mongrel Manhattan in the 1920s*, New York: Farrar, Straus and Giroux, 1995; J. Levin, *The Poetics of Transition*, Durham, NC: Duke University Press, 1999.
14 J. J. McDermott, *The Culture of Experience: Philosophical Essays in the American Grain*, Prospect Heights, IL, 1987; H. Joas, *The Genesis of Values*, Chicago: University of Chicago Press, 2000, p. 209.
15 H. Joas, *The Creativity of Action*, Chicago: University of Chicago Press, 1996, p. 133.
16 J. Dewey, "The Need for a Recovery of Philosophy," in Dewey *et al.*, *Creative Intelligence: Essays in the Pragmatic Attitude*, New York: Henry Holt, 1917, p. 63.
17 See D. H. Hollinger, *Postethnic America*, New York: Basic Books, 1995, pp. 1–2.
18 W. James, "On a Certain Blindness in Human Beings," in G. Gunn (ed.), *William James: Pragmatism and Other Writings*, New York: Penguin Books, 2000, p. 285.
19 This debate is associated with the challenges to traditional belief made by the so-called "Four Horsemen": Sam Harris, Daniel C. Dennett, Richard Dawkins, and Christopher Hitchens.
20 I explore this argument in G. Gunn, *Beyond Solidarity: Pragmatism and Difference in a Globalized World*, Chicago: University of Chicago Press, 2001, pp. 31–8.
21 K. A. Appiah, *The Ethics of Identity*, Princeton: Princeton University Press, 2007, pp. 21–6.
22 J. Dewey, *Art as Experience*, 1934; New York: Perigee Books, 1980, p. 348.
23 Quoted in E. Siskel, op. cit.
24 M. Ignatieff, *Human Rights as Politics and as Idolatry*, Princeton: Princeton University Press, 2001.
25 L. Menand, *The Metaphysical Club*, op. cit., p. xii.
26 I am indebted for this example to Professor Tom Griffiths of Australia National University, who presented an excellent paper on "The Antarctic Treaty System" at the Rockefeller Study Center, Bellagio, Italy, on September 30, 2010.
27 Quoted in T. Griffiths, ibid., p. 5.
28 C. Taylor, *A Secular Age*, Cambridge, MA: Harvard University Press, 2007, p. 710.

4 Culture and the misshaping of world order

1 L. E. Harrison and S. P. Huntington (eds.), *Culture Matters: How Values Shape Human Progress*, New York: Basic Books, 2000.
2 J. Rosenau, "Imposing Global Orders: A Synthesized Ontology for a Turbulent Era," in S. Gill and J. H. Mittleman (eds.), *Innovation and Transformation in International Studies*, Cambridge: Cambridge University Press, 1997, p. 221.
3 R. Dallek, "The Tyranny of Myth," *Foreign Policy* (November 2010), 78–85.
4 Quoted in M. Gladwell, "Cocksure," *The New Yorker*, July 27, 2009, 27.
5 Mark Twain, *New York Herald*, October 15, 1900, reprinted in J. Zwick, (ed.), *Mark Twain's Weapons of Satire: Anti-imperialist Writings on the Philippine-American War*, New York: Syracuse University Press, 1992, p. 5.
6 Quoted in C. S. Olcott, *The Life of William McKinley*, vol. 2, Boston and New York: Houghton Mifflin Co., 1916, p. 11.
7 William McKinley, "Speech before the Ohio Society of New York, March 3, 1900," quoted in ibid., p. 291.
8 L. Trilling, *The Liberal Imagination: Essays on Literature and Society*, 1950; New York: Doubleday Anchor Books, 1957, p. 215. Trilling was referring to a general problem with the moral imagination as a whole, but his insight possesses particular relevance to the operations of the political imaginary in America.

154 Notes

9 Quoted in the *Los Angeles Times*, July 6, 2002, A 17.
10 M. Mamdani, *Good Muslim, Bad Muslim: America, The Cold War, and the Roots of Terror*, New York: Pantheon Books, 2004, pp. 119–260. There are some who have argued with considerable force that this is too simplistic an interpretation of the new kind of terror that gained global attention on 9/11. This mega-terror was not without purpose and point, even if different individuals responsible for it or influenced by it possessed a great variety of different reasons for participating in it. Just as they were responding essentially to political rather than religious factors, so they were motivated by a desire for power. Many of the participants as well as those who admired their actions identified with the emancipatory agenda that portions of radical Islam embraced after the fall of communism in that part of the world. The project was to liberate Islam and the Middle East from the tyranny of the West, and for a variety of reasons political terrorism offered itself as an ideal tactic.
11 M. Juergensmeyer, "The Return of Christian Terrorism," 2012. Available at http://religiondispatches.org/archive/religion–andtheology/2432/
12 In what follows there is no intent to deny that state-sponsored terrorism has been, and remains, a notable feature of political life in the international sphere from the beginning of the nineteenth century to the twenty-first. Nor does the effort of the United States to disguise this fact by securing international support for the opposite view, that terrorism merely applies to violence directed at legitimate states by non-states actors, alter this situation.
13 The most useful study of the relationship between global terror in the present and religion is to be found in M. Juergensmeyer, *Terror in the Mind of God*, Berkeley, CA: University of California Press, 2000.
14 R. Falk, *The Great Terror War*, Brooklyn, NY: Olive Branch Press, 2003, pp. 7–8.
15 J. Derrida quoted in G. Borradori, *Philosophy in a Time of Terrror: Dialogues with Jurgen Habermas and Jacques Derrida*, Chicago: University of Chicago Press, 2004, pp. 98–9.
16 Derrida quoted in Borradori, ibid., p. 101.
17 R. Falk, *The Declining World Order: America's Imperial Geopolitics*, New York: Routledge, 2004.
18 Quoted in M. E. Marty, *Righteous Empire: The Protestant Experience in America*, New York: The Dial Press, 1970, p. 5.
19 See ibid.
20 M. Gorbachev, "Gorbachev on 1989, A *Nation* Interview with K. vanden Heuvel and S. F. Cohen," *The Nation*, November 16, 2009, 14.
21 Quoted in G. Packer, *The Assassin's Gate: America in Iraq*, New York: Farrar, Straus and Giroux, 2005, p. 38.
22 Quoted in J. Schell, "Too Late for Empire," *The Nation*, 14/21, August 2006, 18.
23 F. Scott Fitzgerald, *The Great Gatsby*, in *Three Novels of F. Scott Fitzgerald*, New York: Charles Scribner's and Sons, 1953, p. 137.
24 See D. P. Calleo, *Follies of Power: America's Unipolar Fantasy*, New York: Cambridge University Press, 2009.
25 This is the famous memo in which the head of British intelligence reported on a trip to Washington, where he had learned that the Bush administration was adjusting fact and intelligence to support its claims about weapons of mass destruction.
26 See B. Gellman and J. Becker, "Angler: The Cheney Vice Presidency," the six-part series originally published in the *Washington Post*, and subsequently reprinted in considerable part in three issues of the *Washington Post National Weekly Edition*, Vol. 24, No. 38, July 9–15, 2007, 6–12; Vol. 24, No. 39, July 16–22, 2007, 8–10; Vol. 24, No. 40, July 23–29, 2007, 10–12.
27 The connections between the two presidencies have even raised the prospect that it may be "a long double-presidency." See D. Bromwich, "George W. Obama," *TomDispatch*, August 18, 2011.
28 Quoted in A. J. Bacevich, *Washington Rules: America's Permanent Path to War*, New York: Metropolitan Books (Henry Holt and Company), 2010, p. 12.
29 Ibid., p. 14.

5 America's gods then and now

1. H. Melville, *Moby-Dick or The Whale*, Evanston and Chicago: Northwestern University Press and The Newberry Library, 1988, p. 7.
2. H. Melville, ibid., p. 374.
3. For one of the most interesting recent accountings of such mixing of religion and culture, see D. Chidester, *Authentic Fakes: Religion and American Popular Culture*, Berkeley, CA: University of California Press, 2005.
4. W. Stevens, "The Idea of Order at Key West," *The Collected Poems of Wallace Stevens*, New York: Alfred A. Knopf, 1964, p. 130.
5. M. Kundera, *The Art of the Novel*, New York: Grove Press, 1988, p. 135.
6. A. Wolfe, *The Transformation of American Religion: How We Actually Live Our Faith*, New York: Free Press, 2003.
7. See P. Rieff, *The Triumph of the Therapeutic: Uses of Faith After Freud*, London: Chatto & Windus, 1966.
8. This observation, and much that explains the effect of American individualism on American religion, derives from A. Wolfe's overall argument in *The Transformation of American Religion*, op. cit.
9. Ibid., p. 32.
10. Quoted in ibid.
11. P. Miller, *Errand Into the Wilderness*, New York: Harper Torchbooks, 1964, p. 86.
12. Hellman actually said, "I will not and cannot cut my conscience to fit this year's fashions." L. Hellman, "Letter to HUAC," in Congress, House, Committee on Un-American Activities, *Hearings Regarding Communist Infiltration of the Hollywood Motion-Picture Industry*, 82nd Congress, May 21, 1952, in E. Schrecker, *The Age of McCarthyism: A Brief History with Documents*, Boston: Bedford Books of St. Martin's Press, 1994, pp. 201–2. While there is some dispute about whether Hellman actually lived up to the letter of her line, this does not detract from its usefulness in the present context.
13. The phrase is J. A. Morone's, to whose brilliant and still underappreciated analysis of religion and politics I am much indebted in the next several pages. See *Hellfire Nation: The Politics of Sin in American History*, New Haven and London: Yale University Press, 2003.
14. Ibid., p. 3.
15. Ibid., pp. 10–11.
16. W. R. Hutchison, *Religious Pluralism in America: The Contentious History of a Founding Ideal*, New Haven: Yale University Press, 2003, pp. 1–10.
17. J. A. Morone, ibid.
18. See M. E. Marty, *Righteous Empire: The Protestant Experience in America*, New York: The Dial Press, 1970.
19. R. Suskind, "Faith, Certainty and the Presidency of George W. Bush," *The New York Times Magazine*, October 17, 2004, p. 51.
20. Quoted in A. Cooperman, "A Faith-Based President," *Washington Post National Weekly Edition*, September 20–26, 2004, p. 7.
21. P. Tillich, *The Courage to Be*, New Haven: Yale University Press, 1952.
22. See, in particular, W. A. Clebsch, *Christianity in European History*, New York: Oxford University Press, 1979.
23. S. Žižek, *Welcome to the Desert of the Real*, London: Verso, 2002, p. 20.
24. Quoted in Morone, op. cit., p. 454.
25. J. Stout, *Democracy and Tradition*, Princeton: Princeton University Press, 2004, pp. 2–3.
26. B. Ackerman presents a brilliant analysis of the constitutional consequences of these new reckless and illegal policies and practices in *The Decline and Fall of the American Republic*, Cambridge, MA: The Belknap Press of Harvard University Press, 2010.
27. Quoted in J. Lears, *Something for Nothing: Luck in America*, New York: Viking, 2003, p. 331.
28. Ibid., p. 7.
29. W. James, *Pragmatism and Other Writings*, (ed.) Giles Gunn, New York: Penguin, 2000.
30. Quoted in ibid., pp. 331–2.

31 Ibid., p. 332.
32 S. P. Huntington, *Who Are We? The Challenges to America's National Identity*, New York: Simon and Schuster, 2004, p. 41.
33 Ibid., p. 40.
34 A. Wolfe, "Native Son," *Foreign Affairs*, (83/4), May/June 2004, 120–5; in the exchange under the title "Creedal Passions," S. P. Huntington responded to Wolfe's essay in "Getting Me Wrong," then Wolfe replied to Huntington and Huntington to Wolfe, in *Foreign Affairs*, (83/5), September/October, 2004, 155–9.
35 M. Noll, *America's God: From Jonathan Edwards to Abraham Lincoln*, New York: Oxford University Press, 2005.
36 Ibid.
37 J. Butler, *Awash in a Sea of Faith: Christianizing the American People*, Cambridge, MA: Harvard University Press, 1990.
38 W. Herberg, *Protestant-Catholic-Jew: An Essay in American Religious Sociology*, Chicago: University of Chicago Press, 1983.
39 R. Bellah, *Beyond Belief: Essays on Religion in a Post-Traditionalist World*, Berkeley, CA: University of California Press, 1991.
40 G. Gunn (ed.), *New World Metaphysics: Readings on the Religious Meaning of the American Experience*, New York: Oxford University Press, 1981, pp. xix–xxii.
41 H. Bloom, *The American Religion*, New York: Simon and Schuster, 1993.
42 Quoted, J. F. Wilson, *Religion and the American Nation: Historiography and History*, Athens, GA: University of Georgia Press, 2003, p. 66.

6 War narratives and American exceptionalism

1 Horace E. Scudder (ed.), *The Complete Poetical Works of James Russell Lowell*, Boston: Houghton Mifflin Company, 1897, p. 238.
2 A. J. Bacevich, *Washington Rules: America's Permanent Path to War*, Metropolitan Books; New York: Henry Holt and Company, 2010, p. 27.
3 C. Johnson, *Dismantling the Empire: America's Last Best Hope*, Metropolitan Books; Henry Holt Company, 2010, p. 127. Johnson goes on to note: "Like earlier Base Structure Reports, the 2009 edition failed to mention any garrisons in the Iraq and Afghan war zones, as well as any bases or facilities used in countries such as Jordan and Qatar. By the summer of 2009, for example, there were still nearly three hundred U.S. bases and outposts in Iraq, with the number set to drop to fifty or fewer by 31 August 2010 – President Obama's deadline for removing combat troops from the country. However, the target date and a stated intention to remove all U.S. forces by the end of 2011 were seemingly abrogated months later by his secretary of defense Robert Gates, who admitted, 'I wouldn't be a bit surprised to see agreements between ourselves and the Iraqis that continues a train, equip and advise role beyond the end of 2011.' As a result, don't count on U.S. bases necessarily disappearing from Iraq by 2012," pp. 127–8.
4 See M. Mandelbaum's, *The Frugal Superpower: America's Global Leadership in a Cash-Strapped Era*, New York: Public Affairs, 2010.
5 A. J. Bacevich, op. cit., pp. 12–14.
6 J. W. Dower, *Cultures of War: Pearl Harbor/Hiroshima/9–11/ Iraq*, New York: W. W. Norton and Company, Inc., 2010, p. 440.
7 Kenneth Burke, *The Philosophy of Literary Form*, (rev. ed.), New York: Vintage Books, 1957, p. 3.
8 See D. P. Calleo, *Follies of Power: America's Unipolar Fantasy*, New York: Cambridge University Press, 2009.
9 D. Halberstam, *The Brightest and the Best*, New York: Ballantine Books, 1993; A. J. Bacevich, op. cit.
10 Quoted in C. S. Olcott, *The Life of William McKinley*, vol. 2, Boston and New York: Houghton Mifflin Co., pp. 2, 11.

11 W. McKinley, "Speech before the Ohio Society of New York, 3 March 1900," quoted in ibid., p. 291.
12 M. Hardt and A Negri, *Empire*, Cambridge, MA: Harvard University Press, 2000.
13 Ibid., p. 60.
14 Ibid., p. 400.
15 Ibid., p. 62.
16 *New World Coming: American Security in the 21st Century: Major Themes and Implications: The Phase I Report on the Emerging Global Security Environment for the First Quarter of the 21st Century*. Washington, DC: The United States Commission on National Security/21st Century, 15 September 1999.
17 The full report was submitted to Congress on December 31, 2001. Excerpts of the 2002 classified report were first leaked January 8, 2002 on the website: http://www.globalsecurity.org/wmd/library/policy/dod/npr.htm.
18 I am especially indebted for this interpretation of global civil society as an antidote to war to M. Kaldor, *Global Civil Society, An Answer to War*, London: Polity Press, 2003.
19 Ibid., p. 147.
20 See D. Rieff, *A Bed for the Night: Humanitarianism in Crisis*, New York: Simon and Schuster, 2002, pp. 1–28.
21 M. B. Anderson quoted in ibid., p. 24.
22 Quoted in ibid., p. 333.
23 Ibid., p. 14.
24 B. Woodward, *Obama's Wars*, New York: Simon and Schuster, 2010.
25 G. M. Goldstein, *Lessons in Disaster: McGeorge Bundy and the Path to War in Vietnam*, New York: Henry Holt and Company, 2008.
26 G. M. Goldstein, "From Defeat, Lessons in Victory," *New York Times*, October 18, 2009, WK9.
27 D. Priest and W. M. Arkin, "A Hidden World, Growing Beyond Control", *Washington Post*, July 19, 2010, p. 1. Of this covert world they write: "The top-secret world the government created in response to the terrorist attacks of Sept. 11, 2001, has become so large, so unwieldy and so secretive that no one knows how much money it costs, how many people it employs, how many programs exist within it or exactly how many agencies do the same work."

7 The transcivilizational, the intercivilizational, and the human

1 Y. Onuma, "Promoting Training and Awareness – The Tasks of Education in International Law," *Proceedings of the American Society of International Law*, 75, 1981, 163–7.
2 Y. Onuma, "International Law and Power in the Multipolar and Multicivilizational World of the Twenty-first Century," in R. Falk, M. Juergensmeyer, and V. Popovski (eds.), *Legality and Legitimacy in Global Affairs*, New York: Oxford University Press, 2012, pp. 184–92.
3 These facts have been widely noted in arguments criticizing Huntington's claims, but they have probably been most usefully assembled in A. Sen's *Identity and Violence: The Illusion of Destiny*, New York: W. W. Norton and Co., 2006.
4 C. Geertz, *Available Light: Anthropological Reflections on Philosophical Topics*, Princeton: Princeton University Press, 2000, p. 218.
5 Onuma considers the term "transcivilizational" to be a neologism and only later substituted it for the term "intercivilizational" to define perspective more universal than the "international" and the "transnational." See his "Remarks," *Proceedings of American Society of International Law*, 77, 1983, 163–70. As will become clear later in this chapter, I do not see these terms as interchangeable but rather insist that the distinction between them is crucial.
6 C. Geertz, "On the Nature of Anthropological Understanding," *American Scientist*, 63, Jan.–Feb. 1975, 51.

7 The next several paragraphs follow very closely my argument in G. Gunn, *The Culture of Criticism and the Criticism of Culture*, New York: Oxford University Press, 1987, pp. 111–12.
8 This is Karl Barth's description of God in the radical Reformed tradition of Protestantism.
9 See my rephrasing of the argument between E. Levinas and J. Derrida in G. Gunn, *Beyond Solidarity: Pragmatism and Difference in a Globalized World*. Chicago: University of Chicago Press, 2001, p. 29.
10 E. W. Said, "The Clash of Ignorance," *The Nation (273/12)*, October 22, 2001, p. 12.
11 Quoted in P. Mishra, "Impasse in India," *The New York Review of Books*, 54, June 28, 2007, 48.
12 T. Asad, "Freedom of Speech and Religious Limitations," in C. Calhoun, M. Juergensmeyer, and J. Van Antwerpen (eds.), *Rethinking Secularism*, New York: Oxford University Press, 2011, p. 294.
13 R. Bellah, *Religion in Human Evolution*, Cambridge: Harvard University Press, 2012, p. xviii.
14 See, for example, "Introduction," in C. Calhoun, M. Juergensmeyer, and J. VanAntwerpen (eds.), op. cit., pp. 3–20.
15 A considerable portion of the central argument of C. Taylor's *A Secular Age* (Cambridge, MA: Harvard University Press, 2007) has been distilled in C. Taylor, "Western Spirituality," in C. Calhoun, M. Juergensmeyer, and J. VanAntwerpen (eds.), op. cit., pp. 31–53.
16 H. Blumenberg, *The Legitimacy of the Modern Age*, Cambridge, MA: MIT Press, 1985.
17 R. Bellah, op. cit., pp. 6–7.
18 M. Baxendall, *Painting and Experience in Fifteenth Century Italy*, New York: Oxford University Press, 1972.
19 C. Geertz, Local Knowledge: *Further Essays in Interpretive Anthropology*, New York: Basic Books, 1983, p. 104.
20 C. Taylor, *A Secular Age*, op. cit., pp. 539–93.
21 P. Katzenstein, "Civilizational States, Secularisms, and Religions", in C. Calhoun, M. Juergensmeyer, and J. VanAntwerpen (eds.), *Rethinking Secularism*, p. 161.
22 P. Katzenstein, "Civilizational States, Secularisms, and Religions," p. 156.
23 K. W. Deutsch, "Medieval Unity and the Economic Conditions for an International Civilization," *Canadian Journal of Economic and Political Science*, 10 (1), February 1944, pp. 18–35.
24 A. Appadurai, *Fear of Small Numbers*: *An Essay on the Geography of Anger*, Durham, NC: Duke University Press, 2006, p. 25.
25 D. Brooks, "The End of Integration," *The New York Times*, July 6, 2007, A15.
26 A. Nandy, *Traditions, Tyranny and Utopias: Essay in the Politics of Awareness*, Delhi: Oxford University Press, p. 54.
27 R. Falk, "Toward the Revival of Principled Politics in America," *Tikkun: A Critique of Politics, Culture, and Society*, September/October 2004, 39; U. Beck, *Power in the Global Age*, Cambridge: Polity, 2006, p. 308.
28 A. Nandy, op. cit., p. 54.
29 T. Asad, *Formations of the Secular: Christianity, Islam, Modernity*, Stanford: Stanford University Press, 2003, p. 135.
30 The Universal Declaration of Human Rights, quoted in Asad, ibid., p. 137.
31 T. Asad, ibid., p. 158.
32 R. Sennett, *The Culture of the New Capitalism*, New Haven: Yale University Press, 2006.
33 R. Sennett, ibid., p. 86.
34 R. Sennett, ibid., p. 5.
35 I. Ramonet, "The Control of Pleasure," *Le Monde Diplomatique*, May 2000, 35–7.
36 H. D. Thoreau in J. L. Shanley (ed.), *Walden*, Princeton: Princeton University Press, 1971, p. 12.
37 M. Nussbaum, *Women and Human Development: The Capabilities Approach*, Cambridge: Cambridge University Press, 2000.
38 C. Taylor, *Multiculturalism: Examining the Politics of Recognition*, Princeton: Princeton University Press, 1994.

39 R. Rorty, *Contingency, Irony, Solidarity*, Cambridge: Cambridge University Press, 1989, pp. 141–88.
40 Originally employed to denounce the Turkish massacre of Armenians in 1915, this phrase was eventually developed by the international legal scholar H. Lauterpacht and applied by the Allied powers at the Nuremberg Trials in 1945 as a charge against Nazi defendants.
41 O. Patterson quoted in D. B. Davis, *Inhuman Bondage: The Rise and Fall of Slavery in the New World*, New York: Oxford University Press, 2006, p. 30.
42 D. B. Davis, ibid., pp. 2–3.
43 J. Butler, *Precarious Life: The Powers of Mourning and Violence*, London: Verso, 2004.
44 J. Butler, ibid., p. xii.
45 J. Butler, ibid., p. 130.
46 R. Rosaldo, *Culture and Truth: The Remaking of Social Analysis*, Boston: Beacon Press, 1989, pp. 2–7.
47 Butler acknowledges these issues in *Frames of War: When Is Life Grievable?*, London: Verso, 2010, pp. 173–6.
48 O. Patterson, *Rituals of Blood: Consequences of Slavery in Two American Centuries*, Washington, D.C.: Civitas/Counterpoint, 1998, pp. 180–2.
49 M. Juergensmeyer, *Terror in the Mind of God*, Berkeley: University of California Press, 2000, pp. 168–71.
50 R. Girard, *The Scapegoat*, Baltimore: The Johns Hopkins University Press, 1886.
51 See G. Gunn, *Beyond Solidarity*, op. cit., pp. 35–6.
52 J. Lacan quoted in M. Breitwiesser, *American Puritanism and the Defense of Mourning*, Madison: The University of Wisconsin Press, 1990, p. 41.
53 See G. Gunn, *Beyond Solidarity*, op. cit., p. 29.
54 J. Butler has modified, to some extent, her views of Levinas in this connection. See J. Butler, *Frames of War*, pp. 173–7.
55 W. Stevens, "The Idea of Order at Key West," *The Collected Poems of Wallace Stevens*, New York: Alfred A. Knopf, 1954, pp. 129–30.
56 J. Butler, *Precarious Life*, op. cit., p. 151.
57 J. Butler, ibid., p. 46.
58 Ibid.
59 G. Gunn, *Beyond Solidarity*, op. cit., pp. 37–8.
60 Levinas quoted in J. Butler, *Precarious Life*, op. cit., p. 134. Accountability for Levinas involves the temptation to kill and the prohibition against it.
61 See Mark 12:28–33.
62 See Leviticus 19:17–18, 34.
63 K. Reinhard, "Freud, My Neighbor," *American Imago*, (54/2) (1997), p. 169.

8 Globalizing the humanities and an "other" humanism

1 E. W. Said, *Culture and Imperialism*, New York: Alfred A. Knopf, 1993, p. 31.
2 Ibid.
3 Ibid.
4 E. W. Said, *The World, the Text, and the Critic*, Cambridge, MA: Harvard University Press, 1983, pp. 224–5.
5 G. Graff, *Professing Literature: An Institutional History*, Chicago: University of Chicago Press, 1987, p. 252.
6 E. W. Said, *Reflections on Exile and Other Essays*, Cambridge, MA: Harvard University Press, 2002, p. xv.
7 E. W. Said, *The World, the Text, and the Critic*, op. cit., p. 290.
8 Ibid., p. 291.
9 Ibid., p. 292.
10 Ibid., p. 29.

11 E. W. Said, *Humanism and Democratic Criticism*, New York: Columbia University Press, 2004, p. 13.
12 R. S. Crane quoted in ibid., p. 15.
13 E. W. Said, *The World, the Text, and the Critic*, op. cit., p. 168.
14 Said was very clear about the limitations of Foucault's theory of power: "The disturbing circularity of Foucault's theory of power is a form of theoretical over-totalization superficially more difficult to resist because, unlike many others, it is formulated, reformulated, and borrowed for use in what seem to be historically documented situations. But note that Foucault's history is ultimately textual, or rather textualized; its mode is one for which Borges would have an affinity. Gramcsci, on the other hand, would find it uncongenial. He would certainly appreciate the fineness of Foucault's archaeologies, but would find it odd that they make not even a nominal allowance for emergent movements, and none for revolutions, counter-hegemony, or historical blocks. In human history there is always something beyond the reach of dominating systems, no matter how deeply they saturate society, and this is obviously what makes change possible, limits power in Foucault's sense, and hobbles the theory of that power." E. W. Said, ibid., pp. 246–7.
15 Ibid., pp. 29–30.
16 Two of the more important criticism's of Said's use of the notion of "Orientalism" are D. Varisco, *Reading Orientalism: Said and the Unsaid*, Seattle: University of Washington Press, 2007, and R. Irwin, *Dangerous Knowledge: Orientalism and Its Discontents*, New York: The Overlook Press, 2008.
17 Said, *The World, the Text, and the Critic*, op. cit., p. 291.
18 G. Steiner, "Viewpoint: A New Meaning of Meaning," *Times Literary Supplement*, November 8, 1985, 1262, 1275–6. He then elaborated his position at greater length in G. Steiner, *Real Presences*, Chicago: University of Chicago Press, 1989, pp. 137–232.
19 E. W. Said, *The World, the Text, and the Critic*, op. cit., p. 241.
20 J. Dewey, *The Quest for Certainty*, New York: Capricorn Books, 1960, p. 255.
21 E. W. Said, *The World, the Text, and the Critic*, op. cit., p. 29.
22 W. James, *Pragmatism and Other Essays*, New York: Washington Square Press, 1963, p. 172.
23 E. Heller, *The Disinherited Mind: Essays in Modern German Literature and Thought*, Meridian Books; Cleveland and New York: The World Publishing Company, 1959. Heller's other books include *The Ironic German: A Study of Thomas Mann*, London: Secker and Warburg, 1958; *The Artist's Journey into the Interior*, New York: Random House, 1968; *Franz Kafka*, London: Fontana Books, 1974; *The Poet's Self and the Poem*, London: Althone Press, 1976; *In the Age of Prose*, New York: Cambridge University Press, 1984; and *The Importance of Nietzsche*, Chicago: University of Chicago Press, 1988.
24 Quoted in E. Heller, *The Disinherited Mind*, op. cit., p. 96.
25 Ibid., p. 16.
26 Ibid., p. 19
27 Quoted in ibid., p. 33.
28 Ibid., p. 26.
29 Ibid., p. 17.
30 W. Stevens, *The Collected Poems of Wallace Stevens*, New York: Alfred A. Knopf, 1964, p. 240.
31 W. Stevens, "The Flyer's Fall," *The Collected Poems of Wallace Stevens*, ibid., p. 336.
32 E. Heller, *The Disinherited Mind*, op. cit., p. 97.
33 Ibid., p. 95.
34 F. O. Matthiessen, "The Responsibilities of the Critic," quoted in E. W. Said, *The World, the Text, and the Critic*, op. cit., p. 161.
35 E. W. Said, *Reflections on Exile and Other Essays*, op. cit., p. xi.
36 Ibid., p. xiii.
37 Ibid., p. 382.
38 Ibid., p. 382.
39 Ibid.

40 E. W. Said, "Globalizing Literary Study," *PMLA* (Special Topic: Globalizing Literary Study), G. Gunn (ed.), 116, 2001, 68.
41 E. W. Said, ibid., p. 68.
42 Though I see these stages operating somewhat differently, they were first delineated in detail by P. Casanova, *The World Republic of Letters*, (tr. M. B. DeBevoise), Cambridge, MA: Harvard University Press, 2004.
43 Several paragraphs here have been adapted from G. Gunn, "Global Literature," *Encyclopedia of Global Studies*, Thousand Oaks, CA: Sage Publications, 2012, pp. 1084–7.
44 Hugo of St. Victor cited in E. W. Said, *Orientalism*, New York: Pantheon Books, 1978, p. 259.

BIBLIOGRAPHY

Abu-Lughod, J., *Before European Hegemony: The World System A.D. 1250–1350*, New York: Oxford University Press, 1991.
Ackerman, B., *The Decline and Fall of the American Republic*, Cambridge, MA: The Belknap Press of Harvard University Press, 2010.
Anderson, B., *Imagined Communities: Reflections on the Origin and Spread of Nationalism*, London: Verso, 1983.
Appadurai, A., *Modernity At Large: Cultural Dimensions of Globalization*, Minneapolis, MN: University of Minnesota Press, 1996.
——, *Fear of Small Numbers: An Essay on the Geography of Anger*, Durham, NC and London: Duke University Press, 2006.
Appiah, K. A., *Cosmopolitanism: Ethics in a World of Strangers*, New York: W. W. Norton and Co., 2006.
——, *The Ethics of Identity*, Princeton, NJ: Princeton University Press, 2007.
——, *Experiments in Ethics*, Cambridge, MA: Harvard University Press, 2008.
Archibugi, D., *The Global Commonwealth of Citizens: Toward Cosmopolitan Democracy*, Princeton, NJ: Princeton University Press, 2012.
Arendt, H., *The Human Condition*, Chicago, IL: University of Chicago Press, 1958.
Arnason, P., *Civilizations in Dispute*, Leiden, Netherlands: Brill, 2003.
Asad, T., *Formations of the Secular: Christianity, Islam, Modernity*, Stanford, CA: Stanford University Press, 2003.
——, "Freedom of Speech and Religious Limitations," in C. Calhoun, M. Juergensmeyer, and J. Van Antwerpen (eds.), *Rethinking Secularism*, New York: Oxford University Press, 2011, pp. 282–7.
Axford, B., "Globalization," in G. Browning, A. Halcli, and F. Webster (eds.) *Understanding Contemporary Society: Theories of the Present*, Thousand Oaks, CA: Sage, 2000, pp. 238–51.
Bacevich, A. J., *Washington Rules: America's Permanent Path to War*, New York: Metropolitan Books (Henry Holt and Company), 2010.
Balibar, E., *Masses, Classes, Ideas*, (tr. J. Swenson), New York and London: Routledge, 1994.
Barthes, R., "From Work to Text," in Josue V. Harari (ed.), *Textual Strategies: Perspectives in Post-Structuralist Criticism*, Ithaca, NY: Cornell University Press, 1979, pp. 73–81.
Bauman, Z., *Globalization: The Human Consequences*, New York: Columbia University Press, 1998.
Baxendall, M., *Painting and Experience in Fifteenth Century Italy*, New York: Oxford University Press, 1972.

Beck, U., *Reflexive Modernization: Politics, Tradition, and Aesthetics in the Modern Social Order*, Stanford, CA: Stanford University Press, 1994.
——, "Cosmopolitan Manifesto," *The New Statesman*, March 20, 1998, 28–30.
——, "The Cosmopolitan Society and Its Enemies," *Theory, Culture, and Society*, 19, 2002.
——, *The Cosmopolitan Vision*, Cambridge: Polity Press, 2005.
——, *Power in the Global Age*, Cambridge: Polity Press, 2006.
——, "Cosmopolitization Without Cosmopolitanism: Towards a Cosmopolitan Sociology," Unpublished paper presented at 17th ISA Congress of Sociology, Gothenburg, Sweden, July 2010.
Bellah, R., *Beyond Belief: Essays on Religion in a Post-Traditionalist World*, Berkeley, CA: University of California Press, 1991.
——, *Religion in Human Evolution*, Cambridge, MA: Harvard University Press, 2012.
Benhabib, S., *Another Cosmopolitanism*, New York: Oxford University Press, 2008.
Bhagwati, J., *In Defense of Globalization*, New York: Oxford University Press, 2004.
Bloom, H., *The American Religion*, New York: Simon and Schuster, 1993.
Blumenberg, H., *The Legitimacy of the Modern Age*, Cambridge, MA: MIT Press, 1985.
Bly, R. (ed.), *Neruda and Vellejo: Selected Poems*, Boston: Beacon Press, 1971.
Borradori, G., *Philosophy in a Time of Terror: Dialogues with Jurgen Habermas and Jacques Derrida*, Chicago, IL: University of Chicago Press, 2004.
Breitwiesser, M., *American Puritanism and the Defense of Mourning*, Madison, WI: The University of Wisconsin Press, 1990.
Brennan, T., *At Home in the World: Cosmopolitanism Now*, Cambridge, MA: Harvard University Press, 1997.
Bromwich, D., "George W. Obama," *TomDispatch*, August 18, 2011.
Brooks, D., "The End of Integration," *The New York Times*, July 6, 2007, A15.
Browning, G., Halcli, A., and Webster, F. (eds.), *Understanding Contemporary Society: Theories of the Present*, Thousand Oaks, CA: Sage, 2000.
Buell, F., *National Culture and the New Global System*, Baltimore, MD; Johns Hopkins University Press, 1994.
Burke, K., "Literature as Equipment for Living," *The Philosophy of Literary Form*, (rev. ed.), New York: Vintage Books, 1957, pp. 253–62.
Burke, K., *The Philosophy of Literary Form*, (rev. ed.), New York: Vintage Books, 1957.
Butler, J., *Awash in a Sea of Faith: Christianizing the American People*, Cambridge, MA: Harvard University Press, 1990.
——, *Precarious Life: The Powers of Mourning and Violence*, London: Verso, 2004.
——, *Frames of War: When Is Life Grievable?*, London: Verso, 2009.
Calhoun, C., "The Class Consciousness of Frequent Travelers: Toward a Critique of Actually Existing Cosmopolitanism," in S. Vertovec and R. Cohen (eds.) *Conceiving Cosmopolitanism: Theory, Context, and Practice*, Oxford: Oxford University Press, 2002, pp. 86–109.
Calhoun, C., Juergensmeyer, M., and Van Antwerpen, J. (eds.), *Rethinking Secularism*, New York: Oxford University Press, 2011.
Calleo, D. P., *Follies of Power: America's Unipolar Fantasy*, New York: Cambridge University Press, 2009.
Casanova, P., *The World Republic of Letters*, (tr. M. B. DeBevoise), Cambridge, MA: Harvard University Press, 2004.
Castoriadis, C., *The Imaginary Institution of Society*, (tr. K. Blamey), Cambridge, MA: MIT Press, 1998.
Cheah, P. and Robbins, B. (eds.), *Cosmopolitics: Thinking and Feeling Beyond the Nation*, Minneapolis, MN: University of Minnesota Press, 1998.
Chidester, D., *Authentic Fakes: Religion and American Popular Culture*, Berkeley, CA: University of California Press, 2005.
Christie, A., *An Autiobiography*, London: Collins, 1977.
Clebsch, W. A., *Christianity in European History*, New York: Oxford University Press, 1979.

Collins, R., "Civilizations as Zones of Prestige and Social Contact," in S. A. Arjomand and E. A Tiryakian (eds.), *Rethinking Civilizational Analysis*, Thousand Oaks, CA: Sage, 2004, pp. 132–47.
——, *The Sociology of Philosophies: A Global Theory of Intellectual Change*, Cambridge, MA: Harvard University Press, 1998.
Conrad, J., *Heart of Darkness*, London: Penguin, 1995.
Cooperman, A., "A Faith-Based President," *Washington Post National Weekly Edition*, September 20–26, 2004.
Cunningham, J. V., *Tradition and Poetic Structure*, Denver, CO: Alan Swallow, 1960.
Dallek, R., "The Tyranny of Myth," *Foreign Policy*, November 2010, 78–85.
Davis, D. B., *Inhuman Bondage: The Rise and Fall of Slavery in the New World*, New York: Oxford University Press, 2006.
Delanty, G., *The Cosmopolitan Imagination: The Renewal of Critical Social Theory*, Cambridge, MA: Cambridge University Press, 2009.
Derrida, J., *On Cosmopolitanism and Forgiveness*, London: Routledge, 2001.
——, "Avowing—The Impossible: 'Returns,' Repentance and Reconciliation, A Lesson," (tr. G. Anidjar) in E. Weber (ed.), *Living Together: Jacques Derrida's Communities of Violence and Peace*, New York: Fordham University Press, 2012, pp. 18–41.
Derrida, J. and Anidjar, G., *Acts of Religion*, London: Routledge, 2001.
Devji, F., *Landscapes of the Jihad*, Ithaca, NY: Cornell University Press, 2005.
Deutsch, K. W., "Medieval Unity and the Economic Conditions for an International Civilization," *Canadian Journal of Economic and Political Science*, 10 (1), February 1944, pp. 18–35.
Dewey, J., "The Need for a Recovery of Philosophy," in Dewey. J., Moore, A. W., Brown, H. C., Mead, G. H., Bode, B. H. G., Stuart, H. W., Tufts, J. H. and Kallen, H. M., *Creative Intelligence: Essays in the Pragmatic Attitude*, New York: Henry Holt, 1917, pp. 3–48.
——, *Experience and Nature*, LaSalle, IL: Open Court Publishing Company, 1971 [1929].
——, *The Quest for Certainty*, New York: Capricorn Books, 1960.
——, *Art as Experience*, New York: Perigree Books, 1980 (G. P. Putnam's Sons, 1934).
Dewey, J., Moore, A. W., Brown, H. C., Mead, G. H., Bode, B. H. G., Stuart, H. W., Tufts, J. H. and Kallen, H. M., *Creative Intelligence: Essays in the Pragmatic Attitude*, New York: Henry Holt, 1917.
Douglas, A., *Terrible Honesty: Mongrel Manhattan in the 1920s*, New York: Farrar, Straus and Giroux, 1995.
Dower, J. W., *Cultures of War: Pearl Harbor/Hiroshima/9–11/, Iraq*, New York: W. W. Norton and Co., 2010.
Eliot, T. S., "Gerontion," *The Complete Poems and Plays 1909–1950*, New York: Harcourt, Brace and Company, 1952, pp 21–3.
Falk, R., *The Great Terror War*, Brooklyn, NY: Olive Branch Press, 2003.
——, *The Declining World Order: America's Imperial Geopolitics*, New York: Routledge, 2004.
——, "Toward the Revival of Principled Politics in America," *Tikkun: A Critique of Politics, Culture, and Society*, September/October 2004, 39: 33–9.
——, "How to Live Together Well: Interrogating the Israel/Palestine Conflict," in E. Weber (ed.), *Living Together: Jacques Derrida's Communities of Violence and Peace*, New York: Fordham University Press, 2012, pp. 275–92.
Falk, R., Juergensmeyer, M., and Popovski, V. (eds.), *Legality and Legitimacy in Global Affairs*, New York: Oxford University Press, 2012.
Fine, R. and Cohen, R., "Four Cosmopolitan Moments," in S. Vertovec and R. Cohen (eds.) *Conceiving Cosmopolitanism: Theory, Context, Practice*, Oxford: Oxford University Press, 2002, pp. 137–62.
Fish, S., "Consequences," in W. J. T. Mitchell (ed.), *Against Theory: Literary Studies and the New Pragmatism*, Chicago, IL: University of Chicago Press, 1985, pp. 106–12.
Fitzgerald, F. Scott, *The Great Gatsby*, in *Three Novels of F. Scott Fitzgerald*, New York: Charles Scribner's Sons, 1953.

Fluck, W., Pease, D. E., and Rowe, J. C. (eds.), *Reframing the Transnational Turn in American Studies*, Hanover, NH: Dartmouth College Press, 2011.
Friedman, T., *The Lexus and the Olive Tree*, New York: Farrar, Straus and Giroux, 1999.
Geertz, C., *The Interpretation of Cultures*, New York: Basic Books, 1973.
——, "On the Nature of Anthropological Understanding," *American Scientist*, 63, Jan.–Feb. 1975, 47–53.
——, "Blurred Genres: The Refiguration of Social Thought," *Local Knowledge: Further Essays in Interpretive Anthropology*, New York: Basic Books, 1983, pp. 19–35.
——, *Local Knowledge: Further Essays in Interpretive Anthropology*, New York: Basic Books, 1983.
——, "The Uses of Diversity," *Michigan Quarterly Review, 25,* Winter 1986, 121.
——, *Available Light: Anthropological Reflections on Philosophical Topics*, Princeton, NJ: Princeton University Press, 2000.
Gellman, B. and Becker, J., "Angler: The Cheney Vice Presidency," *The Washington Post National Weekly Edition*, Vol. 24, No. 38, July 9–15, 2007, 6–12; Vol. 24, No. 39, July 16–22, 2007, 8–10; Vol. 24, No. 40, July 23–29, 2007, 10–12.
Giddens, A., *The Consequences of Modernity*, London: Polity Press, 1990.
Gill, S. and Mittleman, J. H. (eds.), *Innovation and Transformation in International Studies*, Cambridge, UK: Cambridge University Press, 1997.
Gilroy, P., *Postcolonial Melancholy*, New York: Columbia University Press, 2005.
Girard, R., *The Scapegoat*, Baltimore, MD: Johns Hopkins University Press, 1886.
Gladwell, M., "Cocksure," *The New Yorker*, July 27, 2009, 27.
Goldstein, G. M., *Lessons in Disaster: McGeorge Bundy and the Path to War in Vietnam*, New York: Henry Holt and Company, 2008.
——, "From Defeat, Lessons in Victory," *New York Times*, October 18, 2009, WK9.
Graff, G., *Professing Literature: An Institutional History*, Chicago, IL: University of Chicago Press, 1987.
Gray, J., *False Dawn: The Delusions of Global Capitalism*, London: Granta, 1998.
Griffiths, T., "The Antarctic Treaty System," at the Rockefeller Study Center, Bellagio, Italy, September 30, 2010.
Gunn, G., *The Interpretation of Otherness: Literature, Religion, and the American Imagination*, New York: Oxford University Press, 1979.
——, (ed.), *New World Metaphysics: Readings on the Religious Meaning of the American Experience*, New York: Oxford University Press, 1981.
——, *The Culture of Criticism and the Criticism of Culture*, New York: Oxford University Press, 1987.
——, *Thinking Across the American Grain: Ideology, Intellect, and the New Pragmatism*, Chicago, IL: University of Chicago Press, 1992.
——, (ed.), *William James: Pragmatism and Other Writings*, New York: Penguin, 2000.
——, *Beyond Solidarity: Pragmatism and Difference in a Globalized World*, Chicago, IL: University of Chicago Press, 2001.
——, "Introduction: Globalizing Literary Studies," *PMLA*, 116, January 2001, 16–31.
——, "Global Literature," *Encyclopedia of Global Studies*, Thousand Oaks, CA: Sage, 2012.
Haidt, J. and Bjoklund, F., "Social Intuitionists Answer Six Questions about Moral Psychology," in Sinnott-Armstrong, W. (ed.) *Moral Psychology*, Vol. 3: *The Neuroscience of Morality: Emotion, Brain Disorders, and Development*, Cambridge, MA: MIT Press, 2008, pp. 181–217.
Haidt, J. and Joseph, C., "Intuitive Ethics: How Innately Prepared Intuitions Generate Culturally Variable Virtues," *Daedalus*, 133/4, 2004, pp. 55–66.
Halberstam, D., *The Brightest and the Best*, New York: Ballantine Books, 1993.
Hardt, M. and Negri, A., *Empire*, Cambridge, MA: Harvard University Press, 2000.
——, *Multitude: War and Democracy in the Age of Empire*, New York: Penguin, 2004.
Harrison, L. E. and Huntington, S. P. (eds.), *Culture Matters: How Values Shape Human Progress*, New York: Basic Books, 2000.

Harvey, D., *The Condition of Postmodernity: An Enquiry Into the Origins of Cultural Change*, New York: Blackwell, 1989.
——, *Cosmopolitanism and the Geographies of Freedom*, New York: Columbia University Press, 2009.
Held, D., *Global Covenant: The Social Democratic Alternative to the Washington Consensus*, Cambridge: Polity Press, 2004, pp. 170–8.
——, *Cosmopolitanism: Ideals and Realities*, Cambridge: Polity Press, 2010.
Heller, E., *The Ironic German: A Study of Thomas Mann*, London: Secker and Warburg, 1958.
——, *The Disinherited Mind: Essays in Modern German Literature and Thought*, Cleveland and New York: Meridian Books (The World Publishing Company), 1959.
——, *The Artist's Journey into the Interior*, New York: Random House, 1968.
——, *Franz Kafka*, London: Fontana Books, 1974.
——, *The Poet's Self and the Poem*, London: Althone Press, 1976.
——, *In the Age of Prose*, New York: Cambridge University Press, 1984.
——, *The Importance of Nietzsche*, Chicago, IL: University of Chicago Press, 1988.
Herberg, W., *Protestant-Catholic-Jew: An Essay in American Religious Sociology*, Chicago, IL: University of Chicago Press, 1983.
Hikmet, N., "Letters from a Man in Solitary," in C. Forche (ed.), *Against Forgetting: Twentieth-Century Poetry of Witness*, New York: W. W. Norton & Company, 1993, pp. 498–501.
Hodgson, M. G. S., *Rethinking World History: Essays on Europe, Islam, and World History*, Cambridge, UK: Cambridge University Press, 1993.
Hollinger, D. A., *Postethnic America*, New York: Basic Books, 1995.
——, *Cosmopolitanism and Solidarity: Studies in Ethnoracial, Religious, and Professional Affiliation in the United States*, Madison, WI: University of Wisconsin Press, 2006.
Huntington, S. P., *The Clash of Civilizations and the Remaking of World Order*, New York: Simon and Schuster, 1996.
——, *Who Are We? The Challenges to America's National Identity*, New York: Simon and Schuster, 2004.
Hutchison, W. R., *Religious Pluralism in America: The Contentious History of a Founding Ideal*, New Haven: Yale University Press, 2003.
Ignatieff, M., *Human Rights as Politics and as Idolatry*, Princeton, NJ: Princeton University Press, 2001.
Irwin, R., *Dangerous Knowledge: Orientalism and Its Discontents*, New York: The Overlook Press, 2008.
James, W., *Pragmatism and Other Essays*, New York: Washington Square Press, 1963.
——, "On a Certain Blindness in Human Beings," in Gunn, G. (ed.), *William James: Pragmatism and Other Writings*, New York: Penguin, 2000, 267–85.
Jameson, F. and Miyoshi, M. (eds.), *The Cultures of Globalization*, Durham, NC: Duke University Press, 1998.
Joas, H., *The Creativity of Action*, Chicago, IL: University of Chicago Press, 1996.
——, *The Genesis of Values*, Chicago, IL: University of Chicago Press, 2000.
Johnson, C., *Dismantling the Empire: America's Last Best Hope*, New York: Metropolitan Books (Henry Holt and Company), 2010.
Juergensmeyer, M., "The Return of Christian Terrorism," 2012. http://religiondispatches.org/archive/religion–andtheology/2432/.
——, *Terror in the Mind of God*, Berkeley, CA: University of California Press, 2000.
Kaldor, M., *Global Civil Society, An Answer to War*, London: Polity Press, 2003.
Katzenstein, P., "Civilizational States, Secularisms, and Religions," in C. Calhoun, M. Juergensmeyer, and J. VanAntwerpen (eds.), *Rethinking Secularism*, New York: Oxford University Press, 2011, pp. 145–65.
Khalifeh, S., *Wild Thorns*, (tr. T. LeGassick and E. Fernea), New York: Olive Branch Press, 1985.
Kloppenberg, J. T., *Uncertain Victory: Social Democracy and Progressivism in European and American Thought, 1870–1920*, New York: Oxford University Press, 1986.

Kundera, M., *The Art of the Novel*, New York: Grove Press, 1988.
Langer, S. K., *Philosophy in a New Key*, Cambridge, MA: Harvard University Press, 1959.
Lears, J., *Something for Nothing: Luck in America*, New York: Viking, 2003.
Lenz, G. H., "Toward a Politics of American Transcultural Studies: Discourses of Diaspora and Cosmopolitanism," in Fluck, W., Pease, D. E., and Rowe, J.C. (eds.), *Re-Framing the Transnational Turn in American Studies*, Hanover, NH: Dartmouth College Press, 2011, pp. 391–425.
Levin, J., *The Poetics of Transition*, Durham, NC: Duke University Press, 1999.
McDermott, J. J., *The Culture of Experience: Philosophical Essays in the American Grain*, Prospect Heights, IL: Waveland Press, 1987.
McNeill, W. H., *The Rise of the West: A History of the Human Community*, Chicago, IL: University of Chicago Press, 1963.
——, "The Rise of the West after Twenty-five Years," *The Rise of the West*, Chicago, IL: University of Chicago Press, 1991, pp. xv–xxx.
——, "Short History of Humanity," *The New York Review of Books*, XLVII/11, June 29, 2000, 9–11.
Mamdani, M., *Good Muslim, Bad Muslim: America, The Cold War, and the Roots of Terror*, New York: Pantheon Books, 2004.
Mandelbaum, M., *The Frugal Superpower: America's Global Leadership in a Cash-Strapped Era*, New York: Public Affairs, 2010.
Margalit, A., *On Compromise and Rotten Compromises*, Princeton, NJ: Princeton University Press, 2009.
Marty, M. E., *Righteous Empire: The Protestant Experience in America*, New York: The Dial Press, 1970.
Matthiessen, F. O., *The James Family*, New York: Alfred A. Knopf, 1961.
Melville, H., *Moby-Dick or The Whale*, Evanston and Chicago: Northwestern University Press and The Newberry Library, 1988.
Menand, L., *The Metaphysical Club*, New York: Farrar, Straus and Giroux, 2001.
Michaels, W. B. and Knapp, S., "Against Theory," in W. J. T. Mitchell (ed.) *Against Theory: Literary Studies and the New Pragmatism*, Chicago, IL: University of Chicago Press, 1985, pp. 11–30.
Miller, P., *Errand Into the Wilderness*, New York: Harper Torchbooks, 1964.
Mishra, P., "Impasse in India," *The New York Review of Books*, 54, June 28, 2007.
Mitchell, W. J. T. (ed.), *Against Theory: Literary Studies and the New Pragmatism*, Chicago, IL: University of Chicago Press, 1985.
Morone, J. A., *Hellfire Nation: The Politics of Sin in American History*, New Haven and London: Yale University Press, 2003.
Mouffe, C., *On the Political*, London: Routledge, 2005.
Nandy, A., *Traditions, Tyranny and Utopias: Essay in the Politics of Awareness*, Delhi: Oxford University Press, 1993.
Nederveen Pieterse, J., *Globalization and Culture: Global Melange*, (2nd ed.), Lanham, MD: Rowan and Littlefield, 2009.
Needham, J., *Science in Traditional China*, Cambridge, MA: Harvard University Press, 1981.
Needleman, J. and Baker, G. (eds.), *Understanding the New Religions*, New York: Seabury Press, 1978.
Noll, M., *America's God: From Jonathan Edwards to Abraham Lincoln*, New York: Oxford University Press, 2005.
Nussbaum, M., *Women and Human Development: The Capabilities Approach*, Cambridge, UK: Cambridge University Press, 2000.
Olcott, C. S., *The Life of William McKinley*, Vol. 2, Boston and New York: Houghton Mifflin Co., 1916.
Onuma, Y., "Promoting Training and Awareness – The Tasks of Education in International Law," *Proceedings of the American Society of International Law*, 75, 1981, 163–7.
——, "Remarks," *Proceedings of American Society of International Law*, 77, 1983, 163–70.

——, "International Law and Power in the Multipolar and Multicivilizational World of the Twenty-first Century," in R. Falk, M. Juergensmeyer, and V. Popovski (eds.), *Legality and Legitimacy in Global Affairs*, New York; Oxford University Press, 2012, pp. 184–92.
Packer, G., *The Assassin's Gate: America in Iraq*, New York: Farrar, Straus and Giroux, 2005.
Papastergiagis, N., *Cosmopolitanism and Culture*, Cambridge: Polity Press, 2012.
Patterson, O., *Slavery and Social Death: A Comparative Study*, Cambridge, MA: Harvard University Press, 1982.
——, *Rituals of Blood: Consequences of Slavery in Two American Centuries*, Washington, DC: Civitas/Counterpoint, 1998.
Perry, R. B., *The Thought and Character of William James*, Boston, MA: Little Brown and Company, 1935.
Pogge, T. and Horton, K. (eds.), *Global Ethics, Seminal Essays*, Vol. 2, St. Paul, MN: Paragon House, 2008.
Poirier, R., *The Renewal of Literature: Emersonian Reflections*, New York: Random House, 1987.
——, *Poetry and Pragmatism*, Cambridge, MA: Harvard University Press, 1992.
Pollock, S., *The Language of the Gods in the World of Men: Sanskrit, Culture, and Power in Premodern India*, Berkeley, CA: University of California Press, 2006.
Priest, D. and Arkin, W. M., "A Hidden World, Growing Beyond Control," *Washington Post*, July 19, 2010.
Ramonet, I., "The Control of Pleasure," *Le Monde Diplomatique*, May 2000, 35–7.
Rawls, J., *Political Liberalism*, New York: Columbia University Press, 1993.
——, "#15 and #16 of The Law of Peoples," *Global Ethics, Seminal Essays*, Vol. 2, (eds.) T. Pogge and K. Horton, St. Paul, MN: Paragon House, 2008, pp. 431–46.
Reinhard, K., "Freud, My Neighbor," *American Imago*, 54/2, 1997, 165–95.
Rieff, D., *A Bed for the Night: Humanitarianism in Crisis*, New York: Simon and Schuster, 2002.
Rieff, P., *The Triumph of the Therapeutic: Uses of Faith After Freud*, London: Chatto & Windus, 1966.
Robbins, B., *Feeling Global: Internationalism in Distress*, New York: New York University Press, 1999.
——, *Perpetual War: Cosmopolitanism from the Viewpoint of Violence*, Durham, NC: Duke University Press, 2012.
Robertson, R., *Globalization: Social Theory and Global Culture*, Thousand Oaks, CA: Sage, 1992.
Rorty, R., *Contingency, Irony, Solidarity*, Cambridge, UK: Cambridge University Press, 1989.
Rosaldo, R., *Culture and Truth: The Remaking of Social Analysis*, Boston, MA: Beacon Press, 1989.
Rosenau, J. "Imposing Global Orders: A Synthesized Ontology for a Turbulent Era" in S. Gill and J. H. Mittleman (eds.), *Innovation and Transformation in International Studies*, Cambridge, UK: Cambridge University Press, 1997, pp. 220–35.
Roy, O., *Holy Ignorance: When Religion and Culture Part Ways*, New York: Columbia University Press, 2010.
Rueckert, W. H., *Kenneth Burke and the Drama of Human Relations*, 1963, Berkeley: University of California Press, 1982.
Rumford, C., *Cosmopolitan Spaces: Europe, Globalization, Theory*, London: Routledge, 2008.
Ryle, G., *Theory of Mind*, London: Hutchinson's University Library, 1949.
Said, E. W., *Orientalism*, New York: Pantheon Books, 1978.
——, *The World, the Text, and the Critic*, Cambridge, MA: Harvard University Press, 1983.
——, *Culture and Imperialism*, New York: Alfred A. Knopf, 1993.
——, *Out of Place: A Memoir*, New York: Random House, 1999.
——, "Globalizing Literary Study," *PMLA* (Special Topic: Globalizing Literary Study), G. Gunn (ed.), 116, 2001, pp. 64–8.
——, "The Clash of Ignorance," *The Nation*, 273/12, October 22, 2001.
——, *Reflections on Exile and Other Essays*, Cambridge, MA: Harvard University Press, 2002.

——, *Humanism and Democratic Criticism*, New York: Columbia University Press, 2004.
Schell, J., "Too Late for Empire," *The Nation*, 14/21, August 2006, 18.
Schrecker, E., *The Age of McCarthyism: A Brief History with Documents*, Boston, MA: Bedford Books of St. Martin's Press, 1994.
Sen, A., "How to Judge Globalism," *American Prospect*, January 1, 2002.
——, *Identity and Violence: The Illusion of Destiny*, New York: W. W. Norton and Co., 2006.
——, *The Idea of Justice*, Cambridge, MA: The Belknap Press of Harvard University Press, 2009.
Sennett, R., *The Culture of the New Capitalism*, New Haven, CT: Yale University Press, 2006.
Shanley. J. L. (ed.), *Walden*, Princeton, NJ: Princeton University Press, 1971.
Sinnott-Armstrong, W. (ed.) *Moral Psychology, The Neuroscience of Morality: Emotion, Brain Disorders, and Development*, Vol. 3, Cambridge, MA: MIT Press, 2008.
Siskel, E. "The Business of Reflection," *University of Chicago Magazine*, August 2002.
Steger, M. B., *Globalization: A Very Short Introduction*, Oxford, UK: Oxford University Press, 2009.
Steiner, G., "Viewpoint: A New Meaning of Meaning," *Times Literary Supplement*, November 8, 1985, 1262, 1275–6.
——, *Real Presences*, Chicago, IL: University of Chicago Press, 1989.
Stevens, W., *The Collected Poems of Wallace Stevens*, New York: Alfred A. Knopf, 1954.
Stout, J., *Democracy and Tradition*, Princeton, NJ: Princeton University Press, 2004.
Suskind, R. "Faith, Certainty and the Presidency of George W. Bush," *The New York Times Magazine*, October 17, 2004.
Taylor, A., *Secular Age*, Cambridge, MA: Harvard University Press, 2007.
Taylor, C., *Multiculturalism: Examining the Politics of Recognition*, Princeton, NJ: Princeton University Press, 1994.
——, *Modern Social Imaginaries*, Durham, NC: Duke University Press, 2003.
——, "Conditions of an Unforced Consensus on Human Rights," in T. Pogge and K. Horton (eds.), *Global Ethics, Seminal Essays*, Vol. 2, St. Paul, MN: Paragon House, 2008, pp. 405–30.
——, *Dilemmas and Connections: Selected Essays*, Cambridge, MA: The Belknap Press of Harvard University Press, 2011.
——, "Western Spirituality," in C. Calhoun, M. Juergensmeyer, and J. VanAntwerpen (eds.), *Rethinking Secularism*, New York: Oxford University Press, 2011, pp. 31–53.
Tillich, P., *The Courage To Be*, New Haven: Yale University Press, 1952.
Trepanier, L. and Habib, K., *Cosmopolitanism in the Age of Globalization: Citizens Without States*, Frankfurt, KY: University of Kentucky Press, 2011.
Trilling, L., *The Liberal Imagination: Essays on Literature and Society*, 1950; New York: Doubleday Anchor Books, 1957.
US Commission on National Security, *New World Coming: American Security in the 21st Century: Major Themes and Implications: The Phase I Report on the Emerging Global Security Environment for the First Quarter of the 21st Century*, Washington, DC: The United States Commission on National Security/21st Century, 15 September 1999.
Vanden Heuvel, K. and Cohen, S. F., "Gorbachev on 1989, A *Nation* Interview," *The Nation*, Novermber 16, 2009, 14.
Varisco, D., *Reading Orientalism: Said and the Unsaid*, Seattle, WA: University of Washington Press, 2007.
Vertovec, S. and Cohen, R. (eds.), *Conceiving Cosmopolitanism: Theory, Context, Practice*, Oxford, UK: Oxford University Press, 2002.
Wallerstein, I., *The Modern World System*, New York: Academic Press, 1974.
——, *The End of the World As We Know It: Social Science for the Twenty-First Century*, Minneapolis, MN: University of Minnesota Press, 1999.
Waters, M., *Globalization*, London: Routledge, 1995.
White, S., *The Ethos of a Late-Modern Citizen*, Cambridge, MA: Harvard University Press, 2009.

Wieseltier, L., "Washington Diarist: 'Aspidistra,'" *The New Republic*, 228/6, February 17, 2003, 42.
Wilson, J. F., *Religion and the American Nation: Historiography and History*, Athens, GA: University of Georgia Press, 2003.
Wolfe, A., *The Transformation of American Religion: How We Actually Live Our Faith*, New York: Free Press, 2003.
——, "Native Son," *Foreign Affairs*, 83/4, May/June 2004, 120–5.
Woodward, B., *Obama's Wars*, New York: Simon and Schuster, 2010.
Wuthnow, R., "Religious Movements and the Transition in World Order," in J. Needleman and G. Baker (eds.), *Understanding the New Religions*, New York: Seabury Press, 1978, pp. 63–79.
Žižek, S., *Welcome to the Desert of the Real*, London: Verso, 2002.
Zwick, J. (ed.), *Mark Twain's Weapons of Satire: Anti-imperialist Writings on the Philippine-American War*, New York: Syracuse University Press, 1992.

INDEX

Abrams, Elliott 70
Abrams, M.H. 121
absolutism: and pragmatism 49
Abu-Lughod, Janet 4
advocacy revolution 53–4
aesthetics 92
Afghanistan war 64, 71–2, 100, 111
Afro-Eurasian zone of civilization 5, 21
Age of Prose 141
Ahlstrom, Sidney E. 83
aid 110
al-Qaeda 62, 66, 72, 74, 123
American Civil War 44, 95, 95–6
American Creed 93, 94, 95 93–5
American exceptionalism 45, 68, 70, 74, 94, 102–3; and war narratives 99–112
American individualism 79, 81, 84
American nationhood 94, 95, 96 94–6
American Protestantism 68, 79–81, 83, 86, 92, 93, 95–7
Anderson, Benedict 9–10
Anderson, Mary B. 110
anger: and loss 129
Antarctic Treaty (1959) 54–5
anti-globalism 22
anti-slavery movement 34
anti-war narrative 101, 108–11
Appadurai, Arjun 4, 123
Appel, Hans-Otto 22
Appiah, Kwame Anthony 19–20
Arendt, Hannah 21
Arnason, Johann P. 10
art, Christian 120
Asad, T. 126

Asahara, Shoko 65
atheism 49
Aum Shinrikyo 65
Austen, Jane 144
Axial Age 20

Bacevich, Andrew J. 100
Bagram Air Base 72, 74
Bakhtin, Mikhail 131
Balmer, Randall 80
Barthes, Roland 7
Baudrillard, Jean 63
Bauman, Zygmunt 2
Baxendall, Michael 120
Bayle, Pierre 137
Bear Stearns 60, 61
Beck, Ulrich 18–19, 124
Bellah, Robert 97, 119, 120; *Religion in Human Evolution* 118
Benhabib, Seyla 18
Bentham, Jeremy 26
Bhabha, Homi 16
bin Laden, Osama 74
Bloom, Harold: *The American Religion* 97
Blumenberg, Hans 119
Boorstin, Daniel 75
Bosnia 64
Bradstreet, Anne 103
Bremer, L. Paul 72
Brennan, Timothy 16
Brooks, David 123
Brzezinski, Zbigniew 67
Buell, Frederick 4
Burckhardt 142

Burke, Edmund 59
Burke, Kenneth 11, 54, 101, 134
Bush, George H.W. 68, 69
Bush, George W. 68, 70, 71, 73, 85, 86–7, 107, 108
Butler, Judith 125, 127–9, 130, 131, 132
butterfly effect 7

Calhoun, Craig 16
capabilities 32, 126–7
Cassin, Rene 52
Cassirer, Ernst 11
Castoriadis, Cornelius 10
Cheah, Peng 17
Chechnya 64
Cheney, Dick 70, 73
Chesterton, G.K. 81
Christian art 120
Christian Right 89
Christian terrorism 64
Christianity 142–3; Latin 121, 122; and neighbor 132–3
Christie, Agatha 99
citizenship 24
Civil Rights Movement 89
civil society, global 109
clash of civilizations thesis 114–15, 117–18, 123
Clebsch, William 87
Clinton, Bill 71, 85
Coalition of the Willing 62
Cold War 44, 59–60, 61, 64; end of 59, 68–9
Collins, Randall 10, 121–2
colonialism 16, 17
Committee on the Present Danger 69
communitarian position: and global ethics 30–1
community of fate 15
Comparative Literature 146
compromise 27
confidence man, and self-made man 91
Conrad, Joseph: *Heart of Darkness* 58, 141, 144
consciousness 11, 124–5
consequentialism 92
conviviality 17
cosmopolitan politics 22, 110
cosmopolitanism 12–13, 94; and its discontents 14–38; by default 16; origins 20–1
cosmopolitans 110
cosmopolitization 19
counter-war narrative 101–2, 101–5

Cox, Robert 59
Creed of Ontological Invalidity 141
critical inquiry 134–9
Cromwell, Oliver 103
cultural cosmopolitanism 22–3
culture 7–8, 58–76, 116; and economics 60–1; and global/globalization 4–5, 8; and international politics 58–9; and the mind 12; and politics 58–9, 61; and religion 79–80; role of imagination in 120–1; and society 12

Dallek, Robert 60
Davis, David Brion 127
deconstruction 93–4
democracy 24, 93; and religion 89–90; and United States 90
derivatives 88
Derrida, Jacques 23–4, 27, 32–3, 65, 66, 130
Descartes, René 136
Deutsch, Karl 122
Dewey, John 12, 19, 39, 40, 42, 44, 46–8, 50, 135, 140; *Art as Experience* 10–11
Dickens, Charles: *Great Expectations* 26
Dilthey, Wilhelm 45
Dobson, James 98
Doctors Without Borders 31
Doctrine of Pre-eminence 111, 112
Dogma (film) 87
Donald, Merlin 119
Douglas, Justice William O. 82
Dower, John 100
Downing Street memo 72, 88
Durkheim, Emile 97

economic cosmopolitanism 22
economics: and culture 60–1
Edwards, Jonathan 120
Eisenhower, President Dwight David 55, 60, 85
Emerson, Ralph Waldo 79
Empire 104, 104–5
enchantment 120
'end of history' 69, 112
Enforcement Revolution 109
Enlightenment 136
essentialism 15
ethics 128 *see also* global ethics
experimental social psychologists 32

face of the other 128
Falk, Richard 33, 65, 124
fallibilism 31

Falwell, Jerry 64, 85
Ferguson, Niall 62
First Amendment 82
Fitzgerald, F. Scott 70
Focus on the Family 98
Forrestal, James 100
Forward Deterrence 111
Foucault, Michel 136; theory of power 137
Freud, Sigmund 129
Friedman, Milton 22
Fukuyama, Francis 69

gambling 91–2
Geertz, Clifford 6–7, 12, 58, 115, 116, 120
Geneva Conventions 52
Genocide Convention 29, 52, 54, 104
Gilroy, Paul 16–17
Girard, Rene 130
global 3, 9, 17; and cultural 8
global ethics 23–30; communitarian position 30–1; liberal position 30
global governance 2, 14, 18, 22, 24, 61, 67, 75, 104–5, 109, 110–11, 144
globalization 1–6, 9, 25, 123, 144; and culture 4–5, 8; definition 2–3; and humanities 134–47; impact of 2–3; origins 3–5; view of the social 12
Goethe 141, 142, 143
Golden Rule 28
Goldsmith, Oliver: *The Citizen of the World* 137–8
Goldstein, Gordon M. 111
Good Samaritan story 37
Gorbachev, Mikhail 68–9
governance, global *see* global governance
grace 91, 93
Gramsci, Antonio 59, 135
Gray, John 1
grief 128, 129 128–9
Guantanamo 72, 111
Gulf War (1990) 69, 70

Habermas, Jurgen 22
Halberstrom, David 102
Hardt, Michael 104–5
Hart-Rudman Commission 105–6
Harvey, David 9, 16
Hauerwas, Stanley 80
Havel, Vaclav 120
Hawthorne, Nathaniel 81
Hayek, Frederick 22
hazards 15
Heisenberg, Werner 141
Held, David 18, 22

Heller, Erich: *The Disinherited Mind* 140–43
Hellman, Lillian 81
Helsinki Accords 110
Herberg, Will: *Protestant-Catholic-Jew* 97
Hikmet, Nazim 113
history 135, 142
Hobbes, Thomas 26
Hodgson, Marshall G.S. 1, 5
Hollinger, David A. 25
Holmes, Oliver Wendell 42
Holocaust 33, 127
hospitality 27
Hugo of St. Victor 147
Huizinga, Johan: *Homo Ludens* 92
human, meaning of 125–32
human rights 51–3, 109, 110; challenges to positive interpretation of 53; international 52–3, 125; and NGOs 53–4; and United States 103–4
Human Rights Watch 31, 71
humanism: towards an 'other' 134–47
humanitarianism 109–10
humanities 140, 144–5; division between social sciences and 6–7; globalizing of 134–47; and religion 140
Humphrey, John 52
Huntington, Samuel P. 58–9, 69, 93–5, 98, 114; *The Clash of Civilizations* 93; *Who are We?* 93
Hutaree militia 64
Hutchison, William 83

ideal theory 27
ideas 54; and pragmatism 50–1; as symbolic actions 54
imagination 10, 46; role of in culture 120–1
imagined communities 9–10, 125
imperialism: and United States 61–2, 68, 94, 99
impossible, politics of the 34–5
Indian thought 138
individualism 26; American 79, 81, 84
INGOs (International Non-Governmental Organizations) 101
intellectual 145
intercivilizational 114, 117–18, 123–33
intercultural communion 124
interdisciplinarity 7
International Criminal Court 104
International Criminal Tribunal 104
International Geophysical Year 55
international human rights movement 52–3, 125

International Non-Governmental Organizations *see* INGOs
international relations 3
IRA 33
Iran 108
Iraq war 64, 72–3, 100, 108, 111
Islam 30

Jackson, Henry 'Scoop' 69
James, Henry 45–6, 78
James, William 42, 45, 47, 48, 49, 50, 92, 140, 144
Jameson, Fredric 1
Jefferson, Thomas 68
Jesus 37
Judaism 132–3
justice 25–8

Kaczynski, Theodore 64
Kagan, Robert 69, 70
Kaldor, Mary 22, 109, 110
Kant, Immanuel 23, 26, 62; *Law of Peoples* 26; 'Perpetual Peace' 21–2
Karadžić, Radovan 54
Katzenstein, Peter 122
Kennan, George F. 67
Khalifeh, Sahar: *Wild Thorns* 34–7
Khalilzad, Zalmay 70
Khmer Rouge 64
Kissinger, Henry 67
Kosovo 64
Krauthammer, Charles 70
Krugman, Paul 59
Kundera, Milan 79

Lacan, Jacques 88, 130
Langer, Susanne K. 11, 12
languages 20
Latin Christianity 121, 122
Latinos 94
Laye, Camera 144
League of Nations 63
Lears, Jackson 91–2, 93
Levinas, Emmanuel 92–3, 117, 128, 130, 132
liberalism 3, 80, 89; and global ethics 30
Lincoln, Abraham 95, 96
literary nationalism 145–6
literary transformation 145–6
living together 23, 32
loss 127–8, 129, 130
Lowell, James Russell: *The Bigelow Papers* 99

McKinley, President William 61–2, 102
McNeill, William H. 5
McVeigh, Timothy 64
Madrid Protocol (1991) 55
Malik, Charles 52
Mandela, Nelson 56
Margalit, Avishai 27, 28
Marx, Karl 26, 105
Matrix, The (film) 87
Mead, George Herbert 50, 131
Mearsheimer, Donald 67
megaterrorism 65
melancholy 129
Melville, Herman: *Moby-Dick* 77, 144
Menand, Louis: *The Metaphysical Club* 41, 42–6, 49–51, 54
Mencken, H.L. 81
Middle East 21
Mill, John Stuart 26
Miller, Perry 81
Milošević, Slobodan 54
mind 10–12; Dewey's view of 10–11, 12
miracles 79
Miyoshi, Masao 1
mondialization 66
Monroe, James 84
Montesquieu 17; *Persian Letters* 137
moral argument 127
moral cosmopolitanism 21–2
moral crusades 84–5
moral reasoning 32, 89–90
moral sentiments 32
moral universalism 110
morality 28
Morgenthau, Hans 67
Mouffe, Chantal 16
mourning 128–31
multiculturalism 15, 48, 95
multitude 105
Myrdal, Gunnar 93

Naipaul, V.S. 144
Nandy, Ashis 123–5, 131
nation-states: reduction of power 3
National Security Strategy 111
nationalism 14, 118, 122, 145; democratic 18; ethnocentric 15; literary 145–6; militant 63–4; rise of 21–2; and United States 94
nationhood, American 94, 95, 96
Navarro, Alberto 110
Needham, Joseph 5
Negri, Antonio 104–5
neighbor 132–3

neoliberal cosmopolitanism 16
neoliberalism 16, 22, 125–6
Neruda, Pablo 77
Neuhaus, Father Richard John 90
New Deal 85
new world order 68, 69, 71
NGOs (non-governmental organizations) 53–4, 71
Nicaragua 64
Niebuhr, Reinhold 86–7
Nietzsche, Friedrich 48, 139, 142, 143
9/11 (2001) 40, 41, 62, 63, 65–6, 70, 88, 106, 108
Nixon, Richard 85
Noll, Mark 96
non-governmental organizations *see* NGOs
North Korea 108
Northern Ireland 33
Novick, Robert 22
Nuclear Non-proliferation Treaty 107
Nuclear Posture Review 105–7, 108, 112
nuclear weapons 105–8, 111
Nussbaum, Martha 118, 126

Obama, Barack 72, 74, 75, 90–1, 107, 111
Ohmae, Kenichi 22
Onuma, Yasuaki 113–15, 117
Operation Rescue 89
Orientalism 137–8
'other' humanism 134–47

Pakistan 74
Palestinian-Israeli conflict 27, 33–7
Pascal: *Pensées* 141
Patterson, Orlando 127
Paul, St. 132
peace: and justice 27
peacekeeping, international 109
Peirce, Charles Sanders 42, 46, 47, 48
Perle, Richard 70
Philippines 34, 102
Pieterse, Nederveen, Jan 17
planetarity 17
pluralism 25, 124; religious 82, 83; secular 91
Pogge, T. 22
politics: cosmopolitan 22, 110; and culture 58–9, 61; and pragmatism 40–1; and religion 85–6
politics of sin 81–2
Pollock, Sheldon 20
polymorphic globalism 122
Post-Information Age 87
postmodernism 3, 48, 146

poststructuralism 41
potential-war narrative 101, 105–8
power: Foucault's theory of 137
pragmatism/pragmatists 39–57; anti-absolutism 49; decline and reasons in postwar period 44–5; deficiencies 49–50; and Dewey 46, 48; as a general perspective 47–8; and ideas 50–1; and James 47; and Menand 41, 42–7, 49–51; and multiculturalism 48; and Peirce 47; and philosophy of difference 48–9; and politics 40–1; a theory of situated creativity 46; and truth 47, 48
Pre-emption Doctrine 111
profane: and sacred 78, 142
Project of the New American Century 70
Protestant Reformation 91
Protestantism 79; American 68, 79–81, 83, 86, 92, 93, 95–7
public sphere 89
Puritans 86, 97, 102, 103
Pynchon, Thomas: *The Crying of Lot (49)* 81

Quattrocento painting 120
Qutb, Sayid 59

rage in grief 129
Ramonet, Ignacio 126
Rawls, John 22, 25–6, 90; *A Theory of Justice* 25
Reagan, Ronald 63, 69
Realpolitik 45
recession (2008) 61, 73, 88
reductionism 15
religion 28–9, 49, 118–19, 139–40; commodification and marketing of 78–9; and culture 79–80; and democracy 89–90; and humanities 140; and politics 85–6; and secular 118–23, 135–6; and state 82; and violence 49
religious criticism 136, 140, 141
religious pluralism 82, 83
Report of the U.S. Commission on National Security/21st Century 105–6
Rich, Adrienne 16
Rieff, Philip 80, 110
rights 114, 126–7 *see also* human rights
Rilke, Rainer Marie 142, 143
Robben Island 56
Robbins, Bruce 17
Robertson, Pat 64
Robertson, Roland 4
Roe v. Wade 85

Romanticism/Romantics 119
Roosevelt, Eleanor 52
Rorty, Richard 40, 41, 49, 90, 119
Rosaldo, Renato 129
Rosenau, James 59–60
Rowlandson, Mary 103
Rumford, Chris 10
Rumsfeld, Donald 70, 72

sacred: and profane 78, 142
Saddam Hussein 70, 72
Said, Edward 39, 117–18, 134–7, 139, 140–7; *Orientalism* 137–8; *The World, the Text, and the Critic* 39, 136
Salih, Tayeb 144
Sandel, Michael 25
scapegoating 129–30
Schopenhauer 142
science 141
secular 119, 139, 140; and religion 118–23, 135–6
secular criticism 136, 140, 141
self-made man: and confidence man 91
selfhood 50, 132
Sen, Amartya 5, 26–7, 37, 126
September 11th *see* 9/11 (2001)
Shiavo, Terri 98
Shulsky, Abram 70
Sklar, Judith 59
slavery 95, 127
Smith, Adam 19, 26
social-contract theory 26
Social Gospel movement 85
social movements 108–9
social sciences: division between humanities and 6–7
Social Scriptorum 50
society: and culture 12
solidarity 25
South: dividision between global North and 123
South Africa 34; postapartheid 56–7
Southern Poverty Law Center 64
sovereignty 67, 104, 109
Soviet Union 68, 69; collapse of 8, 34, 69
Spanish American War (1898) 40, 61, 102
Steger, Manfred 2, 4
Steiner, George 138–41
Stevens, John Paul 39
Stevens, Wallace 79, 92, 131, 142, 143
Stiglitz, Joseph 1
Stoics 17, 21
Stout, Jeffrey 89, 90, 92

subaltern cosmopolitanism 16
Superman 143
Suskind, Ron 85
sustainability argument 126

Taliban 71–2, 74
Talmud 27
Taylor, Charles 25, 29, 56; *A Secular Age* 119–20, 121
Taylor, James 54
Tea Party movement 89
terrorism 63–6, 73, 123; and 9/11 40, 41, 62, 63, 65–6, 70, 88, 106, 108; Christian 64; definitions 63; difference between 'old' and 'new' 64–5; megaterrorism 65; response to by United States 63–4
Terry, Randall 89, 98
theory: criticism of by Said 135
Thiong'o, N'gugi wa 144
Thirty Years' War 67
Thoreau, Henry David 126
Tillich, Paul 86–7; *The Courage to Be* 87
Tocqueville, Alexis de 19, 81
torture 73, 91
totalitarianism 44
transcendence 119, 121, 138–9, 142
transcivilizational 113–33
transnational perspectives 113
Trilling, Lionel 62
true order, desire for 142–3
truth 143; and pragmatism 47, 48
Truth and Reconciliation Commission 56
Twain, Mark 61, 78

United Nations 52, 104, 110, 123; Convention on the Rights of the Child 104; Development Program report (1999) 2
United States 60, 61–4, 67–76; and 9/11 62, 63, 65–6; deconstruction of 94; and democracy 90; expansion of power 71–2; genealogy of imperial destiny 61–2; and human rights 103–4; and imperialism 61–2, 68, 94, 99; and Iraq War 72–3; moral crusades 84–5; and nationalism 94; near economic collapse 73; and nuclear weapons 106–8; and religion 77–98; response to terrorism 63–4; territorial acquisitions after Spanish-American War 102; war narratives and exceptionalism of 99–112; *see also* American
Universal Declaration of Human Rights (1948) 52, 104, 125

universal hospitality 23
universalism 20, 25

Velvet Revolution 34
vernacular cosmopolitanism 16, 17, 20
Vico 136
violence: and religion 49; and scapegoating 129–30; and sorrow 129
Voltaire 137

Wallerstein, Immanuel 4
Waltz, Kenneth 67
Walzer, Michael 24–5
war crimes trials 54
war narratives: and American exceptionalism 99–112
War on Terror 42, 68, 71
Washington consensus 100
Washington Post 73
Waters, Malcolm 4
wealth disparity 2, 79, 110
weapons of mass destruction 111
Weber, Max 45, 78–9, 120
Westphalia, Peace of (1648) 3, 22

Westphalian system 3, 14, 67, 113, 118, 123
White, Stephen 18
Whitman, Walt 97
Williams, Raymond 134, 137
Wilson, John 97
Winthrop, John 68, 102–3
Wittgenstein 2–3
Wolfe, Alan 95
Wolfowitz, Paul 69, 70
Woodward, Bob 111
world order 67
World Social Forum 124
world systems theory 8
World Trade Organization 123
World War II 102
World Writing 146
worldliness 144, 147
Wright, Chauncy 43

Yeats, William Butler 117

Žižek, Slavoj 87–8
zones of prestige 121–2

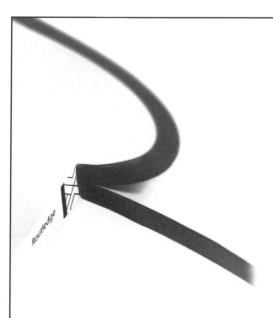

Routledge Paperbacks Direct

Bringing you the cream of our hardback publishing at paperback prices

This exciting new initiative makes the best of our hardback publishing available in paperback format for authors and individual customers.

Routledge Paperbacks Direct is an ever-evolving programme with new titles being added regularly.

To take a look at the titles available, visit our website.

www.routledgepaperbacksdirect.com

ROUTLEDGE
Revivals

Are there some elusive titles you've been searching for but thought you'd never be able to find?

Well this may be the end of your quest. We now offer a fantastic opportunity to discover past brilliance and purchase previously out of print and unavailable titles by some of the greatest academic scholars of the last 120 years.

Routledge Revivals is an exciting new programme whereby key titles from the distinguished and extensive backlists of the many acclaimed imprints associated with Routledge are re-issued.

The programme draws upon the backlists of Kegan Paul, Trench & Trubner, Routledge & Kegan Paul, Methuen, Allen & Unwin and Routledge itself.

Routledge Revivals spans the whole of the Humanities and Social Sciences, and includes works by scholars such as Emile Durkheim, Max Weber, Simone Weil and Martin Buber.

FOR MORE INFORMATION

Please email us at **reference@routledge.com** or visit:
www.routledge.com/books/series/Routledge_Revivals

www.routledge.com